The Rivals

THE RIVALS:

A TALE OF THE TIMES

OF

AARON BURR,

AND

ALEXANDER HAMILTON.

BY

HON. JERE. CLEMENS,

AUTHOR OF "BERNARD LILE" AND "MUSTANG GRAY."

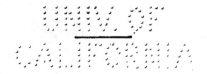

PHILADELPHIA:

J. B. LIPPINCOTT & CO.

1860.

COLONEL JOHN READ,

HUNTSVILLE, ALABAMA.

MY DEAR SIR:—

In dedicating this volume to you, I have not been influenced by the high character and stern integrity of conduct which have marked a long and useful life. Nor even by the consideration that you are the father of that dear wife who has been to me a solace and a support in every trial and every sorrow which have come upon me. It is a tribute rather to domestic virtues—to the kind and genial nature which makes your fireside the abode of happiness, and consecrates the domestic circle to home enjoyments.

In you, a green and healthy old age has followed a youth of industry and virtue; while your heart, instead of hardening by contact with the world, has grown more gentle with advancing years, and CHARITY, the great virtue of the Apostle, abideth evermore within it. May your days be long in the land, and may my last years of life resemble yours.

JERE. CLEMENS.

1*   (v)

PREFACE.

In the preparation of this work I did not confine myself to the life of Aaron Burr, as written either by Davis or Parton. Both are unjust to him—Parton least so. But even he, while writing with an evident desire to do justice, approaches the subject with a degree of timid hesitation which proves that he dreaded to encounter the tide of undeserved reprobation which is yet beating against the tomb of the illustrious dead. The work of Matthew L. Davis is a libel upon the man he professed to honor, and whom he called his friend in life. I went beyond these and collected many old pamphlets and documents relating to Burr and Hamilton, and endeavored to extract from them enough of the truth to enable me to form a just estimate of the characters of both. That estimate once formed, the book was made to correspond with it, the main historical facts alone being preserved, while all the rest is the offspring of imagination.

The history of the war proves conclusively that there was no better soldier, or more devoted patriot, in the long list of revolutionary heroes, than Aaron Burr; and all contemporary testimony agrees that no man ever lived of a more genial, hospitable, and kindly nature. Yet this man, unsurpassed as a soldier, unrivaled as a lawyer, pure, upright, and untarnished as a statesman, became, from the force of circumstances, the object of the bitterest calumnies that malice could invent or the blindest prejudice could believe. Persecution dogged him to his grave; and, although the life of a generation has passed away since then, justice still hesitates to approach the spot where the bones of the patriot-soldier repose. Under the garb of fiction, I have endeavored to contribute my mite toward relieving his memory from the unjust aspersions which imbittered his life. If I accomplish nothing more than to induce a portion of the rising generation to search the records of that life, I shall be amply repaid for the labor it has cost.

Of Alexander Hamilton I have written nothing of which I do not believe he was capable, after the fullest examination of his own writings and those of others. That I have entertained strong prejudices against him from boyhood, is true; that those prejudices may have influenced my judgment, is possible; but I tried to discard them, and look at his character in the light of reason alone. The more I studied it, the more I became convinced that the world never presented such a combination of greatness and of meanness, of daring courage and of vile malignity, of high aspirings and of low hypocrisy. Shrewd, artful, and unscrupulous, there were no means he would not employ to accomplish his ends—no tool too base to be used when its services were needful. Loose in his own morals, even to licentiousness, he criticised those of Thomas Jefferson with a severity no other antagonist ever equaled. Slander was his favorite weapon, and no one stood in his way who did not feel the venom of his tongue and pen.

All that part of the work now submitted to the public, which is not history, is based upon these views of the characters of the principal actors, and wherever I have trusted to imagination, its flight has been restrained within the boundaries of what I believed each to be capable.

The causes which led me to write this book, and the objects I had in view, other than those stated, are of no concern to the public. It has been composed, for the most part, in the midst of many and pressing engagements, and the last part of it was not even read over before it was sent to the publishers; but I ask no charity on that account. The critic is at full liberty to exhaust his powers of satire upon it; and, so far from being offended at the freedom of his strictures, I will thank him for pointing out defects which I may thus learn to amend in future.

It is my purpose to continue the story of Aaron Burr, from the time of his duel with Hamilton to that of his death. The last days of that remarkable man, it seems to me, present a better field for romance than his earlier career. At all events, it is one that is yet untrodden, and therefore possesses an interest in itself which may cause the reader to overlook any deficiency of plot or any faults of style that would otherwise challenge his criticism.

THE AUTHOR.

AARON BURR.

BY FRANK LEE BENEDICT.

AY, come to the grave where they laid him to sleep,
   And left him in shame's mocking silence so long;
The hard and the haughty may now pause to weep,
   To pity his errors and call back the wrong.

The world's bitter scorn hath so heavily lain,
   And cast down its night on his desolate tomb—
At least let the broad-visioned Present refrain,
   Nor scatter the ashes that lie in the gloom.

The spirit of vengeance hath followed the dead,
   And deepened the shadows that slander hath cast;
Ah! sweep back the mists which have shrouded his bed;
   That the starlight may fall on his bosom at last.

Remember the anguish, the sorrow, the grief,
   The long years of exile, of darkness and woe;
The swift-fading sunlight, the glory so brief,
   And weep o'er the grandeur forsaken and low.

The genius that dazzled—the eagle-like mind,
   The passionate heart which still led them astray,—
The greatest of earth in its mists wand'ring blind,
   The spirit of fire shackled down by the clay.

Oh, think of the age that came on in its night,
   And flung down its snow on his greatness o'erthrown:
Wrecked, wrecked on the ocean—no haven in sight,
   His bark going down in the tempest alone.

Ah, leave him to slumber, nor, blind in your rage,
   Still desecrate ashes which lie in repose;
But stamp a new record on history's page,
   That tells of his virtues and numbers his woes.

Let the mosses that cling o'er the waste of his grave,
   Be types of the tribute which soften his name;
Like the fragrance of blossoms that over him wave,
   The thought of his sorrows shall brighten his fame.

The debt should be sacred!—Oh, leave him to rest,
   Nor trample in scorn on the prayer-hallowed sod;
The green turf is holy that covers his breast—
   Give his faults to the Past—leave his soul to his God.

THE RIVALS.

CHAPTER I.

"A world lay moveless on wide ocean's breast—
In sleep profound reposed the mighty West—
An age of ages lonely, wild, immense,
The giant wonder of Omnipotence.
From sacred hills no fragrant incense rose;
Vast, dreary deserts lowered on trackless snows,
And silence reigned, save when the savage yell
Waked shuddering echo from her viewless cell."

In the year 1486, a stranger appeared at the splendid court of Ferdinand and Isabella. His garb was that of one whose circumstances did not admit of any display, but his bearing was as lofty as that of the proudest grandee of Spain. Heroes themselves, and tracing back their descent from a long line of heroic ancestors, the nobles of Spain were at that day the haughtiest in Europe; yet the poor sailor moved among them unawed and unabashed. His patent of nobility was conferred by the Sovereign of sovereigns. Genius stood by at his birth, and crowned the infant in his cradle for immortality. The deep enthusiasm of his character; the vast knowledge he had accumulated; and, above all, the unmistakable sincerity of his zeal for the church, captivated the pious queen, whose prejudices were soon enlisted in behalf of the Genoese, and whose clear judgment readily comprehended the possibility of success in the mighty undertaking to which he had come to urge the sovereigns of Aragon and Castile. The king

2   (13)

turned a colder ear to his pleading. Granada was still held by the Moors, and the stars of the Crescent still floated above the palace of the Alhambra. Anxious as the queen was to aid in carrying out the conceptions of the great navigator, she could find no sufficient answer to the arguments of her politic husband, who insisted that the safety of their united kingdoms imperatively demanded the reconquest of Granada, and that the most acceptable service they could render to God would be to drive the followers of a false religion from the land they had obtained by violence and desecrated by idolatry. Years went by. The conquest of the Moors had been achieved, and the Prophet was no longer worshiped in Granada. The long contest, however, had exhausted the treasury, and the cautious Ferdinand found in the poverty of the exchequer a new answer to the solicitations of his queen. At length, the high-hearted Isabella, fully alive to the glory of so grand an enterprise, proposed to pledge her jewels to raise the requisite amount. From the mortification of this step she was saved by the generosity of one of her subjects. Santangel advanced the money, and on the 3d day of August, 1492, three little vessels set sail from the insignificant port of Palos, upon a voyage whose stupendous results are even yet undeveloped. On the night of the eleventh of October, land was discovered, and on the twelfth, Christopher Columbus set foot upon an unknown world that had for ages slumbered between the waters of the Atlantic and the Pacific.

The brilliant success of the Genoese stimulated other nations, and adventurer after adventurer crossed the seas in search of undiscovered lands. The continent of North America was repeatedly visited by the English, but no permanent settlement was attempted until the year 1607, when a colony was established at Jamestown. The next settlement was at Plymouth in 1620, by a band of pilgrims, numbering one hundred and one. Between these emigrants and the Spanish conquerors further south there was a wide difference of character, and a still wider difference in the objects sought to be attained. The Spaniard made his way by fire and sword. Impelled by the love of gold, he set his armed heel on the naked breasts of millions; desolated provinces, and annihilated empires without pity or remorse. The English, on the other hand, came as tillers of the soil. Actuated by a sincere and fervent piety, they sought a home where persecution for opinion's sake was unknown, and where they might bend the knee to God, unshackled by these legal restraints, which, to them, seemed little less than blasphemy. In the heart, as well as upon the lips of every one, there abided a holy zeal for the religion they had embraced, and for which they abandoned the comforts and luxuries of civilized life for a dreary abode in the dark wilderness of the West. Night and morning their orisons ascended to Him who holds the winds in the hollow of his hand. Night and morning they repeated the solemn anthem,—

"Be Thou our guard and guide!
Forth from the spoiler's synagogue we go,
That we may worship where the torrents flow,
And where the whirlwinds ride."

Peaceful in their inclinations—avaricious neither of gold nor extended dominion, there was yet among them a readiness to repel violence by violence, and a contemptuous disregard of danger in every form, that soon impressed upon their savage neighbors the advantage of cultivating the most friendly relations. Their descendants, born in the wilderness, inherited the virtues of their sires, and acquired from their pursuits a deeper aversion to restraint. Accustomed to liberty, the slightest pressure of a yoke was intolerable, and they instinctively grasped their rifles at the bare mention of an illegal exaction.   Such was the origin, and such the character of the men from whom the materials of this story have been drawn.

Gradually they grew in numbers and in wealth.   Art and science brought their gifts to lay upon the altar of the infant empire, and along the whole belt of the Atlantic coast the dreary forest was metamorphosed into a smiling garden.   Hitherto neglected by the mother country, the colonies now became a subject of earnest debate in the Cabinet and Parliament of Britain.   The interest thus manifested would have been commendable if it had been based upon a parental solicitude for these young communities, instead of a sordid calculation of pounds, shillings, and pence.   The amount of taxation they were able to bear, and the form in which these taxes should be imposed, were the subjects of inquiry.   As early as 1755 a resolution passed the British Parliament, asserting the right to lay stamp-duties in America.   The right thus asserted was permitted to slumber until 1765, when it was for the first time embodied in a law.   The repeal of this statute in the following year, and its re-enactment during the year afterwards, exhibit a degree of vacillation that must be attributed to a consciousness of wrong.   Year after year the disputes between Britain and her colonies became more acrimonious, until the month of April, 1775, when the battles of Lexington and Concord put an end to all hope of a peaceful accommodation.

CHAPTER II.

"Amid the ancient forests of a land,
Wild, gloomy, vast, magnificently grand."

At the period to which we have brought the reader, there was a slender and delicate boy residing in the family of his brother-in-law, in the town of Litchfield, Connecticut, almost wholly unknown beyond the circle of his immediate friends and relatives, and scarcely appreciated at his just value even by them. Left an orphan while he was yet in his nurse's arms, he became the inheritor of a considerable estate, and the baneful privilege of regulating his conduct according to the bent of his own inclinations. At the early age of sixteen, he graduated at Princeton College, in his native State, and soon afterwards devoted himself to the study of history—particularly those portions which detailed the achievements of the great military commanders who had from time to time played their busy parts upon the theater of the world. Even at that day he foresaw that a period was at hand when his country would need all the knowledge thus acquired, and shaped his studies in accordance with the dictates of patriotism. Too young to take any part in the discussions to which the alarming enactments of the British Parliament gave rise, he yet made himself familiar with all the points of the controversy, and his resolution to peril life and fortune in the cause of the colonists was the result of a deliberate conviction that justice was on their side. The battle of Lexington, followed in less than two months by that of Bunker's Hill, hurried him away to Cambridge, where the

American army was then encamped. Possessing all the
theoretical knowledge necessary to make an accomplished
soldier, he was wholly without experience, and the high
idea he had formed of the order and discipline essential
in an army were grievously shocked by the license of the
raw militia, upon whom the colonies chiefly depended to
carry them successfully through a bloody contest with the
mightiest empire of Europe. What such troops can accomplish when animated by an ardent love of liberty is
even yet a mystery to the mere tactician; and it is not to
be wondered at, that, at a time when regular armies alone
decided the fate of nations, a youth like Aaron Burr should
have indulged in gloomy forebodings, when forced to witness the idleness, confusion, and dissipation that pervaded
every rank of the early Continental troops. Their courage,
their energy, and their patriotism he knew to be unquestionable; but, reasoning from the result of military operations
in former times, his heart sickened at the conviction that
these high qualities might serve no other purpose than to
give a bloodier character to the struggle. So great was
his mental disquietude at the total want of subordination
and training among the men, that shortly after his arrival
in camp he was stretched upon a sick bed, and for the first
time in his life suffered for the want of those physical comforts
that wealth is generally able to purchase for the invalid.

The career of the soldier is a hard one at best. The
daily drillings, long marches, incessant fatigue duties, and
often hunger and thirst, are but a portion of the evils
he has to encounter. When the body sinks, as it sometimes must, under these heavy assaults, he is thrown into a
hospital, surrounded by a hundred groaning comrades, as
if to add to his sufferings, by compelling him to witness
the agonies of his friends. When an army is in the field,
these hospitals are nothing more than large tents, where

the men are placed upon beds of blankets, in long rows, through which the surgeon passes once or twice a day, making hasty prescriptions as he goes, that the hospital steward administers or not according to his own convenience. There was enough in this beginning to have damped the ardor of a less enthusiastic patriot; but so far from any wavering in the cause in which he had embarked, Burr seemed only to gather a fresher determination to endure all, and peril all for his country. In a few days he exhibited to his astonished comrades one of those remarkable instances of the mastery of mind over matter —of the mental over the physical man, which sometimes astonishes the disciple of Æsculapius. Tossing on a feverish bed, he overheard a conversation between two officers of his acquaintance, from which he gathered the fact that Benedict Arnold was preparing an expedition for the invasion of Canada and the capture of Quebec. The news acted like healing medicine on his debilitated frame, and, rising from his bed, he announced his purpose to join the expedition. Remonstrances were in vain. The commands, and then the entreaties of his uncle and guardian, were alike in vain. All the kindly arguments of friends and relations were answered in a spirit equally kind ; but his determination was unshaken.

"You are not well enough to leave your room," urged his physician.

"I will be to-morrow," was the reply.

He did leave it. By a mere effort of will he shook off disease as a loose garment, and, enfeebled and emaciated as he was, went forth to brave hardships and dangers from which the stoutest frame and the boldest heart might have shrunk without disgrace.

In the early days of the French Revolution, when courier after courier was arriving at Paris with the news of some fortress taken by the enemy or some battle lost, instead of yielding to despondency, the National Assembly resolved "that the armies of France *shall* win victories." The nations of Europe laughed at the seeming folly of the resolution, but their smiles were soon changed to tears. The soldiery read it at first with astonishment, and then with enthusiasm. They, too, *resolved* to win victories, and from that day triumph after triumph gilded the banners of France until a whole continent trembled at her frown. So in individual life, more than half our battles for existence are won by courage and determination alone. Many more victims have been destroyed by fear, or rather weakness, than by all the diseases, combined, to which the human system is subject. There is an Eastern story which represents a countryman meeting the Evil Spirit and entering into conversation with him :—

"Where are you going?" asked the countryman.

"I am going to the city," was the reply, "to destroy ten thousand of its inhabitants."

Six months afterwards they again met. The countryman reproached him, saying :—

"Thou lying Spirit, thou didst say thou wert going to the city to destroy ten thousand of its inhabitants, whereas thou didst slay sixty thousand."

"Not so, my friend," was the reply. "I killed my ten thousand only. Fear destroyed the remainder."

The fable was founded upon a deep knowledge of the wonderful organization of man. Hundreds, to whom medical science brought no relief, have risen from the brink of the grave simply because they were determined not to die. Aaron Burr, who had never been blessed with robust health, and who was then suffering from the effects of recent fever, took his place by the side of the rough frontier men, to whom hardship had been a familar companion from infancy, and the strongest among them was equaled in iron endurance by the stripling boy.

On the twentieth of September, Arnold's command sailed from Newburyport to the mouth of the Kennebec, where they found a number of light batteaux prepared to aid their ascent of the stream. River and forest were alike unknown to the desperate adventurers. The hum of commerce had never been heard upon the waters of the one, nor the footprints of civilized man pressed the rich mold that had been gathering for centuries beneath the dark shadows of the other. Stretching far away to the St. Lawrence were thicket and brake; the stunted undergrowth, and the lofty tree, presented their rough barriers to the advance of the troops, and exacted a heavy toll in toil and suffering from the worn and wearied soldiery. Onward, still onward, through snow and ice; through the dense shadows that the noonday sun had never brightened, that patriot band pressed upon their desperate errand. After a time the natural difficulties of a march through the piercing sleet and the pathless forest were increased by another and a mightier foe. Gaunt hunger brought its troops of gnawing demons, to wither the strength and crush the spirit that danger and fatigue had failed to conquer. Boat after boat, containing the provisions and ammunition of the little army, was lost among the unknown rapids and dangerous obstructions of the stream. Hitherto the men had marched along the bank, drawing occasional supplies from the boats, but they had now reached a point where it was necessary to strike into the forest; and, as they were destitute of a transportation train, the little provision that was left was abandoned. The presence of so large a body frightened the game to more distant haunts. The cold and the snow had driven the feathered tribe to their sheltered nests, and silence, deep and dread, brooded over the gloomy wilderness. A few dogs had accompanied their masters on the expedition. A few reptiles were discovered on the march. This was their loathsome food, and when it was exhausted, other expedients were resorted to. Amid all these trials, the boy-volunteer, who had been raised in the lap of luxury, accustomed to the most delicate fare and to pillows of the softest down, bore up with a degree of cheerful firmness which was long afterwards the subject of wondering comment among his surviving comrades.

"Come," he said on one occasion to Matthias Ogden, afterwards a colonel in the revolutionary army, "come, Mat, to my camp-fire to-night and partake of my supper." Supposing that he had really something to eat, Ogden gladly accepted the invitation, and, at the appointed time, was punctual in his attendance. He found Burr engaged in boiling something in an old tin bucket, over a huge wood fire, which, on inspection, turned out to be the top of one of his boots. "Let us eat," he remarked, in a cheerful tone, when he judged the cooking process had been sufficiently prolonged to extract whatever of substance the tough leather contained. "We have both partaken of more savory suppers, but no French cook will ever invent a seasoning for his soup to equal the relish that starvation gives to this filthy slop."

On another occasion, while trudging along by the side of a sturdy backwoodsman, cheering and encouraging the men, who were drooping under the weight of privations whose termination they could not see, he observed the eyes of the soldier following his movements with wondering astonishment.

"How does it happen, Mr. Burr," at length he said, "that you are the most cheerful man among us, when a few days ago I would have sworn that ten such striplings as you are would have perished if called upon to endure one-half I can undergo?"

"You would have been right, Crosby, in one respect at least. If we were required to dig trenches, throw up breast-works, or perform any other duty demanding the exercise of physical strength, I should sink from exhaustion before you would begin to feel the effects of fatigue. From early boyhood I accustomed myself to long and tiresome walks, and believing that it would facilitate the acquisition of knowledge, I adopted and rigidly adhered to the rule of living on the smallest possible quantity of food; so that the ills we are now suffering are precisely those I am best fitted to bear. Let me add, too, that there is a great deal in a firm resolution to drive away every approach to despondency. Try it. I am sure the happiest effects will follow."

"I have tried it," was the reply, "and it does not ease the pangs of hunger."

That night Crosby complained of great drowsiness, and, as soon as the fire was lighted, stretched himself on his blanket before the cheerful blaze. There was nothing to eat, and Burr soon followed his example. Sleep, the sweet sleep which is almost always the reward of toil and temperance, fell upon him. No fearful dream disturbed his repose. No nightmare warned him that man's most dreaded foe was crouching by his side. The morning *reveille* roused him from his long repose, and he shuddered to find his arm encircling a lifeless corpse. The strong man had passed away. The sinewy frame had withered at the touch of hunger; and his boy-comrade, dragging the cold body a little ways off, spread his blanket over it, heaped upon that a mound of snow and ice, and left him to his cold and lonely sleep in the gloomy woods.

Thus day after day rolled off, until, at the end of a little more than seven weeks, the gaunt and famine-stricken remnant of that gallant troop caught sight of the battlements of Quebec. They had performed a march unparalleled in the annals of the world. One-half of their number had perished by the way, and the hollow cheeks and sunken eyes of the remainder told a terrible tale of suffering no pen is adequate to record.

In sight of Quebec, Arnold made a careful inspection of his command, and even that daring leader, who rushed to battle as the tiger rushes to its bloody banquet, was forced to abandon the idea of an immediate assault upon the enemy's works with the spectral forms about him. To communicate with General Montgomery, and obtain his co-operation, was the only course. It would be honor enough for that remnant of an army, originally only eleven hundred strong, to maintain its position until succor arrived.

To open a communication with Montgomery, it was necessary that the agent selected for that purpose should traverse one hundred and twenty miles of a territory peopled by foes whose vigilance was aroused, and whose fears were excited to the utmost by the appearance of a hostile army from a wilderness hitherto deemed impassable. Aaron Burr was selected by his commander as the one best fitted for the task. Heretofore he had given unmistakable evidence of courage, firmness, and endurance. Now he was called upon for the exercise of higher qualities—self-composure, tact, skill, and sagacity; these, and these alone, could avail him. Disguising himself in the coarse robes of a Catholic priest, he went directly to a convent of the order of St. Francis, and, knocking at the gates, demanded admittance and shelter from the peltings of the pitiless storm that was raging without. The shades of night had fallen upon the earth; the air was filled with flakes of snow; and this, together with the cowl drawn closely about his head, effectually concealed his features from the prying gaze of the servitors who answered his summons at the gate. Whatever may be said of the Catholic clergy in other respects, it is certain that the duties of hospitality are among the last they have ever been known to neglect. The doors of their religious houses, in all ages and in all countries, have been open to the weary and heavy laden. Nowhere and at no time have hunger and suffering appealed to them in vain. The young priest, as he was supposed to be, was ushered to the private room of the Superior, and all the convent could supply of refreshments was ordered for his use, before a question was asked as to his name, his business, or his destination. After the grateful meal was concluded, and the attendants had left the apartment, the Superior for the first time manifested a desire to learn something more of his guest than that he was a tired and a hungry man.

"You are very young, sir," he said, in a tone of inquiry, "to have taken holy orders."

"It is a secret I purpose to confide to your keeping; and I do so the more cheerfully from having been taught long ago that he who trusts to the honor of a Catholic priest is as safe as if his words were only breathed to the mountain rock."

His gaze rested upon the features of the monk so intensely, while speaking, that it seemed as if he had power to unvail the very thoughts within his bosom. The good father felt the influence of that glance that in after years, on the battle-field, at the bar, and in the fierce partisan conflicts that followed the Revolution, never failed to awe an enemy or to cheer a friend. Large, dark, and lustrous, there was no passion that eye could not express, no mood it could not subdue. When he chose, it was soft and melting as that of the cooing dove. When angry passions stirred his soul, it flashed with a lightning glare, before which the boldest

3

quailed. No secret was safe; no cunning was proof against
its magical power. Men's minds were to him an open book,
wherein he read whatever he wished to learn; and craft and
hypocrisy, with all their manifold arts, tried in vain to be-
wilder or deceive him. The priest instinctively drew the
hood over his face, for none of us like to find that another
is becoming too familiar with our secret thoughts.

"You have," he answered, "been taught aright, my son.
All human errors, nay, all human crimes, save only that of
sacrilege, may find a safe depository in the humblest servant of our holy church. Yet I do not understand how
this can be of any present interest to you. Your looks be-
lie you greatly, if you have sinned so deeply as to doubt of
forgiveness."

"My crime, father, is not against divine, but against human law. I am a soldier, not a priest. A traitor to the
English crown, and a sworn foe to its government. It rests
with you to determine how soon I may become a victim to
its tyranny. If you aid me, I hope to accomplish a great
mission. If you refuse, that mission may be terminated by
a halter."

The Superior was a Frenchman, and therefore a heredi-
tary enemy to England. He was a Catholic, and therefore
felt bound to wage an eternal war against the power that
had dealt such terrible blows at his church. He was a
man, and the genuine enthusiasm which sparkled in every
feature of Burr's face won its way to his heart, and from
that hour the young adventurer had a friend no misfortune
could drive from his side. Resting his head upon his hand,
it was several minutes before the monk made any response
to the frank communication he had received.

"I will serve you," at length he said, "to the extent of
my ability. But to render that service effectual, you must
trust me fully. Half confidences are almost always danger-

ous, and the parties to them not unfrequently find themselves unintentionally playing at cross purposes."

"Such is my own judgment, father; and if you will give
me your attention for one half-hour, you shall know all."

Burr then rapidly recounted the causes which led to the
American Revolution; described the scene at Lexington,
and the battle of Bunker Hill. In words of fire he related
the daring scheme that Arnold had formed of penetrating
the wilderness, and storming the heights of Quebec, at a
season of the year when the extreme cold would prevent
any reinforcements from reaching the garrison. The dangers and miseries over which the American force had thus
far triumphed were concisely stated, and he ended by in-
forming his astonished auditor that he was charged with a
verbal message to Montgomery, without whose co-operation success was impossible and all that had been accomplished would be worse than profitless.

It was a scene worthy the pencil of one of the great
Italian masters. The venerable priest, his form bent and
his locks whitened by the frosts of seventy winters, leaning
his elbows upon the table and listening in rapt attention to
the boy orator and soldier, while he gave voice to a people's wrongs, and proclaimed their unalterable purpose to
conquer, or perish in the attempt. The varied play of his
features gave evidence of the mingled feelings which were
struggling within him. The film of age passed from his
eye, and when the narrative ended, he struck his hand upon
the table with uncanonical energy and exclaimed,—

"You will conquer, my son! Such men are ever victors.
A people animated by the love of liberty, and endowed
with the courage and energy you have already exhibited,
require little training to become invincible. The colonies
are lost to Britain."

"I rejoice, father, to hear you speak so hopefully of our

cause. To the over-wise and the fearful it looks dark enough. Do I trespass on forbidden ground by inquiring if you have always been a priest?"

"No. In my youth I bore arms in a cause less holy than yours. The wild excitement of battle, the gloom of defeat, and the fierce joy of victory, have been experienced in turn; and none of them are entirely forgotten, though years of penitence and prayer have done much to blot out their footprints. But it avails not to recur to such things now. By morning I will find a messenger who shall bear your tidings to General Montgomery."

"Pardon me, reverend sir, I must be that messenger myself."

"You! Why if you could elude the British scouts, who will be sure to be on the watch to intercept any communication between the two American commanders, you could not bear the fatigue and exposure that must be undergone; and if you attempt it, your slight frame will wither before half the distance is accomplished."

"You forget that I have just traversed five times that distance through an unpeopled wilderness, and may well consider the journey before me as a pleasure trip in comparison. Remember, too, that my honor as a soldier is involved. I have no right to transfer to another a duty assigned to me. Whether he failed or succeeded, men would call me coward, if they did not name me traitor. It was not for such a purpose that I sought your convent. Only give me the information you possess of the country, the woods, and the people, and I shall go on my way with a light heart and a grateful memory of your kindness."

Father Pierre made no immediate answer. He was absorbed in thought. His lips moved, but no sound escaped them. The furrows on his brow deepened, and it was evident that his eye took in no object distinctly. His reverie lasted so long that Burr began to be doubtful and impatient. He felt greatly relieved when at last the old man said,—

"I believe you are right. At least, I am sure that at your age I should have reasoned as you do. Leave all your preparations to me; it is past the tenth hour, and you must be stirring early. Here is your chamber."

So saying, he opened the door of a little room, appropriately denominated a closet, and pointing to a low couch, which was almost its only furniture, bestowed upon the youth his blessing, and left him to repose. Seating himself at the table from which his guest had risen, he was for some time engaged in self-communion. Then he touched a small silver bell, and said to the servitor who answered it,—

"Tell Raoul that I would speak to him."

Very soon a man between forty-five and fifty years of age entered the room, and bent one knee respectfully to the Superior. He was about the medium height, broad in the chest, and round in the limbs. Years had taken away the springy lightness of his step, but there was not the least sign of decay in the manly form, that accorded well with the bold and determined cast of his features.

"Rise, Raoul, and be seated. If I remember rightly, I have heard you murmur at the treaty which ceded Canada to England."

"I fought under Montcalm," replied the man, his eyes glowing with the recollection, "and I hope it is no sin to long for a time to come when France shall send us such another leader to break the chain that galls us."

"France will send no leader here, my good Raoul; but the chain may be broken nevertheless. The English colonies on the seaboard have revolted. If Canada unites with them, our ultimate triumph is certain."

3*

"Hope it not, father. Their raw levies and half-armed militia will be swept away like chaff by the British regulars.'

"Your own experience should have taught you better Raoul, for you have seen these same raw levies save a British army from utter annihilation."

"So I did, in the woods and among the mountain glens. On the open plain the result would have been widely different. George Washington and his rangers would not have stood ten minutes before the same troops whose flight they that day guarded."

"I doubt it; but let it be granted. What is there to compel George Washington now to risk pitched battles on open fields? The mountain and the wood still offer their protection, and if he is followed there, Braddock's story may be rewritten on a bloodier page."

"I *hope* you are nearer to the mark than I am. I *know* that whatever one strong arm can do to drive the British lions from America, will be gladly tried. Point out the way, and you will have no cause to murmur at my supineness."

"There was a young priest who sought our halls for shelter, to-night. Did you mark him well?"

"I saw not his features, and only noted his feeble and delicate appearance. It did not seem to me that he could have borne the peltings of the storm much longer."

"Therein you are in error. That boy has just performed a journey that would have taxed your strong frame to the utmost. He is a soldier, attached to the troops now encamped before Quebec, and bears dispatches to General Montgomery. He needs a guide who, to courage and discretion, adds a perfect knowledge of the country. There is not a man in Canada so well fitted for the task as you are, and I have sent for you to request that you will undertake it."

"Your reverence's lightest wish-is law to me. When my comrades, deeming life extinct, left me stretched upon a bloody plain, you had me carried from the field, and nursed me as if I had been your brother, until health and strength returned. When the wars ended, and the soldier, unfit for civil employment, was thrown upon a selfish world, you gave me shelter; you taught me how to earn my bread, and saved me from becoming a mendicant. The hand and brain of Raoul Audigier are therefore yours by a double title. Whatever you command shall be done, if mortal man may effect it."

"Perform this service well, Raoul, and I will hold you acquitted of any debt you may suppose you owe me."

"No, father, no. This is a service in which my wishes go with yours. Gladly on my own account will I pilot the young American to Montreal. Gladly will I stand by him in the battle's front. I have an old grudge against the banner that floats above the walls of Quebec, and I would give ten years of life to tear it down. You must think of something else before we cry quits."

"Well, we will talk of that another time. Now leave me, and make the needful preparations for your journey. Before the dawn you must be on the road."

The Frenchman made a low bow of reverential respect, and left the aged priest alone. Placing writing materials on the table, he indited letter after letter until the convent clock told the hour of three. Raoul was then aroused, who proceeded to harness two strong ponies to one of the rough wagons of the country, while the father awakened his sleeping guest.

When everything was ready for Burr's departure, Father Pierre placed in his hands the packet of letters he had passed the night in writing.

"Here," he said, "are letters to every religious house on

your route   If anything should befall you, and you need
assistance, apply without hesitation to the nearest one.   It
will not be needful to repeat all you have communicated to
me, though you may do so safely.   My letters will insure
you a hearty welcome, and whatever protection they can
give."

Burr was not ashamed, Protestant though he was, to
bend his knee to the frozen ground to receive the benedic-
tion of the kind-hearted priest.   It was earnestly bestowed
both upon Burr and his guide, and the two drove off over
the trackless snow at a pace which placed many miles between them and the convent before the sun made his appearance in the east.

The first care of our hero was to learn something of the
temper and character of his guide, whose features he had
not yet seen, and whose many robes of fur hid even the
outlines of his athletic form.   A few brief questions led to
more general conversation, and Burr was surprised to find
that the man who now acted in a capacity scarcely removed
from that of servant was endowed with an intellect of high
order, improved and strengthened by education; to which
was added a knowledge of the world far deeper than he
himself could claim.   He waited impatiently for the appearance of daylight, in order to judge how far the countenance of the man would remove or confirm the impression
his conversation had made.   The snow-storm had ceased.
The wind no longer swept over the dreary waste, but the air
was filled with frost, and the rays of the bright stars which
penetrated to the cold earth seemed as if frozen by the
way, and hung like glittering icicles from the arched vault
above.   Onward, through the deep snow, sped the tough
and wiry horses; and exultingly, in the still night air,
sounded the voice of Raoul Audigier, as he narrated the
wild adventures and the obstinate battles in which he had

borne a part, when the lilies of France waved over the province of Canada and along the banks of the Ohio.

"It was in the year '55, before your birth, as I should judge," he said, "when Braddock, at the head of a gallant army, came to drive us from a little fort we had erected at the junction of the Alleghany and the Monongahela. We had early notice of his movements, and formed at leisure our plans for interrupting his march. It was in the month of July, and the sun came scorchingly down, even through the leafy covert where we lay in ambush. Afar off we saw the scarlet uniforms and bright muskets of the British regulars flashing in the sunbeams, and over them the lion-banner floating in stern and haughty defiance. My heart was softer then than it has become, after undergoing the hard knocks of more than twenty years, and although they were foes, I felt a cold sensation creep over me as I watched them moving unconsciously upon certain destruction. There were no scouts in front, none upon the flanks; and, to crown the madness and folly of all his dispositions, Braddock had placed the Virginia Rangers in the rear, and assigned the advance to a body of light horse, utterly unfit for service in the thick woods and among the mountain glens. We were not over eight hundred and fifty strong, and had gone out mainly for the purpose of delaying the British march. When our commander, De Beaujeu, observed the order in which Braddock was approaching, he could scarcely credit the evidence of his own senses. Very soon two or three of our scouts came up from either flank and made hurried reports. A glad smile lighted up his features, and, turning to an officer who stood near, he said,— 'They have given us a victory, Bienville, when I only hoped to give them a check. Reserve your fire until you hear a rifleshot on the right. That gallant army is doomed.'

"A deep ravine to the right was lined by our Indian allies, and there De Beaujeu hastened, to restrain their impatience until the enemy were completely in the toils. Steadily, in firm order, the English veterans came on. Nothing had occurred to arouse their suspicions, and although within thirty yards of us, they did not dream of a lurking foe. The sharp crack of a rifle now rang through the forest, and the officer who led the advance tumbled from his horse. Before its echoes died away, a heavy volley in front, and from either flank, was poured upon the astonished soldiery, and a yell arose as wild and terrible as if a thousand fiends had broken loose from the regions of the damned. The advance guard was annihilated by that destructive fire. Still Braddock pressed on at the head of his main body, in the vain hope of closing with us and terminating the contest by the bayonet. In attempting to deploy into line, they were thrown in confusion by the inequalities of the ground. At the same moment a leaden hail was showered upon them from three sides at once, and again the wild yell of the Indian warriors shook the forest and reverberated among the mountains. Nobly and bravely did England's soldiers that day maintain the high character they had acquired in many a stern encounter; but what could human courage do against an unseen foe, whose deadly volleys it was impossible to return? They were broken at length—rallied, re-formed again and again, only to be again and again broken by the messengers of doom that continually went forth from our secret covert.

"Up to this time it had been a massacre, rather than a battle; but now the rangers came up from the rear and threw themselves between us and the bleeding ranks of the luckless regulars. The face of affairs was instantly changed. They understood the warfare of the woods as well as we did, and were fettered by no foolish belief in the possibility of prac-

ticing the tactics of Europe in the wilds of America.
Promptly availing themselves of every sheltering object,
they returned our fire with fatal effect. De Beaujeu was
mortally wounded, and our advance so much checked, that
the shattered remnant of Braddock's army was enabled to
recross the Monongahela. But for Washington and his
Rangers, not one British soldier would have escaped to tell
the disastrous tale of that day's battle. As it was, they
lost all their baggage, artillery, and munitions, and our Indian allies carried seven hundred and fifty scalps into Fort
Du Quesne, as additional trophies of victory."

In such conversation the time wore rapidly away. Burr
was conducted from convent to convent by his sagacious
guide, receiving at each one the warm greetings and lavish
hospitality of its inmates. At Three Rivers they observed
a number of persons gathered about the entrance to a public house, engaged in earnest conversation, which they did
not doubt had reference to Arnold's invasion. To attempt
to pass would be to create suspicion and insure detection.
Raoul drove boldly up to the door and inquired the way to
the religious house at the place, of which he pretended to
be ignorant. The confident manner of the man, and the
priestly vestments of Burr, united to deceive them, and,
although a few of the group eyed them suspiciously, they
were permitted to proceed unmolested.

"We have had a narrow escape, monsieur," said the
guide, as soon as they were out of ear-shot. "For five
minutes I could distinctly feel the pressure of a rope about
my neck."

"Was the danger really so great?" asked Burr. "I
thought from your tone and manner that it was trivia.."

"When you have been knocked about the world, as I
have been, monsieur, you will learn that half of our success in life depends upon appearances. The philosopher

at his books—the tiller of the soil, with no thought beyond the profitable sale of his produce—the soldier in the presence of an enemy—the statesman who struggles for power and place—even the priest at the altar, must sometimes seem to be what they are not, or they will be certain to encounter much disappointment. There is nothing more dangerous than one of those tell-tale faces which reveal our inmost thoughts as plainly as if they were written in a book. If Father Pierre had suspected me of any such weakness, he would never have trusted you under my guidance. I saw in yonder group the man whom, of all others, I have most reason to hate. It has been ten years since we met, and I have changed more than he has; but the quivering of a lip, the flashing of an eye, or any other appearance of unusual emotion, would have betrayed me, and subjected us to an examination we might have found it difficult to pass through."

"The examination would have been fruitless," said Burr; "for I have nothing that would betray me. The letters of Father Pierre are so worded as to remove rather than excite suspicion. I have no dispatches or other papers of any description."

"There is beneath that coarse robe," quietly responded Raoul, "a brace of pistols, and a broad, two-edged dagger. The Catholic clergy are not usually so well provided with offensive arms."

"I am indeed armed as you say. How did you know it?"

"I should have done poor credit to my training, if, in traveling so far, I had failed to discover the texture of your under-garments, provided I had deemed it necessary to possess myself of the information. In this case, however, my knowledge was acquired by a more simple process. You have been jolted against me at least a hundred times, and I could not help feeling your arms. But here we are at the convent gate, and here we must remain until to-morrow. In the mean time, I will find out what danger is ahead of us."

The possibility of a considerable detention at this place, and the certainty that when he did go, he would be compelled to leave at an unusual hour and in a clandestine manner, made it necessary, in the opinion of Burr, that the object of his journey should be fully explained to the chief of the establishment, and accordingly he at once solicited the favor of a private interview.

CHAPTER III.

"See—oh! never more, my comrades,
Shall we see that falcon eye
Redden with its inward lightning,
As the hour of fight drew nigh!
Never shall we hear the voice that,
Clearer than the trumpet's call,
Bade us strike for King and Country,
Bade us win the field, or fall!"

THE evening meal had long been concluded, and the convent bells had chimed the hour of nine. Aaron Burr was still in earnest conference with the Superior. A gentle tap on the door announced the appearance of a visitor. He was evidently expected, for the door immediately opened, and the priest, pointing to a chair, anxiously inquired of the new-comer what news he had gathered.

"The country is aroused and vigilant," briefly responded the man, "and patrols of horse are scouring the roads."

"For what? Heard you for what, Julien?"

"There is a rumor of a rebel army encamped before Quebec; and it is said that rebel emissaries are traveling in disguise to create disaffection among the people."

"This is worse," said the monk, thoughtfully; "much worse than I expected. You may go, Julien," he continued, after a pause, "and partake of some needful refreshment—but first send the guide Raoul hither."

"We have need of your advice, my son," said the monk, when Audigier appeared in obedience to his summons. "Julien reports that the country people are alarmed, and horse patrols scouring the roads. You, who are a soldier by profession, will understand what amount of danger is to be anticipated, and what are the best means of avoiding it."

"I *have been* a soldier, father, and remembered so much of my old calling as to go out myself on a scouting expedition this evening. Julien has not reported matters any worse than they are."

"So I feared! so I feared! What do you advise?"

"It seems to me, father, there is but one thing we can do safely, and that is, to remain within your walls until the patrols have disappeared. They will not molest us here, and I hope and believe they will soon get tired of riding about in such bitter weather as this."

The monk fully agreed with the guide, but such an arrangement was exceedingly distasteful to Burr, and he protested vehemently against it. Every hour lost now, he argued, lessened the chances of a glorious termination to the campaign. It gave the enemy time to recover from his first panic, and, which was of more importance, enabled him to add to and strengthen his fortifications. He contended that the patrols were likely to be just as vigilant some days hence as now, and added, that he felt bound to make the attempt to proceed, however great the danger. The guide heard him without interruption, and then calmly replied,—

"I acknowledge the force of much you have said, Monsieur Burr. I know the importance of speedily reaching Montreal, and it is because I do know it that I advise present delay. To proceed now will be to throw yourself into the hands of the enemy; not probably, but certainly. We might gain a few hours by starting at night, but the tracks left in the snow would enable them to follow at speed, and commanding as they could, and would, fresh horses at every farm-house on the road, our escape would be impossible.

We must remain, monsieur, and if your anticipations of the continued vigilance of the horsemen should prove correct, we can take advantage of the first snow-storm which will fill up the tracks behind us, and lessen the danger by that much at least. I am persuaded, however, that much more will be gained. The people of the country have no heart for this business, and the British horse, who have nothing more than vague suspicion to animate them, will soon find, in the severity of the weather, a sufficient excuse for leaving the road and betaking themselves to more comfortable quarters."

The arguments of the guide were warmly seconded by the priest, and Burr was compelled to submit to an arrangement he could not alter. Having consented to remain, he did not, as so many men would have done, see fit to render it disagreeable to his host by an exhibition of fretful impatience. On the contrary, during the three days of his enforced detention he seemed to forget his warlike mission entirely, and directed the conversation into channels the most familiar and the most agreeable to his hearers. Upon subjects of philosophy and religion, he was at home; and the good fathers were astonished as much by the subtlety of his reasoning as by the extent and variety of his learning.

Every night Raoul communicated the information he had gathered during the day. On the third evening, after his usual report, he said,—

"The coast is nearly clear, monsieur, and the clouds betoken a snow-storm before midnight. If you will take a few hours sleep I will have everything prepared to start by the time it sets in."

Burr was so delighted at the prospect of being again in motion, that sleep was banished from his eyelids. He had no preparations to make beyond a careful examination of his arms. These were secured in a belt beneath his monk's robes, and then he began to pace the floor with a quick and nervous tread. After awhile he seated himself in a chair, and, taking up a Latin volume, tried to pass off the time in reading. His efforts to confine his attention to the book were of no avail. The words seemed to run into one another, and he became conscious that, although he had turned over a dozen leaves or more, he could not recall a single expression, and was ignorant even of the subject treated of in the book. Replacing it on the table, he renewed his walk more rapidly than before. Soon his steps grew slower. The furrows impatience had made upon his brow disappeared. He had surrendered the reins to fancy, and, in the buoyant hopefulness of youth, had given form and substance to the dim and shadowy events which peopled the future. Distinctly, as on a mariner's chart, he traced out his own career, and robed it with a glory that never comes to bless the imagination of any but the young and the inexperienced. He heard upon a hundred battle-fields the stirring war-cry, "Give me liberty, or give me death!" and sent back from his own lips an answering echo. Through scenes like these—in the midst of honors fairly won—he rose from rank to rank, until he saw himself the chosen leader of a band of patriot heroes, whose strong arms had shivered the chains of tyranny, and whose bold hearts had led them unflinching through fire and blood to the loftiest triumph mortal courage may achieve. Then a sweet change came over his dream. The stern shouts of contending hosts, the clashing steel, and the deep-toned thunder of the artillery are hushed, and in their stead swell the triumphal anthems which hail a people's champion and proclaim a nation's birth. The ground where lately the life-blood of the oppressor and the oppressed was mingled in a crimson current, is strewed with

4*

flowers; the serried ranks of armed men are swept away; old men and children throng around their deliverer, and, more highly prized than all,—

> "From every casement comes the light
> Of women's eyes, so soft and bright!
> Peering through the latticed bars,
> A nearer, dearer, heaven of stars."

Farther, farther still, beyond the final triumph and its glad rejoicings, did the visions of the young enthusiast travel. He became the lawgiver of a ransomed continent, and under his encouragement the lake, the stream, the mountain, and the plain were peopled by the mighty creations of science. Art added its brilliant decorations; music and poetry poured their melodies into enraptured ears; and, over all, genius spread its radiant wings, gilding that favored spot of earth with the hues of heaven.

Oh, wisely has an impenetrable curtain been drawn between us and the unknown road our footsteps are doomed to pass! Oh, wisely has it been decreed that no craft, no skill, no exertion can tear it away! Moving as we move, receding as we advance, forever near, yet forever beyond our reach, it hides alike the level greensward and the quicksand, the triumph and the fall, which await us to-morrow. No avenging demon stood by the side of Aaron Burr to reveal the destiny to come, and to strike from fancy's grasp its enchanter's wand. He was but twenty, and he could dream. It has been so ordered that all of us, at that age, may dream if we will, and he is a poor, weak fool, who cherishes not the good gift that Providence has bestowed. The narrow-minded devotee of mammon may say, and truly, that the brightest vision never purchased a loaf of bread or clothed a naked foot; but what would King David have said if he had been told to still the swell of grandeur that almost shivered his harp-strings in the cave of Adullam, when the bright dream of his future greatness and glory flashed upon him? Or, what would old John Milton have answered, if he had been told to chase off his visions of Lucifer's rebellion in hea-ven—descend from his kindred home beyond the stars, and grabble in the mire of earth for sixpence? Tell the sol-dier that he must not dream of victories won in his coun-try's cause; the lawyer, of friendless innocence vindicated by his eloquence; the gospel preacher, of lost souls re-stored to a bleeding Saviour's bosom,—and the soldier becomes a mercenary, the lawyer a pettifogging swindler, and the preacher a heartless hypocrite. Dreams, however wild, however extravagant, are the gift of God himself, sent in infinite mercy to cheer the darkest hours of the desponding, and in infinite wisdom to stimulate the mind of man to the grandest and the loftiest of its exertions. Nothing great, nothing good, was ever yet accomplished by him whose aspirations were bounded by the actual—whose efforts were limited by the probable.

Aaron Burr was still building castles in the air, when Raoul, accompanied by the Father Superior, entered the room to announce that the storm had set in, and the hour for their departure had arrived. For the first ten miles or more, their progress was slow. The snow, falling in flakes as big as a man's hand, shut out all objects at the distance of a few feet from the travelers, and rendered the exercise of considerable caution necessary in picking their road. The dreary night gave little encouragement to conversation, and the silence was only broken by a brief question now and then, and an equally brief reply. No indication of a pursuit had been observed, and Burr was beginning to flatter himself with the belief that the dan-ger was over, when, shortly after crossing a little stream

spanned by a covered bridge, his attention was attracted
by a lumbering noise behind them.

"What is that?" he asked quickly.

Raoul turned his head backward for a moment, and
then replied in a voice indicative neither of alarm nor
excitement,—

"It is the sound of horses' feet on the bridge. We are
followed, monsieur."

At the same time he applied the lash smartly to the
spirited ponies, who dashed off at a greatly accelerated
pace. Holding them steadily to their work, Raoul continued,—

"If they have followed us from Three Rivers they must
be skillful riders, or their horses will be blown before they
overtake us. Ours are as strong as when we left the convent, and will bear up many miles without flagging."

"Is it not possible," asked Burr, "that they may be
upon some other errand?"

"*Possible*, certainly; though there are few errands
which would draw men from their comfortable beds on
such a night as this. It is of little moment, however,
whether they seek us, or whether they have other business.
We are upon the road under suspicious circumstances, in
a time of general suspicion, and that is enough to insure
our arrest if we are overtaken. May I ask, monsieur,
whether you propose in that event to surrender, or resist?"

"Resist, by all means!" was the quick and stern reply. "Resist, and to the death. I will not be taken
alive."

"I am delighted to hear you say so. The fact is, I
look upon death by a halter as altogether so vulgar and
disagreeable, that I am afraid I might have been inclined
to oppose your wishes if you had decided otherwise. It

is better though to avoid the alternative, if it can be done, and, as the horses will require all my attention, I must request you to turn an occasional glance backward, in order that we may get the earliest notice of their approach."

Mile after mile was passed over, and still there was no appearance of the pursuing party. Raoul well understood that they might be in a few hundred yards of him nevertheless, and he kept his horses at the fastest pace they could bear without the risk of breaking down. The storm was beginning to abate, and the first streaks of light dappled the east, when Burr thought he discovered the dim outlines of horsemen in the rear.

"They are coming," he said. "Had you not better increase our speed?"

"No. They will overtake us at any rate. It must come to a life and death struggle sooner or later, and we shall gain some advantage by taking it coolly. Can you make out how many there are?"

"I see but three."

"Three only! There must have been more when they started, and some have broken down by the way."

For two miles further the horses were kept at the same steady pace. The day had grown brighter, and the snow was falling less rapidly than it had been.

"They are gaining on us," said Burr, "but it is very slowly. It will be an hour before they can overtake us, even at our present rate of traveling."

"Do you see no more than three now, monsieur?"

"There are no more."

"Then the chances are all in our favor."

So saying, he reined the jaded horses to a slow trot, dropped the buffalo robe from his shoulders, and divested his hands of the thick fur gloves which incased them.

"Get your arms ready, monsieur, and use them promptly. Not only our own lives, but the fate of Quebec depends upon getting the first fire."

A few minutes only elapsed before the pursuers galloped alongside and sternly ordered them to halt. Raoul complied, sullenly inquiring for what purpose peaceful travelers were thus interrupted on their journey.

"Ah, Monsieur Audigier!" answered the leader of the party, "it seems you have forgotten an old acquaintance. You might have remembered Cornet (now Captain) Robert Campbell, of His Majesty's —— Dragoons, and saved yourself the trouble of asking for his authority."

"I remember," said the Frenchman, with a knit brow and a flashing eye, "that you shot down my brother by my side, and that you treated me like a dog when I was a helpless prisoner under your charge; but I did not know that these acts gave you authority to arrest me, or my companion, on the highway. Where is your warrant?"

"Oh!" replied Campbell, drawing a pistol from his holster, "it is seldom that I am unprepared with a sufficient warrant for the arrest of a traitor and a spy."

Quick as lightning, Raoul thrust a hand in his bosom—in a moment a loud report shook the morning air, and Robert Campbell fell without a groan to the ground. The ball had touched his heart. Almost at the same time Burr's pistol was discharged, desperately wounding another of the dragoons. The remaining one seeing how it had fared with his comrades, hastily returned the fire, and, wheeling his horse, betook himself to flight. Two shots were discharged after him, by one of which his horse was so badly wounded that, at the distance of one hundred yards, he stumbled and fell.

"That will do," said Raoul, coolly drawing on his gloves. "Before he can procure assistance and put an-

other pack of blood-hounds on our trail we shall be far
enough beyond danger from pursuit."

It turned out as he predicted, and the remainder of the
journey was unvaried by accident or adventure. Entering Montreal, Burr proceeded directly to the headquarters of General Montgomery, to make his report. That
gallant officer, charmed by the address and daring of the
young volunteer, conferred upon him the military rank of
captain, and assigned him a place on his own staff.

That the reader may clearly understand the events just
narrated, it may be necessary to explain that when Raoul
Audigier drove off from the inn door at Three Rivers, he
was mistaken in supposing that he had not been recognized
by his old enemy, Captain Campbell. It is true, that individual could not at the moment recall his name, or the time
and place where they had met; but both the face and the
voice were familiar to him, and he kept thinking and taxing his memory until the truth flashed upon him. By that
time Raoul and Burr were safe in the convent. Now Captain Campbell had very little respect for either priests or
convents, and would not have hesitated to make an arrest
at the altar's foot, if the orders from his superiors had not
been distinct and positive, that no indignity whatever should
be offered to any of the religious communities, and that
great care should be observed not to offend the Catholic
population, and thus give them a pretext for joining in the
formidable rebellion which had broken out in the other
colonies of British America. He was satisfied that Raoul
was employed upon some errand hostile to English supremacy, and fully believed that his companion was one of
those emissaries who, it was reported, had been sent out by
the Continental Congress to persuade the Canadians to
unite with them in throwing off the yoke of the mother
country. So thinking, he placed a watch on the roads, and

also succeeded in bribing one of the servitors of the convent to bring him all the information he could gather. This was little enough. Burr was careful to keep the object of his journey, and the place of his destination, a secret from all but the Superior, and, as the time of his starting was wholly uncertain, all that the traitor could do was to promise that he would immediately communicate to Captain Campbell any suspicious circumstances that came to his knowledge. Accordingly, when Burr and Raoul departed from the convent, he sought his employer at the inn, where he found him snoring comfortably in bed. By the time he was aroused, and four troopers (all that he could immediately muster) were mounted, two good hours were lost. This made it necessary to press the horses so hard that before he came in sight of the fugitives two of them were completely blown.

Robert Campbell, though little better than a ruffian in heart or manners, was a man of dauntless courage, who had fought his way up from the grade of a private soldier to his present rank. He was accustomed to overcome difficulties, and to pay little attention to odds or danger in the discharge of his duties. The loss of one-half his force had no other effect than to excite him to fury. Uttering bitter maledictions on the clumsy brutes, and bestowing some hearty curses on the men themselves, who he charged with neglecting the proper care of their horses, he continued the pursuit at the head of the remaining two, as indeed he would have done alone, if they also had given out. In sight of the wagon in which Burr and the guide were traveling, he issued stern orders to kill Raoul at the first show of resistance, adding,—

"If he is out on a treasonable errand he will be certain to show fight. I know him of old."

Nothing but the prompt tactics of the pursued saved

them from the imminent danger, and enabled Burr to deliver his message to Montgomery, in Montreal.

On the reception of that message, the dauntless Irishman, undismayed by the excessive cold and the blinding snow-storms of the season, put his army in motion, and, by a succession of forced marches, in a few days joined Arnold before Quebec. His young aid-de-camp had been daily gaining ground in his confidence and esteem. His untiring watchfulness, patient endurance, and exact performance of every duty assigned him, completely won the heart of his experienced commander, and at the first council of war held after his junction with Arnold, Burr was present by express invitation of the general. That council led to results that will long be remembered in the annals of America. It was determined to take the city by assault, and Aaron Burr, at his own request, was appointed to the command of the forlorn hope.

Under his supervision, ladders were made for the "stormers," and the men, fully armed and equipped, were exercised in ascending and descending these ladders, until they were able to execute the maneuver in perfect order and with the greatest celerity. Each night Burr went himself to inspect the fortifications and examine the ground over which it had been determined to make the approach. So incessant was his activity, that it became a common saying among the soldiers that "little Burr" never slept. Unfortunately, from some cause, the original plan of attack was changed, and on the night of the 31st of December, 1775, Montgomery formed his troops, now reduced from fatigue and exposure to nine hundred men, in four divisions, for the final assault. Two of these were not expected to do more than distract the enemy's attention. The third was led by Arnold. The general, in opposition to the wishes and against the earnest remonstrances of his officers, insisted

5

on commanding the fourth division in person. At four
o'clock on the morning of the first of January, the order
was given to advance, and the columns moved forward in
the midst of a snow-storm of unexampled severity. Montgomery marched in front, accompanied by his staff, and
Raoul Audigier as guide. The British were slumbering
in fancied security. The movement of the Americans had
been conducted so noiselessly that no one inside the fortifications dreamed of their approach. The first row of pickets
was cleared away—still no alarm was given. They neared
the second row and began to remove these also, before the
guard became aware of their presence. A hasty fire, that
did no damage to the assailants, was followed by the flight
of the guard; and now, elated by the seeming certainty of
success, Montgomery raised the exulting shout—"Quebec
is ours." • But, alas! in this world the veriest accident,
the most trivial obstacle, not unfrequently changes the destinies of men and nations! Huge masses of ice blocked
up the narrow gorge through which they were advancing,
and in removing these obstructions priceless minutes were
lost. Behind the second row of pickets there was a square
block-house defended by two twelve-pounders. In the confusion of their first surprise, the British soldiers fled from
the block-house without waiting to try the effect of their
cannon on the advancing column. The delay occasioned
by the necessity of removing the masses of ice gave a sailor
time to observe that they were unpursued. Returning to
ascertain the cause, he reached the block-house just as the
Americans were beginning again to advance. Before betaking himself a second time to flight, he touched off one
of the heavily-loaded pieces. Fiercely through the night
air hissed the destroying grape-shot! Forward fell the tall
form of Montgomery, and down sank two of his aids by
his side! Crimson stains were scattered over the white

shroud that covered the earth, and dying groans added their horrors to the wailings of the winter storm! That iron shower, sent forth by a trembling hand, aimless, and without a defined object, had performed a fearful work! Every man who had led the advance, except Burr and the guide, was either dead, or soon to be so. Appalled at the havoc before them, the troops, who were for the most part raw and inexperienced, stopped and hesitated. In vain Burr shouted to them to come on. In vain he urged, entreated, and implored. In vain he assured them that one effort—one vigorous charge would surely carry the place. What, they argued, could a boy like him know of war and its chances. Their general was dead : there was no other chieftain present in whom they had confidence. From doubt they sunk to fear, and fled disgracefully from the bloody scene. Alas! if Arnold had been there to excite them by his sublime fury, and shame them by his desperate example, how different might have been his own fate! How changed the destiny of Canada! But he, the hero then, albeit the traitor afterwards, was thundering against an impregnable height on another side of the town, and chafing like a lioness deprived of her whelps, because, with mortal means, he could not accomplish a feat beyond any mortal strength.

Raoul Audigier was nearly choked by feelings of bitter contempt as he marked the hesitation, and then the hasty retreat of the Americans. To him it was perfectly apparent that one determined charge was all that was needed to win the mighty prize they were throwing away in their cowardly panic. He knew the ground and the defences well, having served in the garrison when it was occupied by the French, and was pursuaded that the remaining difficulties were light in comparison with those that had been overcome. Ten minutes before his heart was beating

proudly in anticipation of tearing down the hated flag of
England from its lofty eminence.   Now this confident hope
was rudely crushed at the very moment he believed its real-
ization inevitable, and to his utter amazement he witnessed
the terror-stricken flight of armed men from a victory already won.   In a tone of mingled sarcasm and irony, he
addressed himself to the only companion who had not deserted him,—

"You and I might take this fortress, captain, but I doubt
our ability to hold it.   There is no alternative, I believe,
save to follow the example of your gallant countrymen."

It was indeed high time to beat a retreat.   The British
had returned to the block-house, and opened a heavy fire
on the fugitives.   Burr, unwilling to leave his bleeding
commander to the insults of the foe, lifted the dead hero in
his arms, and trudged along through the deep snow with his
glorious burden.   Close upon his heels passed the fierce
pursuers, but he clung to that inanimate body as the
mother clings to her sucking babe, until his strength was
exhausted and he literally sunk beneath its weight.

The hopes of the morning had been fearfully blasted,
and throughout that day dismay reigned over the American camp.   Arnold was wounded, and his men repulsed on
the other side of the town.   In every quarter disaster had
befallen them, and the baffled troops shook off the restraints
of discipline, and gathered in gloomy knots to discuss and
lament their losses.

The contemptuous opinion Raoul Andigier had formed
of the republican soldiers was not improved by the demor-
alization that followed their repulse.   Toward evening
he approached the tent of Burr.

"I have come," he said, "to bid you good-by, captain,
and to wish you higher honors than you are likely to win
while associated with the rabble gang about you."

"This is sudden, and unexpected," answered Burr. "I hoped that you would remain with us to the end."

"So I hoped myself, captain; but it cannot be. One night's experience of the mettle of your troops is enough for an old soldier like me. It is difficult at my age to learn new lessons, and I don't think I could make much progress in the art of running away—an art in which your soldiers have attained a degree of proficiency I have no ambition to equal. In the next battle I should almost certainly be killed. In a good cause and to subserve a useful end, that is a fate at which I should not murmur; but I object very seriously to being called to the judgment bar in the company of men whose wounds were all taken behind."

It was to no purpose Burr attempted to explain that the flight of the Americans could not justly be attributed to any want of personal courage or devotion to the cause; that it was one of those sudden and unaccountable panics by which all new levies are liable to be afflicted, and for which there was much excuse in the fall of their general, and the absence of any commanding spirit to take his place. He insisted that the same men would, the next day, march up the same gorge, and brave five times the danger freely and fearlessly, under Arnold's lead.

"I hope so, captain; and for your sake I will try to believe it. Still, there is no inducement for me to remain. When last night's story is told, you may have well-wishers, but you will have no partisans among our people. It is this that stings so deeply, whenever I think of that dastardly flight. If I had not witnessed it myself, I could not have believed that men with beards upon their chins could behave so wretchedly. Why, a band of peasants, carrying no other weapons than flails and pitchforks, might have exterminated the garrison, so completely were they taken by surprise. As it is, whatever success may attend you elsewhere, the fate of Canada is sealed. God bless you!" he continued, extending his hand. "I know *you* to be a soldier, and a brave one. I grieve that I am not able to say as much for your comrades. I shall seek the convent of Father Pierre, and, if the prayers of a good man may avail you anything, I doubt not that his will follow you wherever you go."

Burr grasped his offered hand.

"Good-by," he said, "my brave and faithful friend. I respect your feelings too much to complain of the bitterness of your language. When next you hear of me, I trust the tidings will be of happier import."

The command of the united forces devolved on Arnold, and for weeks he lingered about Quebec, watching an opportunity to strike another blow, and retrieve the losses he had sustained. One of his first acts was to confer upon Aaron Burr the appointment of brigade-major—a distinction he had so fairly won that it excited no murmur of discontent from those over whom he had been preferred. Indeed, from every quarter the young officer was reaping a harvest of golden opinions. At that period of the American Revolution, there was not one whose prospects were brighter; not one whose name was more frequently on the lips of the brave and the fair. Had Montgomery lived, there is no doubt that chivalrous soldier would have exerted his great influence to procure for his favorite a commission equal to his merits. But, alas! the hero-chief had offered up his life as a sacrifice on the altar of liberty, and the voice, so potent once, was hushed in death! Appearances are as often deceptive in the career of a soldier as elsewhere. At first it seemed that the death of the general, by spreading the renown, smoothed the way to the advancement of the aid-de-camp. It was known that he was in the front rank, by Montgomery's side when he fell.

It was known that he was the last in the retreat, and that
he had borne along with him the body of his commander,
notwithstanding the enemy were close at his heels.   This
crowning act gave a wider circulation to the story of his
other achievements, and the general judgment marked him
as a man eminently fitted for a leader in the trying times to
come.   The popular opinion thus freely expressed did not
fail to reach his ears, and give a brighter color to his hopes.
Alas! how little did he dream, in the intoxication of that
first draught from the fountain of fame, how many bitter
struggles, how many grievous disappointments, how many
gnawing cares, were before him!   The malignant demons
who crouched, grinning, along the pathway of coming
years, were hidden from his mental vision.   The warm sun
of May poured its radiant beams around him.   The fierce
tempests of December were unrevealed and uncared for.
There was before him no magic mirror on whose polished
surface appeared an old man, bent and broken by sorrow,
hunted down by unscrupulous power, stung by its reptile
minions, wandering an exile in a foreign land, subjected to
the capricious tyranny of a despot, his rights as an American citizen denied, and suffering even for the bread necessary to sustain existence.   He did not foresee that a day
would come when an American Consul, backed by an
American Minister, would refuse him the poor boon of a
passport to return to the graves of his ancestors, upon the
miserable pretext that he, the Soldier, the Lawyer, the
Senator, and lastly the Vice-President of the Republic,
was a fugitive from its justice!   The ambitious Greek, who
won an immortality of infamy by burning the temple at
Ephesus, has been outdone in later times.   His crime was
untinctured with meanness.   If it exhibits no other redeem-
ing quality, it was at least daring in its sacrilege.   He
aimed no dastard blow at a powerless man, and offered no

insult to the misfortunes of one he dared not look in the face when his hands were untied. This was crawling down to a depth of degradation that was reserved for Alexander McRae and Jonathan Russell alone—names that will be execrated by the just and manly when that of Erostratus is forgotten.

CHAPTER IV.

"Thus lived, thus died she: never more on her
Shall sorrow light, or shame. She was not made
Through years or moons the inner weight to bear,
Which colder hearts endure till they are laid
By age in earth; her days and pleasures were
Brief, but delightful, such as had not stayed
Long with her destiny; but she sleeps well
By the sea-shore, whereon she loved to dwell."

THE failure of the assault on Quebec made the retreat
of the American forces inevitable. Arnold, hoping against
hope, delayed the movement to the latest moment of safety.
Spring was approaching, and with it a powerful army for
the relief of the garrison. He could wait no longer. At
Montreal he halted to rest and recruit his men. Here
Aaron Burr determined to return immediately to the field
of active service at home, and here he formed the acquaintance of a lady, who, by one of those mysterious dispensa-
tions which we first wonder at, and then dismiss from our
minds as incomprehensible, became the innocent cause of
every calamity that saddened his after life. At this time
she was on a visit to her relatives in Canada. The breaking out of the Revolution had found her there, and the
hostile disposition of the Indians had hitherto prevented
her from attempting to return. Learning that Major
Burr, at the head of some discharged soldiers, was about
leaving Montreal for New York, she eagerly availed
herself of this opportunity to return to her home. Thus
began an intimacy which brought many sorrows to
one, and terminated in the madness of the other. Just
eighteen years of age, beautiful as Helen when she first

(57)

listened to the whispered tale of Menelaus; enriched by
many accomplishments, and possessed of an intellect to
which the term genius most appropriately applies, it
would have been natural enough for the young soldier to
have surrendered heart and mind to the lovely being under
his charge. That he did not, may be attributed partly to
the absence of that inexplicable sympathy that all of us
have felt and none of us are able to describe; and partly
to the fact that his country had just entered upon a war
of uncertain duration and equally uncertain results. The
next year, or the next month, according to the chances of
battle, might crown him a victor or conduct him to a
felon's doom. At such a time his thoughts were upon
bloody fields, not bridal raptures; upon iron chains, not
rosy fetters. The hoarse drum and the piercing fife
echoed in his ears; not the soft lute or the melting lyre.
The spells of beauty were counteracted by the incanta-
tions of patriotism, and the dangerous association awakened no emotion stronger than friendship. Not so with
her. Young, ardent, full of hope and health and fervent
passion, she raised the fiery goblet to her lips and drained
it to the dregs. Adelaide Clifton loved; loved as they
love for whom the wide earth has no enjoyment that does
not center in the worshiped idol. That miserable compound of animal appetite, mental weakness, and childish
vanity, so often misnamed love, came not near the clear
mind and strong heart of the gifted girl. She loved
Aaron Burr, not because he told her she was beautiful;
not because he had pleased her vanity, and excited a kind
of sickly gratitude by extravagant eulogies of her many
perfections; but because he was eminently endowed with
those high qualities which make their way to the heart
through the brain, and win esteem before they ask a more
tender regard. To a mind matured beyond his years, he

added the chivalrous bearing, the manly self-reliance, the
exquisite polish, and the habitual deference for the fairer
sex, of a knight of the olden time. To be intimately associated with such a man, and to become, on their rough
journey, the recipient of these delicate attentions that so
plainly distinguish the man and the gentleman from the
brute or the fop, was a trial beyond her strength, and she
discovered, almost without knowing how, that her heart had
gone out from her keeping. Yet her sense of maiden delicacy was so strong, and her secret was so carefully guarded,
that he, with all his tact, with all his precocious knowledge
of human nature, never suspected her of cherishing a feeling that might become dangerous to her peace. Still less
did he imagine that in a few brief months his name would
be associated with hers in a tale of calumny that has come
down to the present day, and is still occasionally repro-
duced by good-natured newspaper editors, from a commendable desire to gratify the public appetite for scandal.
Conscious of having said nothing, and done nothing, that
a courteous gentleman ought to have left unsaid or undone, he could not see the necessity of dropping the
acquaintance of an intelligent friend, because she happened to be also a beautiful woman. Accordingly, upon
the termination of their journey, he continued to visit her
almost daily, and thus gave color to the accusations that
in a short time blackened her character, and attached a
dishonorable brand to his own good name.

On his arrival in New York, Major Burr repaired to
the headquarters of the commander-in-chief, where he had
been previously informed a staff appointment awaited him.
His good conduct on the march through the wilderness,
and the dauntless courage he had subsequently manifested
under the walls of Quebec, had not escaped the attention
of that illustrious man, and the young soldier was promptly

rewarded by the tender of a situation in the general's own
military family. Thus far the success or failure of our
hero had depended upon himself alone. Thus far he had
encountered none but generous rivalries. Henceforth he
was fated to become the subject of envious intrigues and
malignant calumnies, to which there never was a man
whose character and temper made him a more unresisting
victim. Looking down with a lofty scorn both upon the
intriguer and the slanderer, he forgot that creeping things
are sometimes deadly, and permitted the reptiles that had
stung him to crawl away unharmed. Silence was the only
weapon he ever opposed to the most venomous secret assault,—a silence which, however it may illustrate the
grand proportions of his nature, was yet fatal to his character, and deadly in its effects upon his worldly prosperity. More than mortal in his endurance, he paid the
penalty that all must pay for surpassing their kind. Reasoning from their own fretful impatience under unjust
accusation, and judging others by themselves, the large
majority of mankind are apt to conclude that a calumny
unrepelled must be true, and to their minds silence only
proves the absence of available defense. It is not until
the victim has passed away, and much of passion and of
prejudice has died with him, that we begin to understand
how it is possible for a proud man, conscious of rectitude,
and despising from his inmost soul the loathsome character of his assailants, had rather take the chances of an
unjust condemnation than submit to the degrading necessity of establishing by proof his innocence of infamy.

These were the alternatives presented to Aaron Burr.
He chose the latter—unwisely many will say—but whether
wisely or unwisely, it was the conclusion of a mind never
thrown from its balance, and a heart that was never, in
its most unguarded moment, betrayed into littleness. If

he had known who was his enemy, who was the life and
soul of the conspiracy, it might have been different, since
it is certain that he could have had no excuse for a contemptuous disregard of assaults from such a quarter.
The name of that enemy—that rival—has since become
inseparably blended with the history of a continent. A
West Indian by birth, a soldier by nature, possessing
talents of the highest order, a commanding person, and
a most agreeable address, there was no station to which
he might not aspire, as there was unquestionably none to
which his attainments were not equal. Happy would it
be for his own fame, and happier still for others with whom
he was associated, if the pen of history could rest here.
But with that brilliant intellect and manly bearing, was
blended a moral baseness that charity has no mantle broad
enough to cover. With him, every aim, every object, every
aspiration of life centered in self. A soldier of liberty, he
fought not to establish human rights, but to gather laurels
for his own insatiate brow. The intimate friend of General Charles Lee, he deserted and betrayed him upon the
first appearance of a cloud above his horizon. Indebted
to George Washington for a thousand favors, he complained in private of the asperities of his temper, and
questioned his justice. The avowed partisan of John
Adams during his presidency, he yet denounced him in his
private correspondence as "unfit and incapable," and
habitually spoke of him to leading Federalists in terms of
harsh injustice. Boasting of his chivalry, he did not hesitate to pollute the marriage bed, and add to the crime of
debauchery the despicable infamy of betraying the woman
who had trusted him. Whatever might have been her
guilt,

"Her treachery was truth to him;"

6

and when he rewarded her erring affection by pointing her
out as a mark for the public scorn, he became himself an
object too low for scorn to reach.   Jealous, vindictive,
unscrupulous; ready to employ any means, however vile,
or resort to any artifice, however disreputable, Alexander
Hamilton was a man whose enmity it was dangerous to
excite, whose friendship it was equally dangerous to trust.
Aaron Burr was already regarded by him as a formidable
rival in the race for glory, and this was sufficient of itself
to gain his enmity, and insure his detraction.   To this
was soon added the revengeful venom of a rivalry of another kind.   At the house of a friend he accidentally met
Adelaide Clifton.   His judgment was taken captive by
the brilliancy of her conversation, and his West Indian
blood was turned to fire by her extraordinary beauty.
The acquaintance thus formed was not permitted to lan-
guish.   Every moment of relaxation from his military
duties was devoted to her.   Day after day he was by her
side.   Day after day he exerted to the utmost those fas-
cinating powers that he had as yet found no woman able
to resist.   That she was pleased with his society, and flat-
tered by his attentions, admitted of no question, and her
practiced wooer spared no exertion to improve the favorable position he had gained.   Quietly and artfully he had
extracted from her a knowledge of her tastes, and her
favorite pursuits; of the books she read, the authors she
most admired; the virtues most esteemed, and the vices
most abhorred.   With the hand of a master he touched
the chords on which she had unconsciously taught him to
play.   The evident pleasure and the close attention with
which she listened, raised flattering hopes in his bosom;
and, ignorant that her heart was anothers, he exulted in
the conviction that every hour brought him nearer to the
accomplishment of his purpose.   What was that purpose?

Honorable marriage? Oh, no! He had learned, by dili-
gent inquiry, that she was comparatively poor, and destitute of influential friends. It did not suit his ambitious
schemes to link himself, at such a time, to one who would
be a clog upon his advancement; or, if not an absolute
hinderance, at least incapable of pushing him up the ascent
he was beginning to climb. Yet while his ambition controlled his passion so far as to deprive it of all honorable
aims, it diminished none of its fiery intensity, and only
served to divert it into the channels of criminal gratification.

Weeks passed away. In the year 1776, there were
in the City of New York such things as gardens, and
flowers, and shady walks, in places that have since been
converted into the dusty thoroughfares of commerce.

Latterly, Alexander Hamilton had impatiently watched
for an opportunity to declare the passion that consumed
him, and his very soul was burning to hear the blushing
avowal of its return, that he doubted not would follow.

The opportunity he had longed for came at length, under
circumstances as favorable as he could desire. The hour
was twilight—the time the dreamy month of May, when
the heart is always full, and the blood dances gladly through
the throbbing veins. The broad moon had just risen above
the horizon, bathing spire and cupola in its mellow rays—
mingling sweetly with the opening bud and the blooming
flower, and clothing in robes of richer beauty the green
turf on which it rested. Seated in a bower of fragrant
honeysuckles, Adelaide Clifton was listening in rapt attention to the music of his eloquence. Turning from the
scenes about him, he transported her to the sea-girt isle in
which his infant eyes had first opened to the light of day,
and the happiest years of his youth flew over on sinless
wings. He painted for her a clime where frosts never
come, and the year knows no changes, except from the

balmy spring to the glorious summer; where the green
tree never sheds its leaves, and the rose that drops from its
stem, scorched and withered at noonday, is replaced before
morning by another, sweeter and lovelier, that the dews
of night have nourished into life; where the plumage of
the birds that throng the deep woods, and feast on the
luscious fruits of the tropics, are variegated as the rainbow,
and the rich music of their songs swells like a choral anthem
from the spirit-land; where the maiden slumbers by bubbling
fountains, in gardens of perfume, until the evening shadows
have relieved the fiery sun, and the moon and the stars in-
vite her forth to revel in the glorious beauties of heaven and
dream of the wilder raptures of earth! All the pictures
his memory supplied of that luxurious clime, were placed
before her. Nor did he pause here. He knew the power of
sympathy over the female heart, and gradually led his willing
listener among the varied scenes that had grown familiar
to him in his adventurous life. He described the sea when
the tempest was unchained, and the strong bark shivered,
and the stout mast reeled and cracked at the whirlwind's
breath. He told her of nights upon the trackless deep,
when the heavens were hung with black, and not a star
looked down upon the inky flood; of the wild roar of the
breakers as the doomed vessel dashed among their foamy
crests; of the despairing cries of the struggling victims;
and finally, of the delirious joy of the fortunate few whom
the waves had thrown, stunned and bruised, upon the sandy
beach!

The genuine pathos of his narrative was heightened by
its truth, and its effect was the more marked because he
painted nothing that he had not seen, and gave voice to no
emotion that he had not felt. A stray moonbeam had
stolen through the trellised vines and rested on the cheek
of Adelaide Clifton. By its light Hamilton saw that

she was in tears—tears for his sufferings, his perils, his escape.

"How little do we know," he went on, without seeming to notice them, "the changes that are before us! Eighteen years had not darkened the down on my lip when I exchanged the dreamy isle for the boisterous ocean; the luxurious couch for the hard bed on the rocky shore. Other changes also came; and now, at an age when the boy is scarcely merged in the man, the merchant's pen is thrown aside for the warrior's arms. Perhaps the next change will stretch me upon a bloody field, over which the gorged vulture flaps his lazy wing. All beyond to-morrow is unknown. Of one thing only can we be always sure. Future joys may glide away like the cooling waters that rose to the lips of Tantalus, whenever we attempt to taste them; but the *present* is ours. Ours, not only in the enjoyments it offers to-day, but in the memories it sends with us to gladden the coming time. Grief and pain, sickness and wounds, are robbed of their bitterness when there is one blessed hour upon which we can look back and feel that it is beyond the power of fate to deprive us of the raptures it brought."

"It may be as you say, Captain Hamilton," she replied; "but what are they to do for whom the past has no raptures?—whose eyes, turned back upon the vista of years, rest only upon images of sorrow?"

"To one whose years had really been so saddened, I would say,—look forward, forward evermore, and conquer the gloom of yesterday by anticipating the brightness of to-morrow. But why do you ask? The question can be of no interest to you."

"More," was the mournful rejoinder, "much more than you, perhaps, imagine."

6*

Then, as if afraid of having disclosed more than she wished to reveal, she added,—

"Just now you yourself painted the future as unknown and uncertain. What right have I to claim exemption from the common lot? Why to me, more than others, should the sunshine come unmingled with tears?"

"Because you are better, and fairer, and lovelier. Because the Creator permitted you to stray from your home among the angels, in mercy, not in anger. Because you came to chase away the bitterness of earth, not to partake of its sufferings."

"Captain Hamilton," she replied, "must pardon me for doubting the soundness of an argument which he found it necessary to clothe in such extravagance of flattery."

"Flattery!" he exclaimed. "Oh, Adelaide! it is not unfrequently the curse of men who feel as I do, to have the feeblest expression of their sentiments mistaken for the language of compliment. Flattery! Great God! Does the Persian dream of flattering the Sun when he kneels before his fire-crowned altar, and, in the gorgeous poesy of the East, hymns the praises of his burning idol? Yet in what Persian breast ever throbbed a wilder idolatry than mine? From the first moment I beheld you, my soul went out from my keeping. I did not love; no, Adelaide, I worshiped! And when I wished to tell you of it—when, again and again, the strong impulse was upon me to ask you to listen, I paused and hesitated, because it seemed to me that language had no words to syllable the intensity of that adoration. Even now," he continued, taking her hand in his, "I am tortured by the dark fear that I have but poorly made you comprehend how entirely every thought, and feeling, and desire, save one, have been swallowed up. How completely one word of yours will bless, how hope-

lessly one other word will blast, the morning of my existence."

The hand he had seized remained for a moment in his
clasp. The fragile form of the lovely girl shrunk and shivered like the aspen when the north wind is blowing. A
flood of tears came to her relief; and, snatching her hand
hastily away, she exclaimed, in tones of earnest, deep, and
strong emotion,—

"Forgive me! oh, forgive me, Captain Hamilton! for,
as Heaven is my witness, I never dreamed of this. I do
not—cannot love you; and if I have done anything to
encourage your hopes, I have been deeply criminal. Pity
me, and forgive me!"

"There is nothing to forgive, Adelaide. I was a slave
before I had time to think of encouragement. Mine is a
love that would have blossomed alike under cheering smiles
or menacing frowns. It came unbidden—it will abide with
me here; and when the curtain drops upon the stage of
life, it will travel with me through the countless ages of the
world to come. But you are too deeply agitated to listen
further now. In a few days I shall see you again. Until
then, I will try to drive off despair. Good night, and
may the angels send messengers of bliss to people your
dreams!"

What were the feelings of that bold and gifted, though
eminently bad and dangerous man, as he traversed the streets
of the silent city? Stung, wounded, almost maddened, by
the repulse he had met, he walked rapidly on, trying to think,
yet feeling that thought was impossible. Arrived at his
own quarters, he extinguished the light, and threw himself,
dressed as he was, upon the bed.

"At least," he said, when the chaos of his feelings had
assumed some degree of order, "at least I have made no
unnecessary or embarrassing disclosures. She thinks my

purposes were honorable, and, come what may, my character is safe."

From this villainous consolation, he turned to other views of his situation. He ran over in his mind all that had occurred since their first introduction. He recalled every look, and tone, and gesture. He remembered the minutest shade that had passed over her expressive countenance. He taxed his ingenuity to find some plausible ground to hope that perseverance might still be rewarded by success. It was in vain. The earnest truthfulness of her words and manner—her agitation—her unconcealed distress—left no room to believe that the avowal of his passion had excited any feelings but those of unmixed pain.

"How," he inwardly asked, "could I have deceived myself so egregiously? I would have sworn that she was prepared for, and expected a declaration. Surely I have not been such a fool and puppy as to imagine a preference where none existed!"

Captain Hamilton was well aware that the most astute and self-possessed of human beings are not unfrequently enticed into grave errors by that little bewitching demon, Vanity; and therefore he suspected himself of construing mere evidences of friendship into manifestations of a warmer regard. The more he reasoned, the more apparent did it become to him that he had been unwittingly hugging a charming delusion to his bosom. In his mortification at the discovery, he passed to the opposite extreme, and bitterly cursed his own stupid blindness. Captain Hamilton did himself injustice; a fact that we chronicle the more readily, because it was not one to which he was often addicted. Adelaide Clifton did prefer his society to that of the men who were constantly about her, and she had taken no pains to conceal it. A man less under the influence of

passion than he was, and therefore more capable of reasoning clearly, might easily have mistaken the character of the
preference unquestionably exhibited, and have acted upon
that impression without subjecting himself to the suspicion
of inordinate vanity.

The character of Alexander Hamilton was too strong
and decided to admit of long indulgence in unavailing reproaches. He did not yet despair of eventual success, and
his thoughts were occupied in endeavoring to devise some
means of extracting a triumph from apparent defeat. He
was conscious that a renewal of his suit at present would
be useless; but he knew the value of perseverance, and
hoped that the high opinion she evidently entertained of
his character and acquirements might be improved and
strengthened, until love took the place of friendship, and,
in some unguarded moment, virtue fell a victim to passion.

Morning found him tossing upon a pillow that sleep had
not visited. At daybreak he went forth as usual to attend
to his military duties. He had fixed upon no plan, and
resolved for awhile to trust to the chapter of accidents.
For two days she did not see him. On the third he purposely called at an hour when he was almost certain of
meeting other visitors. He was desirous to avoid the
embarrassment of a *tête-à-tête* at the first interview after
the rejection of his suit, and selected his hour accordingly.
As he hoped and expected, he found that she was not
alone; but her visitor was the last man on earth he desired
to meet in that presence, as he was certainly the one whose
rivalry he most dreaded both in love and in war. Perfectly unconscious of the secret feelings of Hamilton,
Major Burr rose to greet him with easy courtesy, on his
entrance, and exhibited neither surprise nor curiosity at
the embarrassment he could not help remarking in his
manner. Adelaide Clifton was a little flurried and excited,

but Major Burr gave the conversation a direction that put them both at ease.

At this time, and indeed throughout the revolutionary war, the duties of General Washington, his cares and anxieties, were by no means confined to the army. The affairs of a whole continent were on his shoulders, and every important resolution of Congress, upon every conceivable subject, was more or less influenced by his suggestions. Under such circumstances he was necessarily compelled to impose upon his aids a life of incessant labor. No leisure was left them to pay visits of courtesy or friendship, and it thus happened that Hamilton had not heretofore met Major Burr at the house where Miss Clifton was sojourning; nor was he previously aware that there was any acquaintance between them. He now learned for the first time that she had traveled from Canada under his protection. Jealousy is a keen sharpener of the vision. Shakspeare tells us that—

> "Trifles light as air,
> Are to the jealous confirmations strong
> As proofs of holy writ."

And that great master of the human heart might have added, that these trifles are not always wrong indices to the truth. Sometimes they must—very often they may—lead us widely into error; but there are other times when they invest the judgment with the quickness and the certainty of intuition. His thoughts once directed into the right channel, Hamilton perceived what Burr himself had never suspected. The cause of Miss Clifton's extraordinary distress on hearing a declaration of love from his lips was now easily understood. Giving to his rival no higher credit for virtuous self-denial than he was conscious of possessing himself, and believing that the same reasons that prevented him from offering his hand to Adelaide Clifton in lawful marriage would have the same influence over Major Burr, Hamilton persuaded himself that the lovely girl had become a victim to the arts of a seducer, or, if not already degraded, that her ruin could not long be delayed. The wound inflicted by the persuasion of his rival's bad triumph carried along with it a balm. It furnished an excuse for relentless hostility. If anything should occur to expose the vindictiveness of his hatred, he had only to point to the murdered innocence of Adelaide Clifton for his justification. It was not pleasant to have the keen eye of Burr resting upon him while such thoughts filled his mind; and, pleading indispensable business as an excuse, he rose to take his departure. Burr also took his leave; and Hamilton noticed with a pang that while his own adieus were politely returned, she extended her hand to Burr, saying,—

"You are so infrequent a visitor that I must bid you a more earnest good-by."

For nearly the length of a square they walked on together, conversing about the probable movements of the enemy, and agreeing in the opinion that General Washington would soon be compelled to evacuate the city. They separated on terms of apparent cordiality—Burr to return to headquarters, Hamilton to mature the dark scheme that was just beginning to assume a distinct form in his busy brain. A perfect master of the arts of dissimulation, he generally contrived to conceal from the public the terrible passions by which he was often shaken. Few were aware of the malignity habitually cherished by the polished gentleman and the dashing soldier, and none suspected the low intrigues and the vile expedients to which he was capable of resorting to injure an enemy or supplant a rival.

It was not many days after the last meeting between Burr and Miss Clifton, before he perceived that the manners of the commander-in-chief were growing cold and distant. He felt this the more keenly because the position he now held had been in a manner forced upon him. He had been called into the general's military family in opposition to his desires, and had only accepted the appointment on account of the importunities of his friends. The clerkly labors to which so much of his time was devoted were not to his taste. He felt that he had the capacity to perform other and higher services. He panted for a commission in the line, which would give him a wider field for exertion. Still, however distasteful might be his present duties, he was conscious of having discharged them well and faithfully. He could imagine no cause for General Washington's displeasure, and was far too high spirited to make inquiries, or volunteer explanations unasked. By degrees a report gained currency at headquarters that General Washington was seriously offended by the scandal of an amour in which, it was said, one of his staff had borne a disreputable part.

No one was pointed out as the guilty individual, and Burr took no notice of the report. Others did not exhibit a like independence of character. Each one was anxious to exculpate himself, and very soon it was settled that Aaron Burr was the member of the staff to whom allusion was made. His school-boy reputation for gallantry was remembered, and recited with the usual embellishments and exaggerations, and a hundred other circumstances, unimportant in themselves, were so arranged as to give probability to the charge. It was not an offense punishable by military law, and it was probably on that account that the general made no public inquiries. It may be, also, he expected that the accused party, from a desire to retain the good opinion of his commander, would seek an opportunity to exculpate himself if possible, and not wait to be ques-

tioned or formally accused. Judging from what would
have been the conduct of ninety-nine men in a hundred,
this expectation was reasonable. In Burr's case it was unreasonable: first, because he had never heard the accusation until after he had been deeply wounded by the extreme, and to him unaccountable, coldness of the general.
In the second place, if he had heard it, he would have
scorned to enter the lists against an anonymous slanderer,
or engage in the task of repelling charges that could be
traced to no responsible source. Angry and indignant at
being suspected on such testimony, or rather on no testimony, he drew about him a mantle of haughty reserve
which had very much the air of defiance, and was certainly
so construed. His situation was thus rendered so disagreeable that he resolved to leave the army, and wrote
Governor Hancock to that effect.

While things were in this state of quasi hostility between him and the commander-in-chief, he happened to be
present when a communication was received from a com-
mittee of Congress. Burr was standing immediately behind General Washington's chair. Accidentally turning
his head, and observing the position of his aid, the general
suspected that he had been reading the document over his
shoulder, and instantly demanded,—

"How dare you, sir, venture upon the liberty of reading
a paper in my hands?"

Already goaded to the extreme limit of endurance, this
second insulting suspicion was more than the high-spirited
soldier could bear. Drawing up his slender form, and looking his commander full in the face, he sternly replied,—

"When your Excellency puts to me such a question in
such a tone, the only reply that self-respect permits me to
make is, that Aaron Burr *dares* do anything!"

Then, turning on his heel, he sought his own quarters, for

7

the purpose of drawing up and tendering his resignation.
There he found a letter from Governor Hancock, protesting against his leaving the service, and offering to procure
him a more agreeable situation on the staff of General Putnam. Under the circumstances, Governor Hancock's prof-
fer was gladly accepted, and Burr and the commander-in-
chief parted with feelings of mutual dislike that were never
eradicated.

The first blow, and a mighty one, had been struck. Dealt
by an unseen hand, it fell with crushing power on the victim at which it was aimed. Hamilton had accurately calculated, from the known strictness of Washington's principles, that the surest method of bringing down his
displeasure upon any individual was to blacken his moral
character. His own base designs upon Adelaide Clifton
furnished him a hint that he was not slow to improve. It
is probable, also, that he really believed Burr's intercourse
with the fair girl had not been guiltless. But whether
such was his own belief or not, it was the chord he knew
would vibrate most harshly in the bosom of the commander-in-chief; and to that he addressed himself with a skill
that Talleyrand, at a later day, might have envied. Dark
hints and innuendoes were followed by more distinct
charges, and these were supported by an array of circumstances that would have astonished Burr, if he had been
inclined to enter upon a defense of his character. This
course he refused to take, partly from personal pride, and
partly because another was implicated, whose sensibilities
must be deeply wounded by learning that her chastity had
become the subject of public discussion.

This honorable care for the feelings of an outraged woman turned out to be only a temporary mercy. No society
is free from the tale-bearer. Adelaide Clifton was not
long kept in ignorance that her name had become a hissing

and a reproach. Her delicate nerves were shattered by the shock. Reason tottered on its throne, and the lovely and innocent one was borne back to her home a raving maniac. In the paroxysms of her delirium, her burning love for Aaron Burr found utterance. Sometimes she would imagine he was seated by her side, and for hours she would lavish endearing caresses upon some object that she had mistaken for the idol madness had no power to drive from her bosom. Then again, when fancy changed the picture, and he appeared to her distempered mind cold or unfaithful, agonizing sobs would choke her utterance, and scalding tears blister her faded cheeks. Now she saw him returning victorious from the battle-field, and proud and lofty were the words that welcomed the coming of her glorious hero. Now she was straying with him beneath the mighty elms where she had played in childhood, and recalling all the innocent memories that made it holy ground to her. At last a sadder vision settled permanently on her mind: she imagined that he had been struck down in his early youth, that she could see the crimson stains upon the white shroud that covered him, and busied herself in washing out the sorrowful tokens. They tore her away from the stone bench she had mistaken for a death-couch, and tried in vain to dispel the illusion. Whenever their vigilance relaxed she flew to that one spot, and throwing herself on her knees pressed a thousand kisses on its cold and senseless surface. Refusing all sustenance, she gradually wasted away, until Death, in mercy, touched her with his icy dart.

Not one word did she utter in her ravings to inculpate Burr; yet the devilish ingenuity of malice seized upon her most innocent avowals of affection, and tortured them into damning evidence of his guilt. The dreadful wrong, which had blighted the reason and withered the frame of

one of the loveliest of her sex, drew from the ruin it had
wrought new weapons for future mischief.   The dark penalty of crime fell upon the innocent.   The guilty contriver,
the unprincipled intriguer who had created this waste of
wretchedness, was unsuspected, and went unpunished, so far
as human penalties extend.

CHAPTER V.

"The devil sits in his easy chair,
  Sipping his sulphur tea;
And gazing out with a pensive air,
  Over the broad bitumen sea."

On the staff of General Putnam, Aaron Burr was relieved from the voluminous correspondence that had proved so irksome while in the family of the commander-in-chief. Here he found leisure to devote several hours each day to the study of the military profession, at the same time that his duties in the field were sufficiently active to enable him to turn to practical account the lessons he had learned in the closet. Here, too, he enjoyed a season of comparative repose from the long struggle with calumny that darkened his career from early manhood to the grave. Honored by the warm friendship and unbounded confidence of his hero-chief, even envy shrunk from the exhibition of its spleen, and cautious malice paused in the prosecution of its dark designs. But the venom of the viper remained, though its power to wound was suspended. Sleepless eyes were upon him. His acts were stored away in retentive memories, to be drawn out and distorted by practiced ingenuity, when the motives that governed and the circumstances that justified them had become dim and obscure by the lapse of time. Whether he was at that day aware of the persevering hate that dogged his steps, no one ever knew. Throughout his whole life he carefully avoided an exposure of his own wounds, and, like the Spartan youth who permitted the fox, concealed beneath his garments, to gnaw out his vitals, he drew over each

7* (77)

festering sore a mantle, which hid it alike from the
pitying gaze of friends and the triumphant glance of enemies. In the many trials through which he passed, no
opponent ever had the satisfaction of seeing him writhe
or hearing him groan. During the first years of the
Revolution, his time and thoughts were so fully and so
absorbingly occupied that it is probable he was unsuspi-
cious of any malign influences working for his destruction.
Those influences were never at rest. In the very midst
of the momentous events that crowded the arena toward
the close of 1776, new plans were formed and new con-
spiracies were hatched.   ·

The disastrous affair of the 27th of August was over, and
the Americans, hemmed in, in the city and island of New
York, were daily expecting an attack. The month of September had set in cold and dreary, and the leaden sky accorded well with the cheerless city it overhung. In the
obscurity of twilight, two men were silently moving along the
"Broad Way" (as it was then called) of the City of New
York. Early as the hour was, the regulations rendered
necessary by the presence of an army expecting an assault,
together with the unseasonable severity of the weather, kept
the good people of Gotham within doors, and scarcely a
sound was heard along the almost deserted street, save the
occasional tramp of a patrol of soldiers, or the clatter of
horses' hoofs, as some aid or orderly dashed along with orders for the different posts. Our pedestrians walked rapidly
on, hardly interchanging a syllable, until they arrived at
a hotel of some pretensions, and were ushered into an
apartment prepared in anticipation of their coming. One
of them was a tall man of forty or forty-five years of age,
rather spare made, but muscular and wiry. His forehead
was broad and massive, eyes dark gray, mouth large, and
lips firmly compressed. There was an air of power about

the whole appearance of the man. You felt that you were in the presence of one who had a head to conceive, a will to dare, and a hand to execute, whatever his interest or his ambition might prompt. The other was Alexander Hamilton. Directing some bottles of wine to be brought, the elder of the two dismissed the obsequious host, and both of them drew chairs to the fire, that was burning in comfortable contrast to the chilly dampness without. Hamilton was the first to speak.

"Well, Billings," he inquired, "what news do you bring?"

"Bad enough, Captain Hamilton; the girl is dead."

"Dead!" exclaimed Hamilton, starting to his feet, and grasping the arm of his companion with convulsive force. "Dead! Is this true? for, mark me, man, it would be safer to put your head in the hungry lion's mouth, than to trifle with me on such a subject."

"I have not been in the habit," replied the other, his hand slowly stealing beneath the folds of his vest, as if there was something there to which his grasp was accustomed, and which he desired to clutch, more from habit than from a belief that it would be necessary to use it,— "I have not been in the habit of calculating very nicely what might be safe or unsafe, in my dealings with the world; nor am I much addicted to answering rude questions while a ruder grasp is on my arm."

"This is folly!" muttered Hamilton, releasing his hold. "I mean you no bodily injury. That pistol in your bosom would be a poor protection if I did."

"May be so; and I have certainly no wish to put it to the test, though it has never failed me heretofore, and I have no fears that it will fail me hereafter."

Hamilton resumed his seat in silence. Large drops of perspiration gathered upon his brow, his lip quivered,

and his whole frame was convulsed by terrible emotions.
The fierce struggle endured for more than a minute, and
his voice was choked and husky, as he asked,—

"Did you say Adelaide Clifton was dead? The young,
the beautiful, the good; gone, gone forever!"

"I told you the truth," was the reply; "but it added
so little to the sweetness of your temper, that I have no
inclination to repeat the story."

There was another self-struggle. It ended, and Alexander Hamilton was master of himself.

"I beg your pardon, Billings; I have been foolish and
intemperate. If you knew all, you would excuse it."

"Possibly I may not know all of your share in the business; but I know more of my own than it is agreeable to
reflect upon in a still night and a lonely place. I know
that you invented the calumny, and that I circulated it;
and although neither of us could foresee the melancholy
result, we are none the less guilty of murder."

"Calumny! I tell you, Billings, that as God is my judge,
I believed it at the time. I believed, too, that the story
would never reach her ears, for I knew that she was about
starting for her home in Connecticut, and I hoped it would
die away except in quarters where we might think proper
to keep it alive."

"Then, Captain Hamilton, you have the advantage of
me decidedly; for I never believed a syllable of it, nor did
I ever doubt but that some kind friend would communicate
to her all that was said, together with whatever additions
were necessary to fill up any little omissions in the pleasing
tale. But this is profitless. The question is not what degree of guilt attaches to either of us, but rather how we
are to turn untoward circumstances to the best account.
Before we begin the discussion, you must pardon the liberty
I am about to take in offering you some advice I am

nearly double your age, and there are few phases of the human character I have not had occasion to study. The first step toward success in life is self-control. Such outbreaks as you have been guilty of to-night are disagreeable to your friends and dangerous to yourself. No man will trust his fortunes in the same boat with yours, if they are continually liable to be upset by ill-governed passions. In the path of ambition you have deliberately chosen, you must command your words, your looks, your actions. You must be able to call a gay smile to your lips when necessary, although the devil is tugging with red-hot pincers at your heart-strings. Avoid self-deception, for of all deceptions it is the least profitable. Look at your acts in the light of their consequences. Weigh those consequences before the act is irrevocable, and not afterwards. If the end to be attained is of sufficient importance to justify the ruin of a dozen honest names, or the breaking of as many gentle hearts—why, ruin or break them; but do it deliberately, and do not fly into a rage with those who may be serviceable, because you are conscious of having been a very naughty boy. Exhibit as much temper as you please; the oftener the better, since it helps to build up a character for frankness; but never exhibit it when you *feel it*, for ninety-nine times in a hundred it will be foolish and imprudent. Genuine feeling is a great drawback, affected feeling a great advantage, to a rising man. Follow this advice implicitly, and there is no eminence you may not hope to attain. History furnishes more than one instance in which a successful soldier, with worse prospects than yours, has won the diadem of a king."

There was much in the cool and villainous counsel of his confederate not altogether unfamiliar to Alexander Hamilton; the concluding sentence, too, pointed to a result that he was beginning to contemplate as possible, and to

cherish with a good deal more pleasure than was becoming
in a republican soldier. Still he was irritated by the tone
of superior wisdom in which it was delivered; and there
was a touch of scorn in his reply, from which he did not
seek to divest it.

"Pray, Mr. Billings, how does it happen that you, who
know so well the paths to success, have yet missed them
so widely?"

"Your question is natural, and the sneer that accompanied it was natural also; though, let me tell you, it was
far from a wise one. It is one of the very indiscretions
against which I have been warning you. A revengeful
man would remember it to your prejudice, and some day do
you a mischief on account of it. I shall only register it
as the second folly of which you have been guilty in the
last half hour. And now, to answer your inquiry, I might
say that I had failed for the want of your genius, your
capacity, or your accomplishments, and your vanity would
accept the explanation. I choose to be more candid. In
my youth, there was no such revolution as this of the colonies in progress, or in contemplation. The opportunities
that you possess were therefore denied to me; and this explanation would be as soothing to my vanity as the other
would be to yours. To another than yourself, it is all that
I would give; but, as I have just warned you against self-
deception, I must not give you occasion to suspect me of
belying my own theory. *I failed, because my knowledge
came after my character was gone.* Put the devil himself upon earth; let it be known that he is the devil, and
he could not mislead a child. At the commencement of
my career, I was in possession of a fair fortune and a fair
character. Both were dissipated in gambling hells, and
other resorts of vice and immorality. What mattered it
that in the mean time I had acquired an amount of knowl-

edge and of self-control that would have been invaluable
a few years earlier! The road to what men call honorable
ambition was barricaded against the broken-down gambler
and debauchee. Instead of a struggle for power and place,
my life became a struggle for bread; and when at last I had
accumulated wealth, the means by which it was acquired
were so questionable, that I did not care to give occasion
for impertinent inquiries by placing my name before the
public. I believe it is not necessary to extend my confession any further, unless you are curious to know my history,
from the period of leaving England up to the time of receiving on board my ship the beautiful quadroon whose
black eyes your respected father erroneously supposed
might prove dangerous to the peace of his hopeful son."

Hamilton writhed like a wounded serpent under this
allusion to his earliest amour.

"Man!" he exclaimed—"man or demon, you try me
too far! If you must talk of the past, give me a history
of your own exploits among the buccaneers?"

There was not the slightest change in the countenance
of the hardened man he addressed; not a quiver in his
voice, as he replied,—

"I do not remember to have seen the name of Billings
in the list of buccaneers; although, like other curious people, I read everything that was published about them. I
suppose, therefore, that your suspicions have originated
from some other circumstance. Will it be taxing your
kindness too much to inquire what it is?"

"No matter," said Hamilton, who had recovered his
composure. "It is no matter. We have both been wrong
in referring to things that had better be forgotten. Let
us now turn to the business that brought us here."

"Very well, if such is your wish; though as it is of interest to me to know how much, and what kind of suspicion

attaches to my name, I shall probably repeat the question
at another time."

An hour glided off; then another, and the two were still
in deep consultation. The drizzling rain without had
changed to a driving tempest, and the wind howled angrily
along the street.

"You will stay here to-night," said Billings, walking to
the window and listening for a moment to the storm.

"No. The British may make an attempt upon the city
at any moment, and I must be at my post. Our business is
arranged, and I can only tarry long enough to take a glass
of wine before I go."

"Your business is arranged, Captain Hamilton, and, to
some extent, mine also. In the future, as in the past, you
find that my co-operation is essential to your success. It
has been freely given, and I trust you will not consider me
unreasonable in desiring to be informed to what circumstance I am indebted for the suspicion of piracy with which
you have honored me."

"You take up a hasty expression too seriously, Billings.
It were better to forget it."

"I am indebted to hasty expressions for getting on the
track of many a truth; and, besides, I know you would not
hazard such an accusation, unless you fully believed you
could prove it."

"In public, certainly I would not; but it was made to
you alone, and at a time when you had pressed sorely on a
very tender place."

"And therefore the more likely to be earnest and sincere.
Come, Captain, let us have the story!"

"I tell you again, Billings, it is better to let it sleep
where it is. Neither you nor I have anything to gain by
raking up the ashes of the past."

"Let us understand each other," replied his comrade, in

a tone of calm but fixed resolution. "I have served you zealously, and propose to serve you still more. Chiefly, I admit, because I believe it my interest to do so. Sometimes I think there is one crazy streak in this usually cloudless brain of mine, and that is the firm belief that you are destined to attain the highest place the new world has to give. Ambition was not crushed in me by the early vices that made its pursuit a folly, and I look forward to the time when you will have honors and titles to bestow, as the period of my own triumph and reward. You hold me, therefore, by a strong chain—but it may be broken. Aaron Burr is not my rival in love, or in war. I have no personal motive to lessen his just fame. I have no wrong to complain of—no revenge to gratify. If the fancy should strike me that my aims might as well be advanced by transferring my services to him, I could crush you in an hour. In what light would you be esteemed by the stern chief who leads your armies, and from whom at present all honor flows, if Carlota's story was whispered in his ears? Or, suppose I should come down to a later day, and draw a picture of a gallant soldier, blackened by calumny, and a gentle maiden driven in madness to the grave, through your contrivances, how would that severely just and upright man reward the conduct of his subordinate? With all his great, and, to me, incomprehensible qualities, he is human at last, and the weight of his displeasure would not be lessened by the reflection that he had been your dupe."

At this point he paused, as if to mark the effect of his words; and Hamilton, striking the table with his clenched hand, fiercely exclaimed,—

"Go on, sir! Let me hear the full extent of your threats!"

"I mean not to threaten; nor do I wish to excite your anger. I only meant to show that perfect confidence be-

8

tween us is essential to the safety of both. When I am certain that you hold in your hands, or believe you do, the secret means of inflicting on me a deadly injury, I may well suspect that you contemplate paying my services in that coin, if my demands should become importunate. This suspicion once fixed, would naturally lead me to strike the first blow, and thus lessen your power, by destroying your character. Remember that I have made no pretensions to disinterested motives, nor would you have believed me if I had. I serve you because I expect to obtain certain desirable objects through you. If you take away that motive—if you lead me to believe that you intend to use, and then discard me, you will not only lose the services of a valuable auxiliary, but gain the determined hostility of a dangerous enemy. I do not think that you have any desire to do either, and I am sure that a little reflection will convince you that it is reasonable and right to give me the information I ask."

The changing features of Alexander Hamilton betrayed the terrific emotions which agitated him, as his merciless ally thus plainly depicted the nature of the bond between them. Anger, doubt, and apprehension chased each other over his mind. Now he was strongly tempted to draw his dagger and silence forever the confederate who was rapidly becoming his master. Indeed, nothing restrained him but the conviction that a murder would as effectually blast his prospects as any revelations Billings could make. He saw clearly enough that violence would do no good—that conciliation must be resorted to—and, humbling as it was to his proud spirit, he commanded his temper so far as to say,—

"Methinks a grave lecturer on worldly wisdom might have remembered that there are more agreeable ways of extracting information from a man than by holding up threats of disgrace as a penalty for silence; and it might have occurred to Mr. Billings, that the bonds of friendship are not strengthened by boasts of our capacity to harm one another."

"From you, Captain Hamilton, I do not ask friendship, as the world understands the word, and I should be practicing a needless hypocrisy if I professed to feel it toward you. We have a more enduring bond of union than the fragile one of friendship. We are necessary to each other; and as we have no antipathies to reconcile, and no cause of quarrel to bring one passion in conflict with another, our alliance ought to be permanent. I respect your intellect, and admire your brilliant qualities. I am well aware that some things I have said this night grated harshly on your ear, and I beg you to believe that it was as disagreeable to me to speak them as to you to listen; but it is no time to deal in dainty phrases, when matters of such moment are under discussion. What I have said was under the impression that it would remove every cause of misunderstanding from our future intercourse. If it was disagreeable, you may afford to bear it, for I assure you it will never be repeated. I am no pertinacious pedagogue, who insists upon beating his lessons into the brains of a pupil, whether he is willing to receive them or not. You understand me, I am sure, and will need no other explanations."

"I think not. You have been sufficiently candid and explicit to prevent misapprehension."

"I so intended. It is always best to have a little rough weather at the beginning of a voyage, than to encounter opposing gales near its close. May I hope that you are about to follow my example?"

"I shall certainly no longer refuse a request so pertinaciously preferred; although it may give you some annoyance, and can be of no profit. At the time you were engaged in traffic between New York and the West Indies, there was one Roland Williams, a porter in our house at St. Croix. Believing the man might be serviceable, I saved him from the consequences of more than one *indiscretion*, for which he paid me with a kind of bull-dog gratitude—that is, he was ready enough to tear any one to pieces at my bidding, though it was by no means sure that his memory of the kindness was strong enough to prevent him from setting his fangs in my own flesh, if irritated too much. When Carlota was carried away in your vessel, I was angry enough to contemplate a deadly revenge, and I sought Williams's aid to carry it into effect. To my surprise he manifested some reluctance, and at length I drew from him that he had been a pirate, and sailed under your orders. Your real name, he said, was Wheeler, and he believed that you had once been an officer in the British army. You never returned to St. Croix during my residence on the island, and before I met you again I had abandoned my purposed vengeance for a thing in which, after all, you might have been blameless. That is all. I have no other proof, and never sought for any more."

"And this Williams, what became of him?"

"I do not know. I left him on the island. Perhaps he is there yet. If it is desirable I can easily learn."

"It is unnecessary. If it should become important hereafter I will trace him up myself. I do not remember the name, and suppose it was an assumed one. It is probable," he continued, "that we may not again have occasion to refer to bygone events; and in order to remove every possible cause of heart-burning, I desire to say that in the matter of Carlota I was not, as you supposed, an agent employed to thwart your wishes. I purchased her on speculation, for two hundred guineas, knowing nothing of your amour at the time. I sold her for three hundred, and the last I heard of her she was happy, and contented with her lot."

The conversation had reached a point where neither seemed disposed to continue it, and, after a few words of commonplace civility, Hamilton left the hotel, to repair to his post. James Billings seated himself before the fire, and, leaning back in his arm-chair, mused long and deeply upon his eventful life. The specters of the past flitted rapidly but distinctly before him. One by one the opportunities he had misapplied, the talents he had wasted, the character he had thrown away, rose up before him; but he neither quailed nor trembled at their presence. Hard as iron in his original nature, he had grown harder and more stubborn with advancing years, and looked back not to regret what was lost, but to calculate how much yet remained to be accomplished. No thought of repentance and no twinge of remorse was permitted to sadden the retrospect. Yesterday was to him nothing more than a volume of instructions for to-morrow. Slowly and deliberately his thoughts traveled down to the present time.

"I am playing a doubtful game," he muttered, "for a heavy stake. Hamilton is an unscrupulous, a bold, and a shrewd man; so far well. He is gifted with a high, if not the highest, order of genius; that is better. But his temper is as fiery as his own West Indian sun, and that may spoil all. I have faith, however, that this fault may be amended. At all events, I must cling to him. There is not another man in the American army who has the smallest chance of rising to power, from whom I have anything to expect. There are many, doubtless, to whom the mention of a diadem would be no unpleasing sound; but they either want the iron inflexibility to grapple with the diffi-

8*

culties that throng the road to its attainment, or they are
troubled by weak scruples about the means to be employed,
or they are afflicted by childish dreams of the happiness to
be found in republican equality.   There is not one who can
be trusted to develop schemes like mine; for he who walks
in the paths to which I point should have an ambition as
boundless as Lucifer, a will as unchangeable as fate, and a
conscience as unimpressible as adamant.   He should cast
from him honor, virtue, feeling, love of country, love of
everything but power.   Does Hamilton possess these requisites?   Perhaps not; but no other does; and he approxi-
mates to the standard, if he does not exactly come up to its
measure.   In this world we cannot have things as we wish,
and the deepest art is displayed in making the best use of
the materials at hand.   He may fail, and some more fortunate soldier may succeed in converting his sword into a
scepter.   In that case, I shall have played the wrong card,
and must mend it as I may.   The rebellion may be crushed
out by Great Britain, and a scaffold become the common
doom of the chief adventurers.   That chance is a remote
one, and, at any rate, it is one against which I cannot provide.   If successful, he may do as others have done before
him, and repay my services by consigning me to exile or a
dungeon.   That is the least of my apprehensions; not because I have faith in his gratitude, or the gratitude of anything but dogs and elephants, but because it will be poor
management if I do not make myself indispensable to him,
no matter to what height he may climb.   Let him attain the
goal of his ambition, and mine will be likewise won."

Here the dark schemer rose to his feet, placed his elbow
against the mantle-piece, rested his forehead in his open
hand, and seemed to gaze intently on the sparks that flew
upward from the blazing brands.   After awhile he turned
to the table, poured out a glass of wine, which he sipped

at intervals until it was emptied, and, replacing the wine-glass on the table, resumed his former attitude.

"I may be traveling too fast," he said, beginning his self-colloquy where he had left off. "I may under-estimate the danger to be apprehended from Hamilton's want of faith. He treasured up that story of the pirate Williams too care-fully, and was altogether too reluctant to tell it. That was a rod he was keeping in pickle for my benefit, in the event that I grew restive; and in truth it would have done more to tame me than he is aware of, if Adelaide Clifton's brain and heart had not been made of such sensitive material as to wither at the breath of an improbable calumny. I do not think he will use it now. I could retaliate fearfully by revealing the cause of her melancholy fate. Yet it shows he may prove treacherous when his safety allows it. Oth-ers, too, over whom he has no influence, may get wind of the story. Williams must be hunted up. I must make a journey to St. Croix, and happily the probable occupation of this city by the British will leave me leisure enough. Whatever Captain Hamilton may know, he shall not retain the power to prove anything dangerous to my safety, if gold or steel will suffice to silence his witness."

His mind once made up, James Billings wasted no more thought upon the subject. Helping himself again to the wine, he sought his couch and slept as soundly as if no dark crime stained his past life, no present scheme troubled his subtle brain. The habit of watchfulness created by a lifetime of dangers, asserted its supremacy even in sleep, and his very dreams were regulated at pleasure. No fear-ful groans, no incoherent expressions, no contortion of the features, betrayed what was passing in that marble breast. His body, like the mausoleum of the dead, gave no out-ward token of the gnawing worm or the decaying carcass. Who can tell how much of this was insensibility?—how much was the mastery of a steady will over the body's weakness and the mind's infirmities? According to the creed of the moralist, torturing thoughts ought to have been his companions in every hour of solitude. Perhaps they were; for he was no infidel, no believer in the dark creed that whatever we do has been appointed beforehand; that no free will is granted us; and no sin attaches to the darkest of our crimes. He believed in the existence of a God; he believed in a hereafter; and sought by no sophistical reasoning to escape the conviction that he was to be judged there according to the "deeds done in the body." His calmness may therefore have been nothing more than the art of concealing well—an art more easily acquired than we are willing to believe. There is no greater mistake than the commonly-received opinion that guilt will show itself in the countenance. An inexperienced offender who, in an unguarded moment, has been hurried into crime, is indeed apt to permit the blush of shame to mantle his cheek; but it is the most uncertain of all the evidences of guilt, for that blush is just as likely to be called up by indignation at a wrongful accusation as by confusion at detection. The hardened criminal, who has long trod the mazes of vice, defies your scrutiny and laughs at the crack-brained theories of Lavater. There is a higher perfection of wickedness still. There is an adamantine hardness of heart, which frightens away the wholesome though painful reflections that are sent in mercy to turn the sinner to repentance. It lives on unawed, unshaken, in the midst of horrors that would blast a bosom less deeply cursed, and smiles at pangs it never felt. For such spirits earth has no punishment: their sentence is reserved for the world to come.

As we have said, James Billings was sleeping like an infant, although his mind had been for the last three hours completely occupied by crimes committed or intended. He had just informed his guilty confederate of the death of one victim of their dark plottings, and agreed with him upon a precisely similar scheme, which might have a precisely similar result. The story of the seduction of Adelaide Clifton had produced so marked an effect upon the fortunes of Major Burr, that it was supposed a like accusation, supported by plausible circumstances, would completely and forever alienate the commander-in-chief from that dreaded rival. The devil, they say, is always at hand to help his children at need, and, unfortunately, Major Burr was again surrounded by circumstances that materially aided the machinations of his enemies. Such at least was the conclusion of James Billings and Alexander Hamilton, after a careful survey of the whole ground of operations, and mature consideration of the consequences of every step to be taken. To ordinary minds it would have appeared that a stratagem once successfully practiced could not safely be repeated. They reasoned differently. They argued that the very fact that Major Burr had once been accused of a similar offense, would predispose the public mind to believe the new accusation; and they hoped, not unreasonably, that the scornful silence with which he had treated the former charge would still be persevered in. Toward General Washington especially, they calculated that Major Burr would maintain a haughty reserve; and, in the worst aspect of the case, they had provided a mode of escape for themselves, by shifting the paternity of the story to other shoulders. No specter rose up to warn them from the purposed wrong. In a cozy room of a comfortable hotel, a dark and villainous plot was concocted; and when the deed was done, the two companions, in seeming unconcern, pledged each other in a cup of rosy wine, and separated with careless words upon their lips—the one to mingle unabashed with the gallant defenders of a holy cause, the other to enjoy the dreamless sleep of peaceful innocence.

CHAPTER VI.

"Oh, love! what is it in this world of ours
Which makes it fatal to be loved? Ah! why
With cypress branches hast thou wreathed thy bowers,
And made thy best interpreter a sigh?
As those who doat on odors pluck the flowers,
And place them in their breast—but place to die—
Thus, the frail beings we would fondly cherish,
Are laid within our bosoms but to perish."

By one of those chances common in civil wars, Margaret Moncrieffe, the daughter of a major in the British army, had been separated from her father, and was detained as a kind of hostage within the American lines. The proud, spirited girl, irritated by the *surveillance* to which she was subjected, annoyed by a suspicion, that had somehow gained currency, that she was engaged in communications with the enemy, and mortified by the want of pecuniary means, determined to appeal directly to General Putnam. The kind-hearted old soldier, appreciating her situation, and sympathizing with her feelings, promptly forwarded an invitation to take up her residence in his family until he could procure her permission to return to her father's protection. At this period she was not more than fourteen years of age, although a woman in physical, and more than a woman in intellectual development. Divinely beautiful, witty, and vivacious, she at once became the charm of the general's family circle, and attracted crowds of admirers to his doors. Domesticated in the same family, her intercourse with Aaron Burr was necessarily frequent; and, as day by day each discovered some new charm in the

(94)

other's society, it rapidly grew into intimacy, and then as
rapidly ripened into love,—a love as yet unspoken, and,
perhaps, unacknowledged by either. It was her practice,
as she writes in her memoirs, to ascend, in the evening, to
the gallery on the top of the house, for the purpose of
watching, through a telescope, the "wooden walls of Old
England," whose frowning batteries threatened the republican city. After awhile, that secluded spot was invested
with other attractions. It had become a trysting place.
The floating bulwarks that rose and fell with the briny
waves, and the white tents that dotted Staten Island, were
unheeded. A new and absorbing passion had subdued her
natural pride, and abated her natural confidence in British
prowess. She had learned to listen for the coming of a
rebel step, and hang with rapture upon a rebel's voice. It
was impossible that such an intercourse could long continue
without finding words to syllable the emotions that filled
the heart of each. Suddenly and unexpectedly to both,
the avowal came. For many minutes there had been
silence; for many minutes they had been holding communion with each other in the sacred stillness of thought.
Turning his gaze from the white waves of the Sound, it
rested on the heavenly beauty of the sweet creature by
his side. At the same moment her soft eyes were raised
lovingly to his. In that one glance was conveyed all the
burning passions teach; and the young lover, forgetting
that he belonged to his country—forgetting that a wall of
adamant grew broad and strong between them—forgetting
all the dictates of prudence—threw himself madly at her
feet and uttered words which, like the poetry of David,
were "spangled with coals of fire." The deep blush which
spread over her cheeks, rich and rosy as the glorious paint-
ing of the sun upon the morning sky, was a whole world
of bliss to him; and the soft hand she laid in his, thrilled

through every fiber with electric force, and sent the wild currents back upon the heart loaded with joy. No word was uttered. No word was needed to the full fruition of his hopes. One hand detained its willing prisoner, and one, encircling her voluptuous waist, drew her toward him until their lips met and grew together. Oh, happy had it been for both if in that hour the thunderbolt had fallen! Happy had it been if, linked in each other's arms, their souls had taken flight while yet the bloom of innocence was upon them, and neither guilt, nor care, nor torturing sorrow stained the opening bud or the springing tree! Better would the grave have been for her, far better than the guilty pleasures, succeeded by the vain regrets, that checkered her after days! And better would it have been for him to have passed away with his young laurels fresh upon his brow, than to have run a career, splendid indeed at its noon, but, like the hot sun of the tropics, scorching and blasting in its brilliancy, and going down at last behind clouds, and storms, and falling tears!

But what did they care for to-morrow? What warning could break the spell of that ungovernable transport? They were riding in a frail and leaky boat, upon the foamy crests of a tempest-shaken sea; but the angry voice of the great deep was unheeded, and the shrieking breakers, as they rushed madly to the iron-bound shore, sounded low and soft as a mother's lullaby over her first-born infant's sweet repose. And who could blame them for the mental *abandon* of that delirious hour? Such moments come but once, and not always once, in our pilgrimage below. Aaron Burr and Margaret Moncrieffe caught the nectar as it rose, and if death should follow the potent draught, it was a death that came on balmy wings, and pointed his destroying dart with rapturous joys. Side by side they sat upon the rough bench that ran along the gallery—their hands clasped, their eyes bent down until the drooping lashes rested on their cheeks, their lips mute and motionless, their hearts full and eloquent of unutterable joy. Who shall say that days of sorrow, nights of mourning, or even long, long years of anguish was too high a price for all they felt in that unearthly trance?

Twilight deepened into night before the spell was broken, and they rose to return to the family circle.

"You will meet me here to-morrow?" she said, in a tone of gentle inquiry.

A warm clasp of the hand, and a murmured "Yes, sweet one, yes!" was followed by another of those long, lingering kisses that send the blood leaping in fiery currents through the veins, and shed around the soul an incense so sweet that we cannot believe that it was born to die.

Another day was added to the cycle of time. During that day the mind of Aaron Burr had been like the wintry moon, over whose broad disk the clouds are chased in broken columns by the hoarse and angry wind. Troubled thoughts and fitful resolves, and now and then a clear, bright ray of hope, were all confused and jumbled together. As the chaos of his feelings subsided, the barriers to his love, forgotten yesterday, became painfully apparent. He had not thought of them heretofore, because he had indulged no purpose to avow his attachment; and vainly trusted that the tongue could be ruled into silence when the heart was bursting to be heard. A little more experience of his own heart might have taught him that it would be easier to dam up a torrent with sand, than to maintain the cold silence he had imposed upon himself while lingering near the object of his passion. It is a pity that our knowledge so often comes when it is too late to profit by it. If we could only begin life with the same amount of experience that is beat into us before its close, what a

9

world of mistakes and troubles would be avoided! If we
could only know ourselves a little earlier, and a little better, earth might become a very attractive dwelling-place.
But we walk on, believing ourselves stronger and wiser
than we are, until some unexpected pitfall opens before us,
and away goes the man and his hopes forever. Aaron
Burr had been like a blind man wandering in a wilderness
of sweets, who forgets, until he feels its sting, that a viper
may nestle among the roses. He did not remember that,
no matter how beautiful,. and gifted, and virtuous, Margaret Moncrieffe might be, it was impossible for his love to
end in happiness; and it was not until that love was
spoken, and its return avowed, that all the objections to
it that had been floating vaguely and dimly before him,
assumed the form of sturdy, substantial realities, and chilled
his sanguine nature into despair. One day had sufficed to
reveal to him the hard and naked truth; and when the hour
for the meeting of the lovers arrived, Margaret Moncrieffe
stood alone in the gallery. Her heart bounded when at
last she heard his well-known step, and a glad smile illu-
mined her countenance. Upon his visage no such joyful
expression rested. He approached her slowly, and, taking
her hand, pressed it to lips bloodless from agony, then
dropped it and said,—

"We have been like unthinking children, Margaret, and
must pay the penalty for our folly. A lovely flower was
growing on the outmost verge of a precipice, and in our
eagerness to gather it we have fallen into the abyss below."

"What is the matter?" she exclaimed wildly. "Oh,
what terrible thing has happened?"

"Terrible indeed!" he mournfully replied. "Yet it was
lovely and sweet in its coming. You and I have been
guilty of the deep sin of loving one another. You and
I, between whom there is a gulf as wide as hell, have

permitted our heart-strings to intertwine, and when they are torn asunder, as they must be, peace and happiness will bleed themselves to death."

"But why should they be torn asunder? Why may they not remain intertwined forever?"

"Look there!" he said, pointing to Staten Island. "With your naked eye you may discern the tents of England's soldiery; with the telescope you may mark the very spot where floats the regimental banner of your father. Think you that haughty officer will give his daughter to one who is fighting with a halter about his neck? Who, if he wins, may be termed patriot; but if he loses, will certainly be branded as a traitor, and conducted to a traitor's doom?"

"Oh, yes! He is too just not to make allowances for this unhappy quarrel; and when he comes to know you well, he will cheerfully sacrifice any remaining prejudices to his daughter's happiness."

"Never, Margaret—never! Besides, that is the least obstacle in our way. To-morrow, or the next day, or any day, may witness an assault on this city. When that time comes, I shall be in the front rank of its defenders. If I meet your father then, my sword will be directed at his heart, as certainly as at that of the vilest mercenary under his command. Could I approach you and ask this hand while my own was still red with the blood of your parent? No, Margaret: we must part. It was madness— nay, worse, it was dishonor—to go on as I have done, shutting my eyes to consequences an idiot might have foreseen. To have crushed my own peace was bad enough; to have aimed a deadly blow at yours, is a sin no repentance can atone."

The young girl listened in speechless woe. The rose fled from her cheek, and a dull film gathered over the soft blue

eye that had just been eloquent with the happiness of requited love.   But hope has its natural home in the bosom
of woman, and soon a cheering light flashed upon the ray-
less gloom of her despair.

"There are trials before us, my own love," she replied, in
a voice sweeter than the lyre of Orpheus. "Trials and
troubles and bitter hours; but they are not so dreadful as
you think.   This war must have an end; and when you
have passed through it, successful as I trust, and honored
as I know you will be, the vows of yesterday may meet
their fulfillment, and we shall bless the delay that prepared
for us a more entrancing gladness."

Her lover folded her passionately to his breast, and
imprinted a warm kiss on her polished brow.

"Bless you, sweet one, for those words of hope; and
bless you for the soft heart that spared the reproaches
I know I deserve! I will even do as you bid me, and hope
to find trees of frankincense and beds of spices beyond the
gloomy present, to welcome the traveler who faints not by
the way."

Gradually the conversation changed to other themes.
The day-king traveled on his fiery path, and sunk to rest
behind the dark forest that stretched away toward the unknown regions of the West.   The shadows of night fell
upon the earth, and the beauteous stars came forth as if
robed for a heavenly bridal.   Still that lingering, loving
interview was prolonged.   The cloud that had come between them and the sun was for the time forgotten.   In
the light of each other's eyes the darkness disappeared, and
fancy led them to a fairy-land, where the green pastures were
sleeping in a dreamy atmosphere, and the murmuring streams
leaped gayly from the hills.   Each word was music, and
each sigh was eloquence to them.   The honey-dew upon
the lip of love imparted a wilder ecstasy from each recur-

ring draught, and the broad earth supported on its bosom no creatures so happy as that tempest-threatened pair.

All things human must have an end, and our sweetest enjoyments are always shortest lived. Aaron Burr and Margaret Moncrieffe were recalled from the paradise in which they were roving, to the world of reality, by a summons to join the family circle below.

"For your sake," he said, as they descended, "for your sake, Margaret, General Putnam must know all."

"Be that my care," she replied. "The good old man has exhibited for me the kindness of a father, and is entitled to a daughter's confidence in return. I love him as if I were one in reality."

"And well does he deserve it; for a nobler, truer soul never animated a human frame; and that lion-heart which would lead him on a hundred bayonets at his country's call, is soft as that of the fluttering dove when weakness or distress appeals to its assistance or its sympathy."

On entering the common sitting-room they found the wife and daughters of General Putnam engaged in spinning flax for the use of the soldiery. Turn not away, gentle reader, from the homely spectacle! It was a sight upon which the angels might have looked with approving smiles. The wife and daughters of a major-general laboring with their own hands to clothe the half-naked recruits who had answered to the call of liberty. No wonder that soldiery triumphed! No wonder that when hunger and cold, disaster and defeat, were heaped upon them, their spirits rose above the depressing weight, and with the blessed example of female patriotism before them, they sprung to their duties with a new and vigorous alacrity that eventually led to a glorious victory!

General Putnam was seated at a table, having an open map before him, on which he had marked in pencil the position of the British troops. Various lines traced from this point indicated that he had been studying their proba-ble movements, and endeavoring to anticipate the precise place where the principal attack would be made. At his invitation, Burr seated himself at the table, and was soon as much absorbed as the general, in military speculations.

Margaret Moncrieffe had directed her steps to the part of the room occupied by Mrs. Putnam and her daughters, saying as she did so,—

"I hope it is no treason to King George to assist in your labors."

"Thee may be sure," replied the Quakeress, "that it is no treason to the King of kings."

Several days went by, and Miss Moncrieffe had as yet made no communication to General Putnam. The task that seemed easy in the distance, grew more difficult when she came to perform it. Sometimes he was busy; some-times he looked perplexed by troubled thoughts, and she did not like to disturb him. When a favorable opportunity did present itself, her heart failed her, and she shrunk with the instinctive bashfulness of a young girl from revealing the secret of her first love, even to so kind and noble a friend as she knew him to be. At last she determined to adopt the less embarrassing plan of addressing him by let-ter. After many trials she succeeded in framing one to her own satisfaction, which she placed, herself, in his hands. It ran as follows:—

"DEAR AND HONORED SIR:

"When I was a stranger, and you knew me only as the daughter of your country's enemy, you took compassion on my distress, invited me to your home when I had no other, and received me as tenderly as if I had been a favorite child. From you, therefore, I ought to have no secrets; and to you I feel that the circumstances in which I am now placed should be frankly avowed. Under your roof I met Major Burr. I will not tire you with details that are without interest to any one except ourselves. It is enough that we loved, and that it has been confessed on both sides, notwithstanding the barriers that we are well aware exist between us. Those barriers will readily suggest themselves to your mind, and the object of this note is to appeal to you for your advice, and your assistance in removing the difficulties that environ us. Do not fear to pain me by any suggestions you may think fit to make. Whatever they are I know they will be just and sincere, and I know, too, that they will be dictated by a heart whose manly qualities are almost hallowed by the delicate sensibilities with which they are intertwined.

"You will pardon me, I hope, if I cause you trouble or annoyance, when you remember that it is your own goodness that emboldens me to address you in the absence of the parent who, under other circumstances, should alone guide and direct my steps.

"Accept my warmest thanks for all that you have done to render the abode of the prisoner delightful, and believe that I shall ever remain your attached and grateful friend,

"MARGARET MONCRIEFFE."

Major Burr, who was ignorant of the mode of communication adopted by Miss Moncrieffe, and, indeed, ignorant that any communication had been made, was busy with the regimental reports of the day, when General Putnam hurriedly entered his apartment.

"What madness is this, major?" he exclaimed, extending the letter he had just received as he spoke. "Where, in the name of all the saints, have your wits been wandering?"

"It was madness, indeed!" replied Burr, sorrowfully, his

eyes merely glancing over the letter; "but a madness which brings its own punishment. In an evil hour I forgot that the galley slave is more free than I am, and dared to dream of happiness amid the rattle of musketry and the clank of chains. Even when the hour of waking came, a sweet voice called back the illusion, and I was the slave of hope once more. It is over now, and I shall prove none the worse soldier since I have learned to look to a bloody bed as a happy riddance of a troubled life."

"Nay, major, it is bad enough, but not so bad as that. It would be unfeeling, and in my judgment, dishonorable, to think of marriage with Miss Moncrieffe, while her father and yourself hold commissions in opposing hosts. Nor do I think it likely that his consent will be given at any time to your union. In his eyes you are a traitor; in his eyes you will remain a traitor, although success may to others convert the rebel into a hero. That is the worst side of the picture. On the other hand, time and patience may do a great deal toward bringing about the fulfillment of your wishes. At all events, your life belongs to your country, and must be cherished for her sake. The folly of which you have been guilty will be converted into crime by a reckless exposure of your life on the battle-field."

"I did not mean exactly that, sir. I only meant that I might be less careful to preserve it. I rejoice that you acquit me of anything worse than folly, and I assure you that in all this I have been hurried on without knowing what I did, and can scarcely be said to have been a free agent."

"Why bless you, man, I know that as well as you do! I know, also, that at your age I should have done the same thing. If you will ask the old lady who sits at the head of my table, she will tell you that there was a time when a petticoat could have lured Israel Putnam to the devil."

The idea of putting such a question to the demure Quakeress, over whose placid countenance no ripple of passion ever seemed to have rolled, called a faint smile to the lips of the aid-de-camp, and he replied,—

"I am afraid I should lose ground in her estimation by asking a question that implied her good lord had ever been different from what he now is—the most clear-headed and practical, as well as the most upright of men."

"Pshaw! she knows better! She knows that I would have jumped from a precipice at her bidding, or performed any other equally absurd exploit. For that matter, she knows I would do it yet; and the chances are, that when I tell her what a fool you have been, she replies, 'Thou wert foolish thyself, Israel, in thy younger days, and must deal tenderly with the maiden and the youth.' But to return to your own affairs. I hope-you see the necessity of an immediate separation between Miss Moncrieffe and yourself. I shall apply to General Washington to-day for an order to change her residence; and I shall worry Congress until they grant me permission to restore her to her father."

"And so," answered Burr, "I am to reproach myself for making her captivity more irksome, by causing her removal from a family where she has met a daughter's and a sister's welcome. Truly, her acquaintance with me has been unfortunate."

"Do not disturb yourself on that account. When she leaves my roof I will see to it that she is conveyed to another as hospitable and as kind. Now you may go. I give you leave of absence for twenty-four hours, and do not wish to see your face within that time."

"Am I permitted to see Miss Moncrieffe?"

"No. You have met often enough, and must not meet again until Congress grants me permission to send her on board a British man-of-war. I will say all that is needful,

and it will agitate her less, coming from me, than from
you."

Major Burr understood the motives of the general, and
acquiesced uncomplainingly in his decision. When he returned to his duties the next day, he learned, without surprise, that General Washington had issued an order for
the removal of Miss Moncrieffe to the family of General
Mifflin, at Kingsbridge. What reasons General Putnam
had for desiring the change, he kept to himself, and General Washington did not seek to pry into them. The rank
of Miss Moncrieffe's father, however, and the course that
Congress had pursued toward her, gave her movements
an importance in the eyes of the public to which they were
not entitled, and speculation was rife as to the cause of her
sudden removal from New York.   Finally, the majority
settled down in the opinion that she had been detected in
communicating information to the enemy—an opinion that
General Putnam neither affirmed nor contradicted.   To
the fertile brain of Alexander Hamilton it suggested another means of wounding his rival, and on the very night
that James Billings had brought him the news of Adelaide Clifton's death, the infamous confederates concocted
another story of seduction, which soon obtained general
circulation, and the character of Aaron Burr as a libertine
became fixed for life.

It was no easy matter to obtain permission from Congress to restore Miss Moncrieffe to her father.

General Putnam, true to his promise, omitted no opportunity of pressing the subject upon their attention, and
finally succeeded. When the order was received he handed
it to Major Burr, and said,—

"You can go now to Kingsbridge, and carry this news.
I place no injunction upon you not to renew the vows you
have already uttered. In affairs of the heart it is often the

best course to leave the heart to its own guidance. Still,
it will be well for you to remember that the probability is,
you will never meet again—that there is nothing more than
a bare possibility of your future union. Excite no other
hopes in her bosom, and cherish none in yours. Encourage
no correspondence, without her father's free consent.
Utter not one word to lessen her sense of duty to him.
Behave, in short, with that high honor which spurns concealment as an approach to meanness, and would rather
endure the tortures of the rack than the shame of deceiving or misleading a loving and a trusting woman."

Major Burr warmly grasped the hard hand of the veteran
soldier—the big tears came into his eyes, and his throbbing
heart almost choked his reply.

"God bless you, my more than friend! Rightly and nobly
have you pointed out my pathway—firmly and undauntedly
will I follow it, if my heart breaks in the effort."

"I do not doubt you," said the general, deeply affected.
"I do not doubt you, and if I did, I would not trust you
as I do. Go in," he continued, "to Mrs. Putnam and the
girls. They will have many messages to send."

Major Burr's arrangements were soon made. The journey to Kingsbridge was a short one, and the distance was
materially lessened by the speed at which he rode. Those
who have ever loved, will understand that other thoughts
than the gloomy ones of an early separation obtruded
themselves on his mind during the ride. He was about to
meet once more the object of his idolatry; to clasp her
warm hand in his; to look down into the depths of her
blue eyes, and wonder from what world of loveliness their
beauties were borrowed. In imagination he was even now
inhaling the incense of her breath, and draining the nectar
of her lips. At such times the demons of doubt and un-
certainty lose their power, and the dark clouds that, one

after another, they spread along the sky, are brushed away by angels' wings, or changed to rainbow beauty by the God of Love.

They met, not as those meet within whose bosoms hope has laid itself down to die; but with the bounding gladness of those who clasp in their embraces all that is dear, or cherished, or remembered of existence. For one brief hour they breathed the air of Eden, and in its wild delights forgot that but an hour interposed between them and a separation that might be eternal., To them there was no past; no future; nothing but an all-absorbing NOW. They thought not of the world around them, and envied not the heaven above, amid the thrilling joys of the heaven below. Sweet privilege of youth! why is it that you abide with us no longer? Why is it that the same sun that lights your coming must also shine upon your grave? Why is it that the last notes of the rejoicing song that hails. your birth are always mingled with the prelude to the funeral wail that mourns your decay? Alas! before the first green blade decked the bosom of earth, an immutable decree went forth that whenever the Angel of Love folded his wings on the footstool of God, he should be followed by the Angel of Grief, and the raptures of one be succeeded by the anguish of the other. The boon and the curse travel always so nearly together, that the lightning is visible before the sunshine disappears. To Aaron Burr and Margaret Moncrieffe it was the rosy daytime now, and eagerly they gave themselves up to its sweet enjoyments, even while the muttering thunder proclaimed that the stormy night was approaching. *   *   *   *   *

The hour of final separation had arrived.

"Will you not go with me to the boat?" she asked, "and give me every possible moment of your society?"

"No, Margaret. It would be torture to you and to me

to have the prying gaze of indifferent spectators fixed upon us at such a time. Let us part where the throbbings of the heart are unrepressed, and eye and tongue have full permission to proclaim that we would not exchange our love, hopeless as it seems, for all the countless spheres that hang above this orb of ours."

"Nor," she added, "nor for a myriad ages of such poor endearments as those with which the Eastern prophet peopled his paradise. Let it be ours to prove that there is a love as deathless as eternity; and if we meet no more until the soul has put off the stained garment in which it is clothed, there, there beyond the sky, in the heaven to which one is called, or the hell to which it is doomed, let us agree that the other shall follow and nestle by its side."

"So let it be, Margaret," he exclaimed, pressing her to his heart. "So let it be. Our compact is sealed."

One burning kiss—one long, long embrace, and then he sprang to his horse and galloped furiously away.

They never met again. The lines of her life ran in tears and in guilt. A father's command consigned her to the arms of an unfeeling husband, and Nature vindicated its outraged laws by making her the instrument of that husband's dishonor. Still in the depths of the infamy to which she sunk, she clung to the memory of her early love, and when her own hand recorded the events of her unhappy life, every word that spoke of him was filled with passionate fire. The mistress of a royal lover, the splendor that gilded her lot could not bring forgetfulness to her heart; and when she came to die, the name of Aaron Burr was on her lips. At that dread hour her fearful compact was remembered, and her last breath was expended in uttering the words,—

"IN HEAVEN OR IN HELL WE WILL MEET AGAIN."

10

CHAPTER VII.

"And is there blood upon my shield?
  Maiden! it well may be!
We have sent the streams from our battle-field,
  All darkened to the sea!
We have given the founts a stain,
  'Midst their woods of ancient pine
And the ground is wet—but not with rain,
  Deep-dyed—but not with wine."

On the twenty-third of August, General Putnam, on account of the illness of General Greene, was assigned to the command of the works on Long Island. Four days afterwards, intelligence was received that the British army was in motion. Aaron Burr, who, in that brief space of time, had made an accurate survey of the ground—who had visited every post and outpost—who had carefully inspected the troops, and made himself acquainted with the state of their mind at the near approach of an engagement, gave it as his opinion that a battle would end in defeat. Probably there was not a general officer in the army, from Washington down, who did not hold the same opinion. But General Washington on this, as on many other occasions, was fettered by the public sentiment of the country. The great mass of the people understood no results except the obvious ones of battles and of victories. They did not understand that every hour gained by the American general was a step toward freedom; that the resources of the enemy were daily diminishing; that our own troops were daily acquiring greater efficiency; and the minds of the people daily approaching unanimity. The sturdy resistance to the British arms at Bunker Hill had spread abroad an extravagant notion of the prowess of raw militia, and men

(110)

unreasonably looked for reports of victories where it was
no small honor to escape absolute destruction. In these
sentiments the majority of Congress unfortunately shared;
and General Washington was thus often compelled to risk engagements that his own clear judgment told him could have
no other result than a useless waste of life. The attempt
to defend Long Island against a veteran army one-third
more numerous than his own, and deriving a powerful support from the near neighborhood of their fleet, would
never have been made, if Congress and the country could
have been induced to leave the commander-in-chief to the
exercise of his own judgment in the conduct of the war.

The British attacking columns, on the morning of the
twenty-seventh of August, were fifteen thousand strong.
To oppose this formidable army General Putnam had an
available force of not more than five thousand untried men.
Courage and devotion may, and often do, accomplish
miracles, but when it is opposed by equal courage, superior
arms, superior discipline, and superior numbers, it is madness to expect anything but disaster. In this light Major
Burr regarded it, and so expressed himself to General Putnam, who, it is well known, perfectly agreed with his aid-de-
camp. General Putnam, however, was too good a soldier
to question the decision of his superiors. He was ordered
to defend Long Island, and he would have made the attempt if only a single company had mustered beneath his
banner. Immediately on hearing that General Howe was
moving along the coast, he ordered Lord Stirling to meet
him; and sent General Sullivan to the heights above
Flat Bush, on the middle road. Lord Stirling promptly
engaged the left wing of the enemy under General Grant,
who, however, manifested no disposition to press the attack. This seeming hesitation, or supineness, soon had a
fearful solution. General Clinton, with Cornwallis and

Percy, had been ordered to make a circuit, and gain the rear of Sullivan. When the sound of their guns announced that this had been accomplished, Grant shook off his apathy, and put forth his whole strength against Lord Stirling. Borne back inch by inch, the gallant Stirling, at the head of the Pennsylvania, Maryland, and Delaware regiments, struggled gloriously against overwhelming numbers, until Lord Cornwallis fell upon his rear and poured a murderous volley into his already shattered ranks. Even then he gathered the fragments of his corps together, and skillfully availing himself of the advantages presented by a marshy creek, retired slowly and in good order behind the American intrenchments. While this was going on, General Sullivan was assailed on the heights above Flat Bush, by Clinton on one side, and De Heister on the other. For three hours the dreadful conflict raged.. For three hours the boom of cannon and the roar of musketry gave evidence of the impetuous nature of the attack, and the bloody obstinacy of the defense. Hemmed in on all sides, his men cut down by scores at every discharge, the dauntless Sullivan still continued the unequal combat, renewed the disordered ranks of his troops, and infused new fire into their flagging spirits. General Washington had crossed over in the mean time, but he dared not weaken himself by sending a man to Sullivan's assistance, and could only watch, in powerless anguish, the butchery of that gallant detachment. Red currents ran in rivulets from the crimson hill, and mounds of mangled bodies were piled upon its sides. Honor and patriotism could demand no more. All that human courage could do had been tried; and all that human endurance could bear had been undergone. Slowly and reluctantly a white flag went up from the Continental ranks. Sullenly they laid down their arms and surrendered themselves prisoners of war.

Throughout that disastrous day, Major Burr was everywhere present. Utterly devoid of fear—if any man ever lived of whom so much may be said—a practiced horseman, young, active, zealous, he carried the orders of the general from point to point, dashing through the thickest hail of bullets, and seeming, like Charles XII., to exult in their hissing music. The next day and the next, brought no relaxation from his exertions. On the twenty-ninth, General Washington resolved on retreating to the city. Major Burr was engaged during the whole night in facilitating the embarkation of the troops, and his untiring assiduity was such as to attract the particular attention of General McDougall, who did not fail afterwards to manifest his high appreciation of the soldierly qualities then for the first time brought to his notice.

This memorable retreat has been reckoned one of General Washington's highest claims to the title of a great commander. In the presence of a victorious enemy, overwhelmingly superior in numbers and in guns, whose parties were advanced to within six hundred yards of his lines, he transported his whole army, numbering altogether about nine thousand men, all his military stores, and nearly all his provisions and artillery to New York in a single night, in such perfect order and silence, that the enemy obtained no notice of his movements until the last boat was crossing. The high praise to which General Washington is undoubtedly entitled for this successful military maneuver, must be shared by his subordinates, since it was one of those movements in which the highest skill of the commander may be put at naught by the cowardice or the stupidity of an inferior. The slightest misunderstanding of an order, the least delay, or even the accidental discharge of a single musket, would have caused an alarm that must have been attended by the most deplorable

10*

consequences. The conspicuous coolness, the quick intelligence, and the unwearied exertions of Aaron Burr, contributed more than that of any other officer of his grade to the happy result, and won for him a crown of laurels that will never fade until the early history of the Republic is unread, and its early struggles forgotten.

After the retreat from Long Island, the wildest terror pervaded the City of New York. The horrors of a bombardment were daily and nightly before their eyes. Nor, it must be confessed, were these terrors confined to the citizens. They extended to the army, and spread through every rank. Desertions became so frequent that General Washington, in one of his letters to Congress, described them as going off "almost by whole regiments, by half ones, and by companies at a time." The insubordination and want of discipline of those that remained were also the subject of frequent and bitter complaint. Despairing of defending the city with such troops, he began his preparations for an evacuation that he foresaw would soon be forced upon him. The stores and baggage least wanted were removed beyond Kingsbridge. Nine thousand men were stationed at Mount Washington and Kingsbridge. Five thousand, under the command of General Putnam, occupied the city; and the residue were posted in the intermediate space, in good supporting distance of either division.

The British, although completely successful in the affair of the twenty-seventh of August, had suffered severely, and manifested no impatience to bring on another engagement. It was not until the fifteenth of September, that General Clinton landed at Kip's Bay. The scene that followed was the most disgraceful that occurred during the whole period of the Revolution. Our men were shaking with dread before a gun was fired, and fled in irremediable confusion at the first appearance of the foe. In the rear of the flying troops, Major Burr found Captain Hamilton, vainly endeavoring to restore something like order, and as vainly appealing to them, in the names of patriotism and manliness, to turn and redeem themselves from everlasting disgrace. Addressing himself to Burr, he said, in a tone of despair,—

"The day is lost, major, and our honor is lost with it!"

"Not yet," was the reply. "Something may still be done."

Gallantly and manfully these two struggled side by side. Freely and boldly they exposed their persons to the hottest of the British fire, and desperately charged almost alone upon the British bayonets. Their threats, their entreaties, their animating example were thrown away upon the panic-stricken men. The shameless race was continued, until the fugitives were sheltered behind the works at Harlæm.

Happy would it have been for Aaron Burr and Alexander Hamilton, if none but the glorious rivalry of that day had ever darkened their lives! On that field, in the midst of the dangers and distractions of a routed army, both gathered a rich harvest of renown; which, to the one was destined to be barren of its legitimate fruits, and was stained by despicable meanness in the other.

After the retreat, or rather flight, had become irretrievable, Hamilton devoted his attention exclusively to his own company of artillery, and, by the exhibition of remarkable skill and courage, succeeded in leading them from the field with the loss of but a single gun. In riding toward Harlæm, Burr discovered a brigade, who, under the impression that their retreat was cut off, had thrown themselves into a mud fort, and determined to defend it to the last. On learning the determination of General Knox, who commanded the brigade, Major Burr protested vehemently against it; assured him that he knew all the by-paths through the country, and that he could and would guide them safely to the main army. His offer was accepted, and the young aid-de-camp, himself riding in advance, led them to Harlæm, unmolested, except by one small detachment, that was quickly dispersed.

If Major Burr had lived in the days of the Roman republic, this achievement would have won for him the highest honor to which a Roman soldier could aspire— the Corona Civica, awarded to him who saved the life of a citizen—an honor so highly esteemed that afterwards, when the republic was converted into a despotism, and the senate had exhausted its ingenuity in inventing honors for Augustus, they crowned the whole by decreeing that the Corona Civica should be forever suspended from the top of his house. The degree of credit to be ascribed to Burr's conduct on this occasion may be correctly estimated when it is remembered that of a brigade of twenty-seven hundred men who surrendered at Fort Washington a short time afterwards, only five hundred, or less than one-fifth, survived the ill treatment they received in the prison ships of England. Partly on account of the unfortunate differences between him and the commander-in-chief, and partly on account of the malign influences that followed him wherever he went, he never reaped from this brilliant achievement any substantial advantages.

That night General Howe camped in front of the Americans, his right resting on the East River, his left on the Hudson. The next day our troops had recovered from their panic, and, in a sharp action of four or five hours' duration, obtained a decided advantage over the British. The spirited conduct of the men in this affair, so different from that of the day before, surprised General Howe, and deterred him from making a general assault on Washington's position. It did more; it inspired him with so much caution, that for three weeks he lay almost wholly inactive in sight of his enemy.

James Billings had followed the retreating army from New York, and on the third day after the occupation of Harlæm, he was seated on one of the guns of Hamilton's battery, apparently watching through a telescope the movements of the enemy. It was not long before he was joined by that officer, who inquired,—

"Why did you not come to my tent, Billings, instead of asking an interview here?"

"Canvas walls," was the cool reply, "are liable to two very serious objections: they obstruct sight, and do not obstruct sound. It might be inconvenient to have our conversation overheard and repeated by a lounging soldier at the back of your tent. I prefer the open air, where you are certain that no one can come near enough to listen without your knowledge."

"A tent is indeed a poor place for the discussion of private matters, and I should not have suggested it if I had supposed you had anything of importance to communicate so soon."

"Nor have I much to tell, if you allude to our plans in reference to Major Burr. Most men have been too busy since our last interview to waste time in listening to stories of private scandal; yet I have not been altogether idle. I have already whispered a pretty little story of the seduction of Miss Moncrieffe, in a quarter where it will be sure to reach the general. By the way, captain, do you know I have a shrewd suspicion that we are much nearer the truth this time than we were before?"

"Why so? What have you seen?"

"Nothing myself; but servants will talk, you know, and

both General Putnam's and General Mifflin's speak of longer interviews and more tender partings than were to have been expected between the daughter of a British major and a rebel in arms against his king."

"I do not believe it. Mrs. Putnam would have turned them both out of the house at the first appearance of impropriety, much less of criminal intercourse."

"Well, I do believe it; but as it will equally favor our schemes whether he is really guilty or we only make him appear so, it is not worth while to discuss the truth of the case. Besides, I do not want to have my belief in his present guilt dispelled. After having been actively instrumental in circulating one false story of the kind, it is a comfort to think that I have discovered a true one at last."

The color faded from the cheek of Hamilton, and his voice trembled, as he replied,—

"Let me beg of you, Mr. Billings, not to refer again to Adelaide Clifton. That tragedy has been played out, and I would rather hear no allusion to it, particularly in your cold and devilish tones. As to Major Burr, I am half inclined to abandon my plans against him. When he came to my side the other day, and generously assisted me in arresting the flight of my panic-stricken men—when I heard his earnest appeals to them not to abandon their guns, and saw him desperately expose his life to save me from that deep disgrace, the memory of the wrongs I had done him smote me like a bolt of iron; and the thought has ever since haunted me that it would be the better, as it is the more manly policy, to discard all underhand intrigues, and trust to superior energy or superior fortune in the race between us."

"There is a little question to be settled, Captain Hamilton, before taking that resolution, which I should be sorry to think you had entirely overlooked."

"Pray what is that?"

How far you have a right to engage men in schemes for your benefit, and then abandon them to the mercy of enemies they have made on your account."

"If I remember rightly, you had the frankness to inform me that your services were rendered chiefly with a view to your own advancement."

"Certainly! I am not so fond of tortuous paths as to tread them without the hope of reward. Still, you must not forget that it was yourself who devised a plan for the destruction of a dangerous rival. In the execution of that plan you sought my assistance. When your views were unfolded to me, I concurred in your opinion, and labored faithfully according to your directions. I had no other interest in it than that of binding you to me by such ties that hereafter you could not decently refuse any reasonable request I might make. You showed me a means of accomplishing the object I had at heart, and I adopted it. If you had shown me any other, it would have been the same. Of my motives I make no concealment. I was willing to work for you now, and take the chances of your paying me hereafter. A part of my work, the most disagreeable and the most dangerous part too, is done. Your bond to ne is uncanceled, and you have no right to lessen my security for its future payment."

"Suppose I admit the force of your reasoning, how will you prove that I jeopard your interests by refraining from further acts of hostility to Major Burr?"

"It needs no proof. The proposition is self-evident. You may remember the fable of the serpent which stung a child and killed it. The father endeavored to destroy the reptile, but only succeeded in striking off a part of its tail. Afterwards a reconciliation took place, and the two engaged in friendly conversation. The man pressed the serpent to come out from his hole; an invitation his snake-ship politely declined. 'Why not come out?' asked the man. 'Are we not friends?' 'Oh, yes! but your dead child and my shortened tail are not; and we should quarrel on their account.' You are in the condition of the serpent. There is that between you and Aaron Burr that makes a truce impossible, and if you leave your hiding-place before you have an opportunity to sting him, you are lost."

Something, not exactly a sneer, nor yet a smile—a compound expression of anger and mortification, curled the lip of Hamilton, and imparted a tone of bitterness to his reply,—

"I presume you do not expect me to thank you for the compliment deducible from your story, and its application. That Major Burr is a true man I know; that he is a man of genius all report agrees; yet I did not know that you held him in such high esteem, or regarded me as so deficient in like qualities, as to render an open contest between us one of certain defeat to me. You will pardon me, I trust, if my vanity prevents me from looking at the picture in the same light that you do. I am loth to believe that I may not couch a lance at his breast on terms of equality."

"Six months ago you might have done so; but within that time events have transpired that put you at perilous disadvantage. What would become of your open rivalry, if he should discover and proclaim your agency in bringing about the quarrel between himself and the commander-in-chief? I will not refer to other matters, as they are disagreeable to you. That alone would be sufficient to blast you in the estimation of your comrades and your superiors. What security can you have that he does not make the discovery? Or suppose he does not, you will be for-

ever haunted by the fear of detection. · Your resolutions
will be vacillating, and your efforts will be timid. Can
you doubt what use a bold and sagacious adversary would
make of such advantages? Be assured that if you mean
to run out the race of ambition in which you have entered,
you must crush Aaron Burr without his knowing the hand
that deals the blow. For you there is no return; and
hesitation is destruction. The ambitious aspirant can hope
for no forgiveness when his errors are exposed; for the
only evidence of amendment that will be received is an
abandonment of the designs he has cherished. You have,
indeed, the alternative of retiring to private life, or of
contenting yourself in a subordinate position. When you
are no longer in the way, men may overlook your former
indiscretions, and extend to you the charity of forgetfulness. If you have made up your mind to this course, it is
but fair that you should take upon yourself the blame for
what has passed, and leave me unimpeded by any other
enmities than those with which you found me. If, on the
other hand, you are resolved not to abandon your hopes
of power and greatness, there is no alternative except a
steady persistence in the plans we have adopted. Major
Burr must be kept too busy in repelling new accusations to
allow him leisure for minute inquiries into the sources of
old ones. In my judgment, this will be easy; for I repeat,
that I believe he is guilty this time, and in his efforts to
hide the real crime, he will be very apt to overlook the
false accusation."

"And I repeat," answered Hamilton, "that I do not,
and cannot believe him guilty; though to you, who are a
doubter of the existence of virtue, my reasons may appear
ridiculous. He is too highly esteemed by General Putnam,
and too warmly loved by his wife, to have committed an act
of such flagrant immorality beneath their roof. I cannot

11

be mistaken. He is as certainly innocent as I am. There may have been some love passages between them, for she is a girl well calculated to inspire the utmost madness of passion ; but if so, they were of an honorable nature, and both General Putnam and his wife have been apprised of whatever has taken place."

"Ah !" exclaimed Billings, in a tone of more surprise than he was wont to exhibit : "ah ! I had not thought of that. It is possible," he continued, after a pause, "that you have hit the right nail on the head ! Upon reflection, I am inclined to think you have. That foolish girl, to whom I paid fifty dollars for watching Miss Moncrieffe and reporting her acts, has been giving me her inferences, and calling them facts ; and I, like an idiot, swallowed her story without investigation, because I wanted to believe it. Another such a blunder will woefully lessen my self-confidence, though, in this case—thank the stars, or the devil, or whatever goblin or sprite had a finger in the business— the mistake is of no great consequence. He will be quite as anxious to protect the fame of his intended wife as he would have been to hide the errors of his victim. Either will give him food for anxious thought ; and the best of it is, that he will be so hampered by pride and delicacy in the one case, or by the consciousness of guilt in the other, that he will take no notice of the report unless it is forced upon him so publicly as to be unavoidable. You have the trumps in your own hand, Captain Hamilton, and if you do not win the game, the fault will be yours."

"There is one view of the case which does not seem to have occurred to you, Mr. Billings, that strikes me as worthy of consideration. Is it not possible that, to win the daughter's hand, he may seek to recommend himself to the father's favor, by turning traitor to his country ? Such things have happened in times not very remote from ours."

"No, captain; I thought of that, and dismissed the idea as altogether improbable. It is possible, to be sure, that a man in love may make an infernal fool of himself in every conceivable way, and Major Burr would save us a great deal of trouble by proving himself no exception to the rule; but he will not do it. It is my habit to study attentively the character and dispositions of those who occupy to me the relations of friend or foe. Major Burr, though properly neither the one nor the other, is in my way, and has not escaped my scrutiny. His heart is in the American cause. He does not adhere to it, as you and I do, because he believes it will triumph in the end. He is bound to it by birth, by kindred, by education, and by association. He comes of the old Puritan stock who first settled the wilderness; and the bones of his ancestors, for generations back, are moldering beneath this soil. It is my fixed opinion that if he were suspended over the pit of hell, and you were to offer him the alternative of betraying his country or dropping into the burning lake, he would choose the latter. I know you are thinking that, admitting this to be so, it does not negative your suggestion, since it would be easier to take this sudden and desperate resolve than to resist the daily and hourly pleading of the passions, when a beautiful woman is the lure. Applied to a nature like yours, the reasoning is undoubtedly correct. Major Burr is of a different stamp. In him patriotism is stronger than love; and if the gifted beauty from whom Socrates took lessons, and of whom Pericles was first the pupil and then the slave, could again revisit the earth, the eloquence which captivated the philosopher, and the charms which enraptured the warrior-statesman would be wasted in the effort to win him to the side of England. I use strong language, for I wish to impress upon you my earnest conviction of the truth of what I utter. We must make our calculations upon winning the game without any assistance from him."

. "You are assuming more than half the argument," responded Captain Hamilton. "You are taking it for granted that I intend to play out that game; whereas I have informed you that I am strongly inclined to throw up my hand and begin afresh."

"I did not think you serious, particularly as I have heard from you no denial of my right to be consulted about a matter which so materially affects my interests."

"I do deny it, and insist that I alone am the rightful judge of the course it becomes me to take."

"You are in error, Captain Hamilton, and your position will not bear argument, if I were disposed to urge it. It would do me no good, however, and afford me no pleasure to convince you against your will. I prefer that your decision should be made according to your own sense of what is due to me and to yourself, only insisting that as I have no fancy for the game of blind man's buff, you will not leave me to grope in the dark, but inform me distinctly what your determination is."

The perfect coolness of the practiced villain, the total absence of every expression of regret, anger, or astonishment, and his studied avoidance of every word that implied a threat, had a meaning for Alexander Hamilton that was perfectly terrible. Until recently, he had looked upon James Billings merely as an unscrupulous knave, who might be used when necessary, and bullied or bought into silence when his services were no longer needed. After he was too deeply committed to recede, he discovered that he was, to a great extent, in the power of a man of vast mental resources, of greath wealth, (how great no one knew;) without a touch of fear, or pity, or remorse; full of ambitious schemes, as yet but dimly disclosed; prepared to commit any human crime that promoted his views, and reckless of any human suffering that might follow his acts. Knowing this man as he did; knowing that with him there was no middle ground—that he must be either an ally or an enemy; knowing, further, that in less than one hour from the date of a rupture between them, he would be plotting his destruction, as earnestly as he was now scheming for his advancement, and remembering how much that was black and damning he could reveal, Captain Hamilton, bold as he was, felt his heart sink within him, and his good resolutions took to themselves wings and flew away.

Oh, it is a bitter, bitter draught, when the haughty son of genius finds that by one misstep, one plunge into crime, a thing to which he had ascribed no more than a reptile's consequence has obtained the mastery over his actions, and whenever his better nature turns in horror from the crimes to which he is urged, there stands the relentless demon beckoning forward with one hand, while the other points to an abyss of infamy behind! Whenever, too, his guardian angel whispers "Return—repent," its low tone is drowned by a louder voice, which says "One step more, and you are safe: one more deed of shame is all that is needed. There, beyond that one deed, lie power, and wealth, and honor. Courage, and they are yours! To turn back is weakness—worse than weakness; it is self-destruction! You cannot recall the past, and you have done so much, that the little more required will scarcely add a feather's weight to your guilt!" And so he goes on from crime to crime, under the delusive belief that each one is the last; that each one is all that intervenes between him and the prize he is losing his soul to win. Hamilton reasoned as thousands had done before him, and fell, as they did, into a moral hell, which is robbed of none of its

11*

tortures by the gilding of worldly success. His reply was an index to the thoughts that oppressed him.

"I have no alternative, I suppose, but to yield to your wishes, or to blow out your brains."

"And the last alternative is one that I trust Captain Hamilton instantly dismissed, since these same brains may be serviceably employed in the promotion of his interests."

"I did dismiss it. Why or wherefore is immaterial. My resolution is taken to go on as we agreed at our last interview in the city. As I understand that you have nothing particular to communicate in reference to that matter, it is best to drop the subject."

"I had no idea when I broached it, that it would lead to so much conversation between us; still, I do not like to leave anything unfinished; and I confess to some curiosity to know what pleasant vision you were indulging a short time since, in connection with my sudden decease."

"Mr. Billings, you spared me the mortification of listening to a threat from you, and I would willingly have exercised a like forbearance. If anything should sound unpleasant in what I am going to say, remember that your inquiry extracted it. The vision I was indulging is one that will remain near me hereafter. The day that I resolve to break off our connection, will be the last of your life. You have the power to injure me deeply, and whenever I suspect that you are about to use it, (and I shall suspect it the moment we quarrel,) I will slay you as certain as there is a God in heaven!"

The words were hissed through his closed teeth, and the bloodless lips scarcely moved when the sound escaped them. The superhuman self-control of Billings failed him for once, and his eye quailed before the glance of fire that was fixed upon him. It required a strong effort to recover from his confusion, and reply in his usual voice.

. "That is a bond between us I had not thought of. By the Lord, there are few friendships so well cemented as ours! A quarrel is death to both. Well, I do not lament the little wrangling that has brought us to so clear an understanding, and I predict that our work will be better and more harmoniously done, since it is manifest that a failure on either side will be followed by consequences so serious. We will, if you please, consider this long episode at an end. I sought you to say that I am going to-night to the City of New York, and from there I must take a journey southward. It will probably be two months or more before you see me again. In the mean time it will be best to let the little seed I have planted grow untended. Indeed, if General Howe is a soldier of as much capacity as he is represented, he will leave you no leisure to attend to private matters. At the head of his force, he ought to drive General Washington from the State of New York in two days. The Americans can make no efficient stand until he is drawn inland, beyond the reach of aid from his shipping, and is weakened by the garrisons he must leave behind. I may have occasion to write to you, and if so, take it for granted that there is not one word of truth in the visible contents. When you are alone, hold it over a hot fire, and whatever then appears upon the third page you may rely on."

"Going to the city, did you say? That is impossible; the enemy's lines extend from river to river."

"Nevertheless I must make the attempt; and I have accomplished more difficult feats before now. Take this glass," he continued, "and examine that skirt of timber to the left. I thought I detected the glitter of scarlet uniforms among the autumn leaves."

Hamilton took the glass, and, after a brief survey of the ground, closed it again, saying,—

"It is nothing but a post of videttes."

"I know it," replied Billings; "but look again. There is a lot of officers coming this way, and there is no occasion for letting them know that our conversation has had reference to anything else than the perfection, or imperfection of General Howe's dispositions. Give me the glass."

Taking the instrument, he adjusted it to his eye, and ran it along the whole length of the British line.

"General Howe," he said, just as the officers to whom he had alluded approached the spot, "General Howe seems to like your company so well, that he is preparing to make a permanent encampment in your neighborhood. You have reason to thank your stars that England did not send out a more energetic commander."

"What do you mean?" asked one of the younger officers. "Do you think General Howe ought to make an attack on these fortified heights?"

"I am not a military man, and my opinion is not entitled to much consideration. General Howe, doubtless, knows his own business better than I do; but if I was at the head of yonder army of red-coats, I think these fortified heights would be mine before the rising of to-morrow's sun, and George Washington a captive or a fugitive. In my judgment, General Howe is over-cautious."

"You speak like a fool!" replied the officer, hotly. "An army of fifteen thousand freemen, behind these works, is more than a match for treble that number of hireling mercenaries."

"I deserve the rebuke," answered Billings, with a bland smile, "for venturing an opinion on a subject of which, I confess, I am ignorant. I shall not hereafter question the ability of the American army to perform miracles. Indeed, I was myself a witness to an achievement of theirs which has few recorded parallels. To my certain knowledge, on

the fifteenth of this present month, they made the distance
from New York to Harlæm at an average speed of about
twelve miles to the hour, and in such remarkable order,
that not a single colonel was able to find his regiment, and
very few captains possessed a more accurate knowledge of
the whereabouts of their companies. Gentlemen, I bid you
good day!"

At the conclusion of this bitter speech, James Billings
made a polite bow, and walked deliberately away.

"Who is he, Hamilton?" asked two or three of the
astonished officers at once.

"Some years ago," he replied, "I knew him as a trader
between New York and the West Indies. Afterwards, I
understood that he had accumulated a fortune and retired
from business. What are his present pursuits I do not
know. I do know, however, that he is a zealous and efficient friend of the patriot cause."

"I should have taken him for a soldier," answered
General Lee, who was among the group. "His voice has
the ring of tried metal, and I will stake more than I could
well afford to lose, that it has been heard above the sound
of clashing steel before this war began."

"I knew him only as a merchant," said Hamilton, "and
never heard him allude to any other service in which he
had been engaged. Your conjecture may be correct,
though I think it improbable. He was too familiar with
the details of the mercantile business not to have passed
many years in acquiring a knowledge of that hazardous
calling."

Captain Hamilton had, in reality, no certain knowledge
of the former occupations of James Billings. He knew
enough to be assured that they had not been of the most
reputable kind, and this made him desirous of appearing
more ignorant than he was. Not knowing to what the

present conversation might lead, he hastened to change it by abruptly inquiring, "What do you think of our position, general? Can we hold it?"

This question led, as he expected and desired, to an animated discussion, in the heat of which James Billings and his biting retort were forgotten.

CHAPTER VIII.

"Whate'er that thought, still unexpressed,
Dwells the sad secret in his breast;
The pride his haughty brow reveals,
All other passion well conceals."

THE retreat from New York was the beginning of a series of disasters that almost annihilated the American army, and spread among the people a feeling of dismay so general that the most hopeful trembled for the result. That was emphatically the time "that tried men's souls." Every messenger that galloped through the country carried tidings of woe. Congress fled in terror from Philadelphia. The tears of the wife mingled with the blood of the husband; and the wail of the orphan rose above the unburied corpse of the father. General Washington, at the head of a miserable remnant of four thousand men, was driven through New Jersey, and beyond the Delaware. Still, undismayed, he kept the field with his little band, and sent General Putnam to Philadelphia, (then the largest city in America,) to make such preparations for defense as the time allowed. In the active discharge of the numerous duties that devolved upon him as the aid-de-camp of General Putnam, the days and nights of Major Burr were fully occupied. General Washington had ordered a line of intrenchments and redoubts to be thrown up from the Delaware to the Schuylkill. The proper performance of this service required a degree of scientific knowledge that General Putnam did not possess, and he was compelled to trust a great deal to his aid-de-camp.

(131)

His confidence was not misplaced. Major Burr was everywhere present, carrying orders, giving directions to the workmen, and encouraging them in their labors. His slender frame was proof against fatigue, and his buoyant spirits neither permitted despondency in himself nor in others. The difficulties to be overcome were greatly increased, from the fact that the command consisted almost entirely of militia. General Washington could spare no others. He had need of all the regular troops he could muster for the brilliant winter campaign he was then contemplating, and which, beginning with the battle of Trenton, in three weeks resulted in relieving Philadelphia, in the recapture of every post the enemy had taken along the Delaware, and in the reconquest of almost the whole of the Jerseys. A campaign so astonishing, that an Italian historian declares it was "regarded with wonder by all nations, as well as the Americans."

From the gloom of despondency the spirits of the army and the people rose to the highest pitch of exulting hope. Philadelphia was no longer in immediate danger; and in the new disposition of his forces, General Washington transferred General Putnam to Princeton, in New Jersey. At this place Aaron Burr was born, and here his childhood was nursed; at this place his father and his mother were buried; at this place his education had been acquired. A few years before, he had gone out from its college walls happy and contented, with no want to oppress him, no sorrow to harass, no wrong to madden. Happy in the possession of his books, happy in the friendship of his associates, happier still in the kindness of his relatives, a life of sunny brightness spread itself out before the student. He came back to it a boy still in appearance, but in accomplishments a soldier of proved ability; and in heart a worn and sorrow-stricken man. He stood alone between the graves of his honored parents, and let his mind run back upon the family history. For three generations it had furnished the most celebrated lawyers, clergymen, and statesmen of the provinces. His father was eminent as the President of Princeton College, and still more eminent as a pulpit orator. His mother was the most accomplished woman of her time, and the daughter of that Jonathan Edwards who is still pointed to with pride, and whose memory is still cherished with fond affection by every genuine son of New England. On both sides, every drop of blood that flowed in his veins came from a fountain of unsullied purity; and in the long retrospect there was not one act to call a blush of shame to the cheek of their descendant. From these proud and pleasing recollections, he came down to his own less enviable lot.

"Not upon me," he said, "can the curse have fallen, that the sins of the parent shall be visited upon the children, even unto the third generation; for the three generations have gone by, and each one has been marked by the upheavings of a piety as fervent as that of Isaiah when the Seraphim had touched his lips with a living coal. Why did I not follow in their footsteps? Why did I not take up the weapons of the church, and do battle for the redemption of souls, rather than engage in the less ennobling strife whose fruits, however sweet, are mortal still; and whose victories, however great, are unsung in that eternal world in which at last the spirit finds its resting-place? What healing balsam can the world's brief triumphs pour on the riven fibers of the heart? From glory's fountain no Lethean waters roll over buried hopes and blasted joys. The higher we climb, the more we become like the Alpine glacier, from which the sun's beams are thrown in frozen radiance, and whose very brightness reveals more distinctly the gaps and rents that warring storms have made.

12

"Not to earthly honors did the venerated dead beneath me look for consolation and support. Not there did the father, the grandfather, and the great-grandfather turn when the trials that afflict the upright as well as the undeserving came upon them. Their thoughts turned upward in adversity, and to them crushed affections became a blessing, even as the bruised petals of the rose exhale a sweeter odor than its opening bloom gave out. To these pleasant fields I also was invited. Was it my fault that I accepted not the invitation? Surely it was in my nature to labor as they labored, and to worship as they worshiped! From my earliest boyhood the Bible has been to me the book of books. Its grand conceptions, its lofty poetry, and its pure morality, apart from the memory of its inspiration, clothed it in raiment of light; and, one after another, my soul drank in its beauties—from the bearded majesty of Moses to the vailed mystery of Malachi; from the fiery eloquence of Paul to the tearful history of John. There was nothing repugnant to my taste in the profession my fathers followed. No habit of idleness to deter—no love of dissipation to draw me from the Christian's walks. Nor were there wanting warm-hearted friends to remind me of their useful lives, and urge me to follow their blameless example. Yet I turned from it to wander through the mazes of a labyrinth that leads I know not where, but which I do know is infested by a poisonous malaria, in whose presence peace and happiness have withered and died. Was the choice mine? or was it the fulfillment of an eternal decree hung up in heaven centuries ago? or have I fallen upon the times when the Evil One, his thousand years of bondage over, is permitted to revisit the earth and lure the creature from the service of his Creator? Oh! much of this must remain unknown until the soul stands up before the illuminated record that is its accuser, its advocate, its witness, and its judge. Until that dread hour, let me be contented with the knowledge that the road to redemption not unfrequently runs through tears.

"In the first flush of youth, life and fortune were freely offered to my country. Another sacrifice was demanded; and even as Abraham journeyed to the mountains of Moriah with the child of his old age, did I bear an offering a thousand times more precious than his, and cast it down upon her altars. But unlike him, there was no voice to stay my hand—no ram, entangled in the bushes, for a substitute. The duty is fulfilled; the suffering remains. Yet to suffer well is to triumph; and, come what may, no tear shall roll over my cheek—no murmur escape my lips."

The self-promise then made was faithfully redeemed. In prosperity and adversity; at the height of power; in poverty and exile, that mighty heart was true to itself. True always. True and unfaltering to the last.

Up to this time his enemies had accomplished a great deal, though not all they expected. Morally they had effectually degraded him in the eyes of the commander-in-chief; but they had not blinded him to Major Burr's military merits. They had strong hopes that when the army came to be reorganized, and Washington (upon whom Congress had conferred dictatorial powers) should come to make his official appointments, Burr would be overlooked. It was impossible for meaner natures to understand fully the character of that illustrious man. They made the mistake of supposing that his private prejudices would influence his appointments, whereas patriotism and military capacity were his requisites, and in these his judgment was rarely at fault. The very persecution to which Burr had been subjected was in this aspect an advantage to him. The eye of the general was drawn more particularly to him, and he was less inclined to judge his conduct from the reports of others. Major Burr himself, knowing the prejudice against him at headquarters, anticipated no appointment. He judged wrongly; as others did.

In July, 1777, General Washington inclosed him the commission of lieutenant-colonel in the Continental army; an honor never before or since conferred upon a man of his age, unless General La Fayette can be regarded as an exception. His new appointment removed him from the family of General Putnam, whose unfaltering friendship and manly sympathy had cheered the darkest hours of his life. The parting on both sides was marked by feelings of warm and earnest regard.

"Good-by, my boy," faltered out the general, wringing Burr's slender hand in his own hard and horny grasp. "Your colonel is one of the best of men, and purest of patriots. He is no soldier, and only accepted the command because his refusal would have been an injury to the patriot cause. If you please him, as I know you will, he will soon turn over the regiment to your exclusive control, and I expect to hear such accounts of you as will make me feel proud of the interest I have taken in your advancement."

"Thank you, general, for this and for all your kindness. If you hear aught of Aaron Burr that does not give you pleasure, it will be that he has fallen in the battle's front, in the full and faithful discharge of his duty to his country."

Returning the warm pressure of the friendly hand, Colonel Burr mounted his horse and rode off to join his regiment. In those days a regiment consisted of an indefinite number of men, according to the success that attended its recruiting officers. Malcolm's regiment, to which Colonel Burr was assigned, was encamped on the Ramapo, and contained only about three hundred effective men. Nothing was easier than for a finished man of the world, and a born soldier like Burr, to obtain a complete ascendency over the mind of a man conscious of his own deficiencies, and sincerely desirous, on his country's account, that the command should be confided to more competent hands. In a few weeks, he became so perfectly satisfied that everything might be trusted to his lieutenant-colonel, that he withdrew entirely from the regiment, and never once interfered with its discipline or led it into battle while Colonel Burr continued in the service.

The rule of Malcolm had been an easy one; and Colonel Burr was surrounded by difficulties at the outset that called forth all his energies. The men were raw and inexperienced. The junior officers, taken mostly from the city, were destitute of military knowledge, and effeminate in their habits. Transferred at once from the indulgent sway of Malcolm to the rigid discipline of a man who was "every inch a soldier," and expected every one under his command to become like himself, the change operated, as such changes almost always do, most favorably upon the men, and unfavorably upon the officers. The soldiers submitted cheerfully to the long drills, the severe inspections, and the strict enforcement of every military regulation, when they saw that their officers were subjected to the same treatment. They respected the commander who was not above inspecting every pound of their rations and every article of their clothing, in order to convince himself that they were not imposed upon in either respect; and they absolutely loved him when they saw him making daily visits to the hospital, to examine the condition of the sick and afford them every comfort it was possible to obtain. This great step gained, he turned his attention to the officers, whose murmurs he had hitherto pretended not to hear. They were now subjected to a rigid examination, and at its conclusion he very quietly ordered a portion of them home, intimating that they had chosen the wrong profession, and

12*

had better remain there. This bold step was illegal, and he knew it; but it was demanded by the necessities of the times; and General Conway, under whose command he then was, cordially approved it. Thenceforward his task was easy. The remaining officers and the men went about their duties with a determination to perform them well. His ranks filled up, order reigned, and he had the satisfaction of writing to General Putnam that there was not a better disciplined regiment in the service.

Just as he had brought his soldiery to this satisfactory state of efficiency, a rumor reached him that a British force, two thousand strong, had marched out of New York and were within thirty miles of his position. Rejoiced at the opportunity thus offered of rendering a signal service to the cause, he put his men in motion to meet them. On the march he was met by an express from General Putnam, advising him to remove the public stores in his possession, and retreat to the mountains.

As the dispatch was in the form of advice, and contained no positive order, Colonel Burr determined to disregard it. A hard march of sixteen miles brought him by sundown to Paramus, where a body of militia had assembled, who, in their ignorance of military matters, were wasting time and labor in building a breastwork of fence-rails. Uniting his own troops with the militia, and putting a stop to the useless work in which they were engaged, he posted the whole command in an advantageous position, gave strict injunctions to guard against surprise, and proceeded himself, at the head of seventeen picked men, to ascertain the numbers and position of the enemy. About ten o'clock at night he learned from a countryman that he was within a mile of their picket guard. His men by this time were so much wearied that he thought it best to give them some repose, and, leading them into a thick wood, he left them there and proceeded alone to reconnoiter. He soon discovered that the information received from the countryman was correct, and further, that the picket of the enemy, entirely unapprehensive of danger, were fast asleep, and guarded by two sentries only. The British, unconscious of the near neighborhood of a hostile force, had laid down to sleep, leaving their camp fires burning. By crawling close up to the sentries, and bringing their bodies between him and the blazing fires, he was able to mark exactly their position, and to obtain a very correct knowledge of the numbers of the sleeping guard. His observations satisfied him that the picket might easily be captured or destroyed. Quickly returning to his own men, who had fallen asleep, overcome by fatigue, he roused them from their slumbers, and, briefly explaining his object, ordered them to follow in perfect silence. Notwithstanding all the celerity he could exert, by the time they arrived at the picket camp the fires had burned so low that the forms of the sentries could not be distinguished. Still he was sure he had marked the place too well to be mistaken. A whispered order was passed along the line, and, throwing himself on the ground, after the Indian fashion, he crawled toward his object. The rustling of a bush within five paces of him, attracted the attention of one of the sentries; his musket was brought suddenly down, and the stern challenge, "who goes there?" echoed through the woods. The answer was a leaden messenger from Burr's pistol, and the unfortunate soldier sank to rest upon his post. Almost at the same moment the order to "charge" rang loud and clear from his lips. Before the drowsy Britons gained their feet, the Americans were among them. In their astonishment, there was no thought of resistance. Only one man attempted to use his arms. He was bayoneted on the spot, and the remainder—twenty-seven privates, two non-commissioned and one commissioned officer—surrendered themselves prisoners of war.

Dispatch is the soul of military operations. The great Napoleon, after his Italian campaigns, declared that he had beaten the overwhelming numbers that were sent against him solely because their generals did not understand the value of minutes. Nothing was ever lost by Aaron Burr for the want of activity. He did not even wait to see that all his prisoners were secured, before sending off a messenger to bring up the forces he had left at Paramus. He had not closed his eyes for more than thirty-six hours, yet he allowed himself no repose. Through the morning, messengers were dispatched to different neighborhoods to bring up all the militia that could be gathered. These messengers spread the tidings of his partial success. It was of course magnified into a splendid victory, and before nightfall he had concentrated an imposing force, with which he resolved to give battle to the invading troops. The enemy, however, alarmed by exaggerated reports, did not wait his approach, but abandoned the plunder they had collected, and beat a hasty retreat. Colonel Burr, intent upon bringing them to an engagement, gave directions for an energetic pursuit. To his great mortification, he was stopped by an express from headquarters, ordering him to march at once to the main army in Pennsylvania, where General Washington was sorely pressed by Sir William Howe.

The defeat of Brandywine had been followed by the bloody repulse of Germantown. Red Bank and Fort Mifflin had been taken. The British army was in possession of Philadelphia, and the Delaware was open to the British shipping, when Colonel Burr joined the main army of the Americans, twelve miles above Philadelphia. To compensate for these losses, Burgoyne's fine army of ten thousand veteran troops had been destroyed or captured by Gates, and thirty-five brass field-pieces were thereby added to the American means of defense. On the whole, the commander-in-chief had reason to be satisfied. He had lost the finest city on the continent it is true, and had been beaten in some bloody encounters. But that was all. His strength was undiminished, and his resources were greater than they were twelve months before. On the other hand, the loss of Burgoyne's army was almost irreparable to England. Sir William Howe, the victor, drew his men into winter quarters, gloomy and discontented. Washington, the defeated, calmly and hopefully erected a little city of huts on the banks of the Schuylkill, and exerted every nerve to straiten and harass his enemy.

In this poor apology for winter quarters, where the men, almost destitute of shoes and blankets, shivered through a dreadful winter, the intrigues against Colonel Burr were renewed. Alexander Hamilton was now upon the staff of General Washington, and had completely gained his confidence. In the preceding two months he had been sent to the Northern army under Gates to hurry forward reinforcements to the main body. In the discharge of this duty, which he performed zealously and well, he took occasion to further his own private ends. General Putnam's warm friendship for Colonel Burr was known and dreaded. In his correspondence with General Washington, the arch-intriguer let slip no opportunity of disparaging the old soldier whom all America now delights to honor. It was his remorseless policy to weaken every hand that might be raised in Colonel Burr's defense, and, in pursuance of that policy, he did not hesitate to avail himself of the confidential relations existing between himself and the commander-in-chief, to bring the most serious private accusations against one of the boldest and purest

of the revolutionary leaders. He charged him with having
neglected or deranged everything in the department under
his command; and, knowing General Washington's sensi-
tiveness on that point, he more than intimated that General
Putnam was concocting a plan for the surprise of New
York, without the sanction, and for the purpose of over-
clouding the glory of the commander-in-chief. He neglected nothing, in short, which could create distrust of the
officer whose influence he dreaded more perhaps than that
of any other soldier in the army of the United States.
Nor was he entirely unsuccessful. He did not, indeed,
accomplish all he desired, but he did raise suspicions in
the mind of Washington which were never completely
removed, and the intercourse between the two generals
was thenceforth marked by less cordiality than ought to
have existed between men so distinguished for patriotic
devotion to liberty and the country.

Upon Hamilton's return from the North, he found James
Billings in the American camp. That bold, bad man, had
made liberal advances to purchase supplies for the army,
and his patriotism was so highly esteemed that he easily
procured permission to put up for himself a house of
superior accommodations within the lines of Valley Forge.
At this house Colonel Hamilton sought his confederate
on the night of the 25th of December, 1777. A blazing
wood fire sent forth its genial warmth from the ample
hearth-stone; bottles and glasses were placed upon a
table drawn conveniently between the two occupants of
the room. As yet the conversation seemed to have been
on indifferent topics, but Billings now sought to direct
it into more serious channels.

"You have not employed your time badly since I left.
To have risen to the rank of lieutenant-colonel, is a great

deal; to have secured the confidence of Washington, a great deal more!"

"I have indeed risen as rapidly as I had any reason to expect; and in one sense my position is more favorable; but these staff duties, while they bring me into constant communication with the commander-in-chief, and are so far favorable, have yet their drawbacks. No opportunities for individual distinction are presented to me. I must move always in the shadow of another."

"True, if you hold it always! but what is there, when your plans are sufficiently ripened, to prevent you from seeking employment in the line?"

"Much! Much more than any one unacquainted with the ever-watchful jealousies of our officers can comprehend. General Washington, from undue respect for the complaints of line officers, has adopted a rule not to give appointments to staff officers that may interfere with their claims to rank. I fear he is immovable, but something may be done."

"Yes! anything—everything may be done by a man who works pertinaciously and intelligently. At present your best place is exactly where you are. When your plans are ripe, sever the knot which binds you to Washington, if you cannot untie it, and take your destiny in your own keeping."

"Such is my purpose, though I foresee many difficulties in the way of its accomplishment."

"There are difficulties between us and every earthly prize which is worth the winning. If we stop to count them we shall never attain our objects. Conquer them as they rise, and do not tremble at their anticipated coming."

"I am not much given to trembling, either at shadows or realities; yet methinks it is good soldiership to anticipate and prepare for all that may happen. There is nothing lost by erecting bulwarks to keep out a danger which we know must come some day, and may come early."

"Granted,—if it brings no despondency, no cessation of effort. But what difficulties do you anticipate other than the jealousies you have named?"

"I may have to leave General Washington in such a way as to forfeit his friendship."

"Trust to a stray bullet to carry him off before that time comes, or, at least, before you become a sufferer from the loss of his regard. If fortune should fail you in that respect, trust to me. I have neither scruples nor remorse, and this hand has seldom stricken a blow which needed repetition. It may prove your best reliance at last."

Colonel Hamilton was startled by the tone and manner, as much as by the words, of his fiend-like confederate. The blood forsook his cheek, his hand trembled, and his hair stood erect, at the bare thought of the dark and terrible deed to which his companion so distinctly pointed. His voice had a strange hoarseness as he asked,—

"What do you—what can you mean?"

"You are nervous, my dear colonel; take a glass of wine, and I will answer your inquiry."

His own glass was filled to the brim. Draining it slowly like a man who enjoys what he is drinking, he replaced it on the table and continued,—

"I mean, that if General Washington was, to-day, the only obstacle to the success of your plans, and his removal would crown you king of this fair domain, it should be my care to remove that obstacle. What I would do to-day it is tolerably certain that I shall have the will to do to-morrow, or any succeeding day. If he lives, the time will come, in all probability, when it must be done, though I believe that time is yet afar off. According to my calculation, John

Bull's obstinacy will prolong this war for ten years to come. The last two years of hostilities will be the proper period for the accomplishment of your ends, *and mine*. Let him go on until an empire is just ready to fall into his grasp, and then"—he paused and drew his breath hard before he concluded—"my last service will be performed."

Astonished, shocked, almost terror stricken at the dreadful villainy so remorselessly contemplated, and so daringly avowed, Hamilton walked to the door and threw it open to let the freezing night air blow upon his burning brow. His throat was parched, his lips dry and hard; and, returning again to his seat, he swallowed two glasses of generous wine in quick succession.

"For God's sake, Billings," he gasped, "never allude to this subject again!"

"I do not intend to do so," was the cool rejoinder. "It is enough to talk of such a matter *once*."

"Too much!" almost groaned Hamilton in reply.

James Billings took no notice of the agitated manner of his companion, but refilled his glass and drank it off deliberately, occasionally holding it before the light to admire its color.

"I find," at length he said, "that Colonel Burr is highly esteemed as a military man, and that he is rapidly growing into favor alike with officers and soldiers. Would it not be well to turn your attention to that point, and cripple him before he obtains too strong a hold on the affections of the army?"

"My attention has been directed to it, and I have done what I could to keep him back without seeming to desire it. But somehow he has the faculty to make, or the good fortune to find, opportunities for distinction where no one else could. Even now, he is applying for permission to

13

lead an expedition against Staten Island, which will be almost sure to add greatly to his reputation as a soldier."

"Thwart him. You can surely find means enough. The men are destitute of shoes and blankets. The weather is terrible; and two days' exposure, you might plausibly argue, would cut off more than a battle."

"I thought of that; but he proposes to take only two hundred of his own best appointed men, and rely upon raising the people of the country in sufficient numbers for his purpose. Besides, I really think the expedition will do great good to the republican cause."

"It will do *you* no good; and the cause is progressing toward a triumphant conclusion quite as fast as your interest or mine demands. If I could have my will, Burgoyne's army would now be comfortably quartered in New York."

"It would be a death-blow to the independence of America."

"Not at all. It would only put it off a year or two longer. If you cannot stop this purposed expedition altogether, why send it forward, but send it with an officer of superior rank to monopolize the glory."

"Burr would not go. I would not consent to act as second in an expedition I had planned myself, and I am sure he will not."

"Let him stay then. His refusal to go may be turned against him. At all events, it accomplishes your object."

"I will think of it," replied Hamilton, "and act according to circumstances."

"I see no objection to that course, provided that at the same time you make up your mind to act according to circumstances, you make it up also to have a finger in shaping the circumstances. To inflict a telling blow on Colonel Burr justifies some risk. He has all the qualities to make a rival dangerous, as I have before had occasion to remind

you.   With a strong and powerful intellect, a mind stored
with much and varied learning, accomplished beyond most
men of his day, utterly fearless, and deeply ambitious, he
is a man to be watched and feared; and whenever a single
feather can be drawn from his pinions, the opportunity
should not be allowed to pass unimproved.   No other
young officer has any chance against you, and as for the
older ones, history, if it teaches anything, teaches us that
the first leaders of a successful revolution rarely ever reap
its highest rewards.   Who would have dreamed at the
beginning of the English civil wars, that the rough and
ungainly Colonel of the Ironsides would be the foremost
man in the kingdom at its close ?"

No immediate reply was made, and the conversation,
when it was resumed, turned to other subjects.   It was
near midnight when Colonel Hamilton rose to depart.

"By the way," he said, taking his overcoat in his hand,
"we have been so deeply interested that I forgot to ask
where you had been since our parting."

"To St. Croix.   I wished to ascertain if that fellow
Williams, of whom you once spoke to me, was really any
one whom I had ever known, and I preferred making the
journey myself to trusting to another who might be intimi-
dated, or make mistakes, or accept bribes from other hands
than mine."

"Did you find him ; and did you know him ?"

"I saw him, but too late to learn anything from him.
As ill luck would have it, the very day after my arrival,
he was found dead in a thicket of mangos; and, up to
the time of my departure, which you may be assured was
not unnecessarily delayed, his murderer had not been discovered."

Colonel Hamilton drew on his coat rather hastily—bade
his companion "good night," and in another moment was

tramping over the frozen snow in the direction of his own quarters.

"That will do," muttered Billings, closing the door, and returning to the fire. "He knows well enough who struck that blow, and will feel that he has one hold less upon me. He must be desperate, indeed, before he resorts to that other alternative which he hissed in my ear on the heights of Harlæm."

James Billings habitually slept but little, and that little at whatever time proved most convenient. He rarely dismissed any of the many problems which, at different periods, thronged his busy brain, before he had worked out a satisfactory solution. It was his habit, always before seeking repose, to think over any conversation of interest in which he had been engaged, and to calculate how far he had succeeded in making the impression he desired. At such times his thoughts almost invariably took the form of words, and he appeared to derive increased self-satisfaction from the sound of his own voice. On the present occasion he drew off his boots, incased his feet in a pair of morocco slippers, lighted a fragrant Havana, and settled himself comfortably down to *think aloud.*

"For a man of sense," so ran his thoughts, "for a man of sense, and very few troublesome scruples, Hamilton was startled more than could have been expected when I hinted at the indispensable necessity of putting George Washington out of the way when our plans were ripe, or nearly so. I am glad I mentioned it so soon. He must grow familiar with the idea before the time comes for putting it into execution. He has gone off now believing it impossible that his consent can ever be given to my suggestion; but I have read the book of human nature too attentively to be deceived in such a case. It is one of those ideas which, when they once obtain an entrance into a man's head, will come back, no matter how often they may be driven away, and every time they present a less forbidding aspect. There will be no necessity for me to refer to it again. It will force itself upon his attention, and, in process of time, he will come to regard it as a very dear and familiar friend, whose society, instead of creating uneasiness, is of exceeding comfort in dark and cloudy weather. On that score I have no fears, notwithstanding his seeming horror at the proposition; and the net I have been so industriously weaving, in that part at least is sound. My chief apprehension is the want of time. Our hopes will be as effectually blasted by an early termination of the war, as by England's reconquest of her provinces. Brother Jonathan comes of a stiff-necked race, who have, before now, taken off the heads of legitimate sovereigns, and he is of a temper to follow the ancestral example, if any premature usurper should attempt to fetter his limbs before he is completely wearied and disgusted by successive years of lawlessness and blood. In that case only will he consent to exchange his dreams of freedom for the government of a prince, albeit that prince should be of his own selection. We are getting along too fast now, and I must contrive to put some clog upon the wheels. An occasional hint to Sir William Howe, such as may enable him to gain partial successes, will do the business—and, by the Lord, he shall have it! This Staten Island expedition offers a good chance for a beginning. If Colonel Burr commands it, a double purpose may be gained by preparing the British to meet him. If he does not, there is still the chance of affixing more or less odium upon him as the original proposer of an adventure which has ended in disaster and defeat. The game seems to me easy enough. All that is needful is so to regulate my information, that it will not serve the British commander any further than just enough to keep up his hopes, by enabling

13*

him to gain immaterial triumphs. The thing, on its face,
is plain and simple; but we never can foresee all the consequences of such maneuvers, reflect upon them as carefully as we may. It is a ticklish business, and few could
be trusted with its management; but there is no great
probability of my losing anything from a want of skill or
nerve, in playing my hand to the best advantage. At all
events, I shall make the experiment. Hamilton need not
know anything about it. Indeed, he must not. He would
be interposing troublesome objections, and would withhold
information that he will communicate freely, so long as he
does not know to what use I intend to put it."

Having decided upon his course, James Billings dismissed the subject from his mind, and sought his couch
with a brow whose unruffled smoothness betrayed no sign
of the dark schemes which had been working within

CHAPTER IX.

"Full in thine eye is waved the glittering blade,
Close to thy throat the pointed bayonet laid,
The level'd muskets circle round thy breast,
In hands as steeled to do the deadly rest."

THE suggestion of Billings was not lost upon Hamilton; and in a few days Colonel Burr received notice that his application for permission to make an attack upon Staten Island had been rejected. Afterwards the mind of the commander-in-chief appeared to undergo a change, and Lord Stirling was sent to perform the service Burr had suggested. Notice of Lord Stirling's designs was communicated to the British commander, through whose agency the reader will be at no loss to determine, and the enterprise in consequence proved to be a failure. Colonel Burr, thus cut off from one road to distinction, soon found another. The cool courage and untiring energy which he had exhibited on the night of Washington's retreat from Long Island had not been overlooked or forgotten, and to that he owed his appointment to a situation where such qualities were indispensable in the commanding officer. Ten miles from the main camp at Valley Forge, there was a pass called the Gulf. If the enemy should leave the city at any time during the winter, to attack him, it was from this point that Washington expected to receive the earliest notice of his movements. Accordingly, he posted a strong body of militia at the pass, instructing the officer in command to keep patrols and spies continually on the alert, so that he might be instantly apprised of any movement in force Sir William Howe might attempt to make. The optics of these militia men were unfortunately endowed with magnifying properties whenever they were required to look at a "red-coat," and the consequence was, that to their vision every little foraging party assumed the proportions of an army, and the commander-in-chief was continually annoyed by false alarms, some of which caused him to draw out his whole force, and expose them needlessly to the bitter blasts of winter. After various attempts to correct the evil, General McDougall advised him to send Colonel Burr to the Gulf, and withdraw all the officers superior to him in rank, so that the whole direction of matters should devolve on him. This advice accorded so well with Washington's own estimate of Burr's fitness for the place that it was promptly adopted, and orders were at once issued to carry it into effect. It is probable that Hamilton made no objection to the arrangement, since it seemed to furnish his rival with little chance for increased distinction.

Placed again in an independent command, untrammeled by other than mere general orders, Colonel Burr devoted himself to the duties that devolved upon him. His activity knew no pause. His vigilance never slumbered. He was always in the right place, exactly at the right time.

Knowing full well the importance of discipline at all times, and particularly under such circumstances, his first care was to establish a rigid system, which he enforced with unflinching determination. Heretofore the excesses of the militia had been winked at, under the impression that there were no other means of keeping them in the service. The consequence was, that they had become more formidable to the people of the country than to the enemy. Colonel Burr believed that they could be reduced to as strict subordination as regular troops, and he determined that they should be. No drill was omitted on account of the severity of the weather, as had previously been the custom. No excuse

was accepted for the non-performance of any duty, and no
criminal was allowed to go unpunished. The men, long
accustomed to the license of freebooters, broke into open
murmurs, which grew louder daily, as one after another
suffered the penalties incurred by their predatory habits.
About this time, James Billings rode over to the Gulf, and
was observed during the day in close conversation with a
stalwart soldier who had been severely punished for some
misdemeanor the preceding day. When they parted, the
soldier's pocket was heavier by several pieces of gold,
though what had been agreed upon between them could
only be inferred from the events which followed. As soon
as night came, the soldier, urged on by the strong incen-
tives of gain and revenge, cautiously passed from hut to
hut, stirring up the worst men at the post, reminding them
of the punishments they had received, and pointing out to
them that there was no hope of any relaxation of the stern
rules to which they were subjected, except in the death of
their present commander. In that army, as in every other,
there were abundance of men ready for any deed of violence,
upon even less provocation than that which they chose to
consider had been offered; and, during that night and the
next day, the conspiracy came to a head. For the purpose
of dividing the responsibility, it was determined that when
the colonel made his appearance at the evening parade, a
dozen muskets should be discharged at him at once. As
the hour approached, one of the number grew nervous, and
disclosed the plot. To arrest and place the mutineers in
irons, was an obvious mode of avoiding the danger; but
Colonel Burr regarded this as a temporary expedient,
which, however it might succeed at the time, would have
little effect in preventing other mutinies in the future. He
wished to give them a more impressive lesson. With this
view, he caused all the suspected soldiers to be detailed for

fatigue duty, and while they were thus engaged, secretly drew the charges from their muskets. When the hour for evening parade came, instead of approaching them in front, he came up on the right flank and walked slowly down the line, eying each man intently as he passed. About the center of the line, the chief mutineer stepped from the ranks, leveled his musket, and shouting, "Now, boys, is our time !" pulled the trigger. The unloaded gun merely flashed in the pan, and, quick as lightning, the saber of Colonel Burr descended upon the right arm of the mutineer, cleaving entirely through the bone, and severing the limb completely from the body. The musket dropped to the ground, and the baffled murderer mechanically obeyed the stern order, "Back, sir, to your place in the line !" Not another word, was spoken. Colonel Burr continued his walk to the extreme left; and then, taking his place in front, went through with the dress parade as if nothing had occurred. From that hour the spirit of disaffection was at an end. Complaints from the country people ceased entirely. That lawless militia were converted into the most orderly soldiers of the army, and not a single false alarm was borne to Valley Forge.

Some expressions dropped by Billings on the day of the mutiny, induced Hamilton to suspect that he had been engaged in fomenting the discontent of the soldiery, and after the failure of the attempt to assassinate Colonel Burr, he sought his house for the purpose of ascertaining how far his conjectures were right. He found that worthy surrounded by the comforts we have described on a former occasion.

"I did not expect," he said, rising to greet his visitor, "the honor of your company to-night; but it is always agreeable. Take a glass of wine, and let me know whether you have merely called on a friendly visit, or whether there is anything you want done."

"There is something," replied Hamilton, "that I wish undone; and I have strong misgivings that you had a greater agency in it than was prudent for you or service-able to me."

Now James Billings did not have the least doubt on his mind that Hamilton alluded to the unsuccessful attempt to murder Aaron Burr; but he wanted a moment for reflec-tion, and, to obtain that, he leisurely took a cigar from the box on the table, deliberately bit off the twisted end, and lighted it before he replied.

"I shall be sorry if anything disagreeable to you has occurred; and more so, if I have had a hand in it. Pray, what is it? I have heard nothing important."

"You have heard, I suppose, of the mutiny at the Gulf, and of Jackson's attempt to shoot Colonel Burr."

"Of course! I could not help hearing what has been the common camp talk for a whole day. It has afforded to our little city of huts so delightful a theme of gossip, that I verily believe one-half of them forgot they were shoeless, and the other half ceased to complain of the thread-bare blankets which covered them."

"This matter is serious, Billings, and I pray you to drop that sneering tone, and let me know what agency you had in it."

"You are entitled to my confidence, Colonel Hamilton, and you shall have it. My agency was very limited. It began without any intervention on my part. I found Jackson in the mood to rid you of a troublesome rival, and I barely intimated that so long as I could assist him he should be no sufferer by his unsolicited kindness. The murder of Colonel Burr was not mentioned by either of us; though, to be entirely frank with you, I was sure he had that pleasant idea in his head. We only spoke of his tyranny, and of the comfort that would result to the soldiers at the Gulf if such a disturbance could be created as would induce the general to recall him. In everything else the blundering fool acted on his own responsibility, and richly deserves the punishment he received, not so much for the crime he meditated, as for the folly of snapping an unloaded musket at the bosom of a man who had a drawn saber in his hand and no little skill in the use of the weapon."

"I wish the blow had fallen on his head, instead of his arm," replied Hamilton. "You have given him a fearful power over you; and who can tell what moment he may use it? Men become excellent subjects for remorse when wounds and pain have reduced them to the weakness of children."

"He has no power over me whatever. If every word I uttered was written down, and submitted to a court-martial, it would be impossible for them to find me guilty of anything but an imprudent expression of sympathy in a case which I, being a citizen unacquainted with military regulations, could not be expected to understand fully."

As he uttered these words, a scornful smile curled the lips of that daring man, and a momentary fierceness flashed from his eyes, which belied his assumed ignorance of the law of arms, and told plainly enough that in his own soul he despised the plea he was urging.

Hamilton noticed it, but made no comment, and went on as if it had been unobserved.

"You might be mistaken in that. There are officers in this army who believe that you have seen more of a soldier's life, and know more that pertains to his duty, than you seem disposed to acknowledge. I heard General Lee offer to lay a heavy wager that such was the case."

"General Lee is a vain, imperious, headstrong fool, who fancies that he knows more than George Washington and all his general officers combined; and who, acting under this belief, will be certain to get himself into serious trou ble before long. My advice to you is to cut loose from his friendship as early and as rudely as possible."

"Well, it is unnecessary to discuss General Lee's char acter at present. From your statement, I am satisfied that the danger Colonel Burr has escaped was of your contriv ance, and I must tell you that your mode of proceeding is rather too decided to meet my approbation. I insist that hereafter you keep clear of treasonable plots; that you leave Colonel Burr to take his chances from the bullets of the enemy, and that you do not again run the risk of com promising me by a like act of damnable villainy."

"Your language is strong, colonel; but, as my little scheme proved a failure, I deserve to hear it so charac terized. As for the future, rest easy. I do not expect to be favored with such another opportunity; and, if I am, your strong repugnance will be sufficient to prevent me from using it. There can be no harm in adding, however, that in my judgment you are wrong, and I would rather have lost a finger than to have made the promise you have now drawn from me."

Hamilton mused for some moments, and then said,—

"I should like to know, Billings, what cause you have to hate Colonel Burr so cordially?"

"Not a particle," was the easy and unembarrassed reply. "Colonel Burr is in my way, and I pursue him precisely as I would a wolf or any other dangerous animal. I never heard of him until after the assault on Quebec. You pointed him out to me as a formidable antagonist. Until then, I had no interest in the man. After that, I studied his character, traced out his history and that of his family; marked his conduct, and weighed his ability. I found that you had not over-estimated him, and made up my

14

mind to destroy him at any cost. On the occasion of his
rupture with the commander-in-chief, I hoped that he
would become disgusted, and abandon the army. If he
had done so, I would have dismissed him from my mind,
or at least ceased to remember him as an enemy. He preferred to adopt another course, which left me no alternative but to consider him still as an obstruction in my pathway, or in yours, which is the same. Again, I hoped that
in the distribution of field-commissions he would be overlooked; that also failed. Then I found the hand of a
desperate mutineer armed against his life, and added a
few arguments to strengthen his purpose. Here, too, I
encountered disappointment. And now, you, who are the
last man in the world who ought to interfere for his protection, have tied me by a promise not to repeat the attempt.
If I was such an idiot as to believe in any destiny except that
which is shaped out by a firm will and unbending purpose,
I should be inclined to give up the struggle in despair."

"There is no necessity for giving up the struggle, and
no necessity for personal violence either. Events that cannot be safely hurried, must be waited on; and there never
was a case to which this truism more forcibly applied."

"Such, I know, has been your policy from the beginning. Mine was sharp and sudden. It failed, as men's
schemes are apt to fail who trust to third persons for their
execution. It is but fair that yours should have a full
trial; and I repeat that I will not again interfere without
your knowledge and consent. But come, my throat is dry,
and I feel strangely depressed to-night. Let us try what
effect this good wine will have upon the spirits. We can
talk of business another time."

For an hour the wine circulated freely, and when Hamilton rose to depart, not a trace of anxiety was visible on
the countenance of either.

CHAPTER X.

"Hark! the trumpet's blast is ringing,
And banners wave along the coast;
Freedom to the field is bringing
The remnant of her shattered host."

THE terrible winter of 1777–78 at length wore away
The season for active operations had arrived, yet both parties seemed willing to repose a little longer on their arms.
The occupation of Philadelphia had proved to the British almost as fatal as that of Capua to Hannibal. Sir William Howe had captured the city at the expense of much toil and blood; but in so doing, he had gained no substantial military advantage. It had indeed supplied him with comfortable winter quarters for his men, but this advantage was more than counterbalanced by the evils which accompanied it. The dissipation which it is impossible to prevent among the conquerors in a conquered city, had enervated a large portion of his men, and others made acquaintances and formed attachments which caused them to desert by the hundred. Dr. Franklin never exhibited a deeper knowledge of human nature than in his reply to the French Minister at Paris, who informed him that General Howe had taken Philadelphia. "Say, rather," replied the doctor, "that Philadelphia has taken him." The prediction was verified. One winter in the city sufficed to demoralize the best army that England had as yet landed on our shores.

In the spring of 1778, General Howe, wisely deeming that British laurels were of rare growth on American soil,

(159)

solicited permission from his government to surrender the chief command in America, and return to England. His request was complied with, and Sir Henry Clinton appointed in his stead. The new commander soon became aware of the evils resulting from the hard-won conquest of his predecessor, and, as he could perceive no countervailing advantage from its occupation as a military post, he determined to abandon it. This was a maneuver that General Washington had no idea of permitting him to execute in peace. His scouts were constantly on the alert, and when, on the eighteenth of June, the enemy crossed the river and began his retreat, the American army was almost instantly in motion. The march of the British was necessarily retarded by the long train of wagons and pack-horses which they had collected for the transportation of their plunder, while the troops of Washington were light, and unencumbered by anything except their arms. A knowledge of this enabled the American commander to calculate with great certainty the time and place where the enemy must be overtaken, and his dispositions were made accordingly. Morgan's Rifles were ordered to gain their right flank; Maxwell's brigade their left; and fifteen hundred picked men, under General Scott, to overtake and gall their rear.

Before reaching Monmouth Court House, Sir Henry Clinton became aware that he must soon be overtaken, and, like a consummate soldier, as he was, immediately changed the disposition of his troops, placing his baggage train in front and his most reliable veterans in the rear. That night, (June twenty-seventh,) he encamped in a strong position, protected by impenetrable marshes on either flank. Though fully aware of the strength of the enemy's position, at five o'clock on the morning of the twenty-eighth, General Washington, who was in the rear of his own army, sent orders to General Lee to begin

the attack; but that officer, from some unaccountable
cause, certainly not from a want of courage, instead
of an attack, began a disorderly and hazardous retreat.
A message from La Fayette brought Washington himself
to the front. Those who saw him on that occasion describe him as animated by a passion that it was fearful
to behold. Every muscle of his usually serene and placid
countenance was alive and working. His eye burned with
a fire that was absolutely scorching, and his voice rang
louder than the trumpet that sounded the charge. Fiercely
he demanded of General Lee the cause of "this ill-timed
prudence;" fiercely he rode among the men and ordered
them to halt, face about, and meet the now exultant and
pursuing foe. His presence acted like magic, and soon,
along the whole line, the roar of artillery, and the regular,
sustained volleys of musketry, told that the retreat was at
an end.

Most of the details of that glorious day have been em-
balmed in more enduring histories than this, and the course
of our narrative only requires special notice of the operations of the left flank, where Lord Stirling commanded, and
under whom fought Aaron Burr.

Anticipating a general engagement, Colonel Burr had
employed nearly the whole of the preceding night recon-
noitering the ground in his front. The sickness or absence
of his superiors had devolved upon him the command of
one of Stirling's brigades, which was, early in the action,
opposed to a superior British force. Steadily and firmly
the veterans of England came on. With equal firmness
the Continentals, under their youthful commander, awaited
their approach. At the distance of fifty yards the British
order to "charge" was given—an order which was immediately answered by that stern shout of the hardy Islanders
which has spread terror through the ranks of their foes in

every quarter of the globe; but now they were faced by men of kindred blood, and the response was a murderous volley, which checked their career and made wide gaps in their bristling line. Another, and another, succeeded; and then, in turn, the clear voice of Aaron Burr was heard above the noises of the battle,—"Forward, and sweep them from the field!" Disordered as the British were by the heavy fires of musketry, they met the onset with all the proverbial courage and stubbornness of the race. Burr's second in command was killed by his side, and his own horse shot under him, before the enemy were borne back, rather than driven back to a morass, where they promptly reformed behind a supporting force.

The issue of the direct attack in front had impressed upon the British officers a useful lesson, and they now endeavored, by skillful maneuvering, to gain his left flank. Here again they were met, and again they were foiled. Throughout the whole of that oppressive day combat succeeded combat, and when night put an end to the battle, Colonel Burr threw himself upon the ground where he had fought, in the midst of his men, with the dying and the dead around him, and impatiently awaited the reappearance of daylight, to renew the engagement. Sir Henry Clinton, however, had fared too badly during the day to willingly risk another struggle. If Washington's order had been obeyed by Lee in the early morning, he must have been totally routed; as it was, his losses were terrible; and, now that his baggage train had gained a day's march, every prudential consideration urged him to decamp, secretly, during the night, and follow after them. The morning of the twenty-ninth revealed to the Americans a camp occupied by none but those whose wounds had converted them from enemies into objects of compassion.

The unremitted exertions of Colonel Burr on the field

of Monmouth, his exposure to the burning sun at noonday, and the chilling dews at night, were too much for his
delicate organization, and he rose from the ground on the
morning after the battle, so cramped and stiffened, that he
was unable to mount his horse without assistance. Yet
his physical sufferings brought no abatement of his patriotic zeal. He refused to let his name be entered on the
sick report, and cheerfully, in obedience to the orders of
Washington, marched to the neighborhood of New York,
to watch the motions and obtain information of the intentions of the enemy. This duty was discharged to the entire satisfaction of the commander-in-chief; and when his
services in that vicinity were no longer needed, he was
ordered to proceed with his regiment to West Point. At
West Point, the disease contracted at Monmouth reap-
peared in an aggravated form. He had taxed his physical
powers beyond their strength, and was compelled to seek
repose. A few weeks, passed among his old friends in
Elizabethtown, improved his health so much that he was
induced to believe a respite from labor, until the opening of
the next campaign, would restore it entirely. The near
approach of winter, and consequent suspension of active
operations, took away much of his reluctance to ask for a
furlough; and on the twenty-fourth of October he wrote to
General Washington, giving an exact account of the state
of his health, and requesting leave to retire *from pay and
duty* until the coming spring. General Washington, always
severely just and upright, did not look at the subject in the
same light that Colonel Burr did. He thought Burr's
fears of the malicious insinuations of enemies groundless,
and believed his feelings of delicacy at receiving pay during
a period of temporary inactivity overstrained. He thought
that an officer was as much entitled to pay during the
period necessary for the restoration of his health, broken in

the service of his country, as when he was actually in the field. and he could not understand how that country could withhold compensation, under the circumstances, without discredit to itself. Jealous of the honor of the Republic, and decided in his own opinion of the right, he replied to Colonel Burr's application in a letter whose pointed brevity is eloquent of the straightforward justice of the man :—

> "HEADQUARTERS, FREDERICKSBURG,
> 26th Oct., 1778.

" DEAR SIR :

"I have your favor of the twenty-fourth. You, in my opinion, carry your ideas of delicacy too far, when you propose to drop your pay while the recovery of your health requires your absence from the service. It is not customary, and it would be unjust. You therefore have leave to retire until your health is so far re-established as to enable you to do your duty. Be pleased to give the colonel notice of this, that he may know where to call upon you, should any unforeseen emergency require it.

"I am your obedient servant,
"G. WASHINGTON."

Burr's military conduct had thus far escaped the misrepresentations of envy; but he was painfully conscious that he had been sorely wounded in other respects, by false and malignant accusations. Notwithstanding the unbroken silence he maintained, no man ever suffered more under the lash of calumny. He shrunk from the venom of an evil tongue as timidly as a blushing girl. He did not know how soon the accuser might enter the sanctuary of his military life, and he trembled at the bare idea. Determined not to furnish the slightest excuse for ill-natured comments, he refused to accept the proffered leave of absence except upon his own terms, and immediately repaired to his post.

Sir Henry Clinton, exasperated by his losses, and believing that a conciliatory policy would only add to the arrogance of rebels who had arms in their hands, determined henceforth to carry on the war upon a system of cruelty and plunder disgraceful to himself and to the country which employed him. Baylor's dragoons were surprised at night, near Tappan, and indiscriminately slaughtered. Pulaski's legion mèt a similar fate at Egg Harbor. Nor were these barbarities confined to men who had taken up arms in the cause of the colonies. Peaceful citizens were remorselessly butchered, helpless females were outraged, and little children driven out houseless in the wintry weather. No part of the country witnessed more of these horrors than Westchester County, in the State of New York. From the very beginning of the war, the divisions among its inhabitants had caused it to be overrun now by Whigs, now by Tories, and now by armed banditti who served whatever party promised at the time the greatest amount of plunder and the greatest license to cruelty. Scenes of rapine and lawless violence increased to such a degree, toward the close of 1778, that, in the language of an eye-witness, "no man went to his bed but under the apprehension of having his house plundered or burned, and himself or family massacred before morning." The British forces in New York made frequent incursions into the country, and it was at all times overrun by their spies and emissaries. To counteract these evils and punish these outrages, various American officers had at different times been stationed upon the lines of Westchester; but all had been either outwitted and cut up by the enemy, or had imbibed the universal proclivity for plunder and murder, and become themselves no better than marauders. General McDougall, who had taken command of the district of country of which Westchester constituted a part, resolved that this state of things should come to an end—that the plundering parties from New York should be met and driven back—that the inhabitants who remained peacefully at home should be protected, and the British emissaries detected and punished. In seeking for an officer upon whom he could fully rely to carry out his energetic purposes, he disregarded the claims of rank, and, overlooking several others who imagined they were entitled to a preference, he called Colonel Burr from Haverstraw, where he was then stationed, and appointed him to the command of the lines from the Hudson to the Sound, a distance of fourteen miles — his headquarters being at White Plains, near the center. In his orders, General McDougall gave still further proof of his unbounded confidence in the valor, the discretion, the activity, the humanity, and the justice of Colonel Burr. After enumerating many things to which he wished particular attention should be paid, he added, in reference to all doubtful cases, *I authorize you to be sole judge.* Thus, at the age of twenty-three, Colonel Burr was vested with almost unlimited powers in the command of one of the most important points in America. After events vindicated the choice of his general, and proved that the confidence reposed in him was not misplaced.

On the day of his arrival at his future headquarters, he found his predecessor preparing to set out on an expedition whose ostensible object was to watch the movements of the enemy near New Rochelle. Ill advised and injudicious as Colonel Burr regarded this enterprise, he did not feel authorized to interfere, further than to enjoin upon Colonel Littlefield a strict regard for the rights of property, and a careful observance of military discipline on the march. The scouting party were gone the whole night, and the next morning, after Colonel Burr had formally assumed the command, he was mortified by seeing them come into the post loaded with plunder. The license of the times and of the

place had made robbery so much a matter of course, that
there was no attempt at concealment. The stolen articles
were openly deposited in a heap, to wait an equitable distribution among the robbers. At this sight Colonel Burr's
feelings of delicacy toward his predecessor vanished. The
whole property brought in was unhesitatingly seized, and
placed under a guard of his own selection. Regarding the
commanding officer as really the most guilty of the party,
he inflicted no punishment upon the men, but instituted
searching inquiries to ascertain from whom the property
was taken; and when this was done, he ordered its immediate restoration to the real owners, without any discrim-
ination between Whigs and Tories. At the same time,
he distinctly intimated to officers and men that a license to
rob was not to be found in the military code, as he understood it, and clearly informed them that offenders in that
line would hereafter be subjected to condign punishment.
Nor was he content to pause here. During that day he
rode to every post, repeating his orders and instructions at
each one, and giving assurances of protection to the peaceful inhabitants as he went.

There were among the troops on the lines of Westchester some who had served under or near Colonel Burr
in former campaigns. These old soldiers knew that he
meant what he said, and would perform to the letter whatever he promised or threatened, and not only dismissed all
idea of indulging in any further license themselves, but
prepared to aid their commander in his efforts to repress it
in others. The people of the country, however, had heard
so many solemn promises of the same kind, and had been
so often deceived, that they distrusted his professions, and
doubted his ability, if he had the will, to protect them;
while the militia, who composed the larger part of his
force, had long been so much accustomed to have their own

way, that they looked almost in derision upon any attempt
to restrain them from the exercise of their favorite pursuits.
Colonel Burr was perfectly aware of the fears of the people and the incredulity of the militia, and calmly awaited
a fair opportunity to remove both.

In the mean time, in order to prevent the intrusion of the
enemy's spies, he issued an order that no person from below
should pass his lines on any pretext whatever. Their complaints, if they had any, and their communications, whatever they might be, were to be deposited at the posts, and
trusty persons were designated at each one to receive and
forward them to headquarters. His next care was to make
a careful reconnoissance of the country, which induced him
to alter his posts and advance some of them three miles
nearer the enemy. Nothing was neglected, and to everything he gave his personal attention. About this time
an opportunity occurred to impress the men and the citizens
with the full conviction of his unflinching determination to
protect the defenseless, and restore peace and order to a
rent and bleeding community. A man by the name of
Gedney was robbed by a party of militia, and his family
grossly insulted. The finale of the affair is thus narrated
by Colonel Burr's biographer :—

"By what means he detected them was unknown; but,
before twenty-four hours had elapsed, every man of the
party had been secured, and a great part of the stolen property recovered. Upon referring to his register, Colonel
Burr found that Gedney was a Tory; but he was known to
have taken no active part against the patriots, and Burr
had promised that all such should be protected. He
therefore caused the robbers to be drawn up in the presence of the troops, laden with their booty, and then had
them conducted by a company of soldiers to Gedney's
house. There he required them, first, to restore the stolen

goods; next, to pay in money for such as had been lost or damaged; thirdly, he compelled each man to present Gedney with a sum of money. as a compensation for his fright and loss of time; fourthly, he had each robber tied up and flogged ten lashes; lastly, he made each of them ask pardon of the old man, and promise good behavior for the future. All these things were done with the utmost deliberation and exactness, and the effects produced by them were magical. Not another house was plundered, not another family was alarmed, while Colonel Burr commanded the Westchester lines. The mystery and swiftness of the detection, the rigor and fairness with which the marauders were treated, overawed the men whom three campaigns of lawless warfare had corrupted, and restored confidence to the people who had passed their lives in terror."

Colonel Burr was not yet ready for active operations against the enemy. He wished first to *accustom* his men to the restraints of a wholesome discipline, as well as to make his own position perfectly secure in every respect. For this latter purpose he established a system of sleepless vigilance, and organized a corps of patrols and videttes so effective that it was impossible for a party of British troops to move in any direction without his immediate knowledge. In this he was greatly aided by the country people, who, satisfied that they had at last found a protector, repaid him tenfold by freely and promptly communicating every species of information that might aid his operations.

In numerous encounters with small parties of the enemy, Colonel Burr had a fair opportunity of testing the mettle of his men, and he was gratified by observing that they feared no danger and counted no odds when he was their leader. As soon as he was fully satisfied that they could be relied on in any emergency, he resolved to employ them

15

on a more dangerous service than any in which they had
yet been engaged. In the lower part of the county the
British had erected a block-house as a rallying point for
their foraging and plundering parties; this, again, was protected by a strong body of several thousand troops, posted
some two or three miles off. To destroy this block-house
would be to deprive them of a safe and convenient place of
retreat, and increase the danger of their forays to such an
extent as to make it probable they would be abandoned
altogether. He had, according to his custom, carefully inspected the work and the grounds about it, and only waited
for a dark and rainy night to put in execution the plan he
had formed. It was not long before the weather proved
as propitious as he could desire, and, selecting forty men,
properly equipped and instructed, just after nightfall he
began his march for the scene of action. At two o'clock
in the morning he arrived in the vicinity of the block-
house. Here he divided his force into two parties the one
commanded by Captain Black, to whom his instructions
had been previously communicated, and the other by himself. The garrison was buried in sleep, and the shivering
sentinels were more intent upon protecting themselves from
the bitter blasts of a northern winter than in looking out
for an enemy of whose presence they did not dream. Suddenly the thick darkness was illuminated by flashes of
light, and loud and clear rang a voice upon the night air,
"Charge, and smoke the murdering bandits from their
den!" There was a simultaneous rush, short ladders were
planted against the block-house, showers of hand-grenades
were poured through the port-holes, and the drowsy garrison started from their slumbers to find themselves surrounded on all sides by fire. The assault had been too
sudden and too well planned to admit of resistance, and
the British soldiers, instead of flying to their arms, yelled

lustily for quarter. This was at once granted, the prisoners secured, and a rapid retreat commenced. The ruddy hue painted upon the heavens by the burning block-house gave early notice at the British camp of the danger of their friends, and a strong body of horse, followed by another of infantry, was dispatched without delay to their assistance. But long before they could reach the scene, their enterprising foe, with all his prisoners, was safe beyond the reach of pursuit. A heap of burning coals and blackened stones greeted their arrival, but no human being was left to point out the pathway of the destroyer.

The next day Colonel Burr sent up his prisoners to General McDougall, and received in return the warm plaudits of his veteran commander. To the common soldiers he had now become an idol. His unwearied exertions to procure them shoes, blankets, and other comforts, his tender solicitude for the sick and wounded, the unvarying urbanity of his deportment, and his perfect readiness to endure whatever he required others to undergo, created an enthusiastic love for his person that was only surpassed by their unbounded confidence in his military abilities. The very strictness of the discipline he enforced made his other qualities stand prominently out on the canvas, and they respected and loved him the more from the fact that they dared not trifle with his orders. Brave men they could find anywhere—humane men, though not so abundant, were yet no rarity; it was the union of courage and humanity, animated by tireless activity, and regulated by the highest intelligence, that seized upon their affections, and, to their eyes, invested the young officer with the attributes of a demigod.

The capture of the block-house was soon followed by an enterprise upon a larger scale. Governor Tryon, of house-burning memory, came out of New York at the head of two thousand men. His main object was to destroy certain salt-works on Long Island Sound, but coupled with this he had it in view to drive off cattle, and indulge his men generally in their favorite recreations of robbery and murder. Colonel Burr, though far inferior in the number of men he could prudently withdraw from their posts, determined to make the governor pay for his amusement. A messenger was accordingly dispatched to General Putnam, who was nearer to the enemy than himself, advising that officer of his intention to get into Tryon's rear and compel him to give battle or surrender. At the same time he earnestly requested the general to make such demonstrations in front as would draw Tryon's attention from his own movements, and facilitate the object he had in view. By means of false information, the British succeeded in misleading General Putnam as to the object and direction of their march, and, instead of complying with the request of Colonel Burr, he sent back his courier to communicate to Burr the supposed fact that Tryon had turned off toward Connecticut. Changing the direction of his own column, Burr followed, as he imagined, in pursuit; but he had not gone far before he ascertained certainly that General Putnam had been imposed upon. Without a moment's hesitation the faces of his men were again turned toward the Sound. About nightfall, after a long and fatiguing march, he came up with the British rear. Inferior in numbers, and wearied as his own men were, he allowed no time for repose, but at once led them on to the attack. The conflict was short. Governor Tryon was thoroughly alarmed by the boldness and impetuosity of the onset, and thought more of escaping than of fighting. In haste and disarray he retired from the field, abandoning all the plunder he had collected, and leaving many prisoners in the hands of the conqueror.

The military career of Colonel Burr was now drawing

to a close.   The disease contracted by his exposure on the
field of Monmouth had terminated in a confirmed and settled malady, under the debilitating effects of which he was
rapidly sinking.   Heretofore the regularity and abstemious-
ness of his habits had been of essential service in enabling
him to undergo the hardships he imposed upon himself,
but constant exposure, in spite of all the precautions of
prudence, did its work at last.   The opening of spring, to
which he had looked for his probable restoration to health,
brought with it increased debility, and he became painfully
conscious that he was no longer able to discharge his duty
in the manner to which he had been accustomed, and in
which he would alone consent to discharge it.   On the
10th of March, 1779, with deep regret, and after long
hesitation, he transmitted his resignation to the commander-in-chief.

No one ever left the service of his country under circumstances more creditable to him, as an officer and as a man,
than did Colonel Burr.   He found upon the lines of Westchester a discontented, disorderly and demoralized rabble,
who hid behind their intrenchments at every appearance
of a British force; who made no distinction, in their ma-
rauding expeditions, between friend or foe; and plundered,
indiscriminately, the unoffending and the guilty.   In a short
time he converted them into a well behaved, disciplined,
almost invincible corps.   Not once did the enemy approach
his lines without being met and repulsed; not one soldier
deserted his standard; not one was made prisoner during
the whole period of his command.   It was his pride to teach
them that a soldier, with arms in his hands, had no apology for surrendering.   He found a distracted and bleeding
people, shivering at every blast, and trembling at every unusual noise, in fearful expectation that the robber and the

15*

spoiler had come to take away the little they had left—
hating the Continentals as cordially as the red-coats, since
both oppressed them alike, and murdering with equal satisfaction the one or the other, whenever a safe opportunity
occurred.   He left them secure in their persons and property—sleeping as peacefully within hearing of the enemy's
guns as if they were a hundred miles removed—devoted
to the Republican cause, and zealously exerting themselves
to promote it.   He found the country overrun by British
emissaries and British spies, who kept the British general
in New York continually advised of every movement of the
Americans above, and enabled him to strike whenever and
wherever our troops were least prepared to receive him.
These emissaries were detected and punished with such
unerring certainty, that, in a brief while, no reward could
induce one of them to venture beyond the British posts.
The enemy's sources of information were thus entirely cut
off, and they were kept in such total ignorance that they
dared not hazard a movement of the least importance.
To show the difficulties over which Colonel Burr had triumphed, it is only necessary to state that Major Hall, an
excellent officer, who succeeded him in the command, was
compelled, in less than one month, to fall back many miles,
to be in supporting distance of the army in the Highlands.
Colonel Thompson, who was sent to command the same
lines, was surprised, taken prisoner, and his forces dispersed or captured.   Colonel Greene was also surprised,
himself and Major Flagg killed, and the greater part of
his troops taken prisoners.   No one could maintain the
position before Colonel Burr took the command—no one
did maintain it afterwards.   The laurels gathered on this,
the last field of his military labors, abided with him through
life, and, in the darkest period of his fortunes, one of the
bitterest of his revilers was forced to testify that a soldier

could nowhere find a leader who would be more certain to conduct him to honor and renown.

General Washington reluctantly accepted his resignation. No one valued Colonel Burr as an officer more highly than he did, and it is well known that he regarded his retirement as a public calamity. His letter, accepting the resignation, contains expressions which the perfect sincerity of the man invests with a meaning not usual in such correspondence. It is dated at Middlebrook, April 3d, 1779, and, after briefly stating his acceptance of his resignation, conveys to Colonel Burr the expression of the general's deep sorrow for the cause which rendered that resignation necessary, and his equally deep regret that the country was to be deprived of the services of such an officer at such a time.

CHAPTER XI.

COLONEL BURR was now free. Four years' service in
the armies of his country had broken his health and seriously impaired his fortune. Liberal to profusion, his purse
was always open to his fellow-soldiers, and those were times
when the most fastidious were frequently compelled to ask
and accept pecuniary favors. In many cases he advanced
sums of money to his acquaintances when he could not
have had the most distant hope of repayment. He was
now poor, his constitution shattered, and the pathway to
military renown closed against him; but the heaviest blow
was yet to come. A few days before his final departure
from the lines of Westchester, an officer came in with a flag,
to treat for the exchange of prisoners. Through that
medium he received a letter from Margaret Moncrieffe.

"I know not when this will reach you," she wrote, "or,
indeed, whether your eyes will ever rest upon these pages;
but I should go mad if I did not make the attempt to convey to you some knowledge of what I feel and suffer. For
many months I have submitted to the cruel silence imp
upon us. For many months I have submitted to the
injunction that bade me hold no intercourse with r
enemy, however little that father was entitled to
ter's obedience. Even now that silence would

(176)

unbroken, if an unnatural tyranny over the affections had
not doomed me to become the bride of another. In surrendering everything else, I reserved to myself the sad
luxury of addressing a farewell letter to the idolized being
to whom my virgin vows were plighted, and who now holds
supreme dominion over my heart. I did not wish you to
learn first, through the veracious report of a bribed newspaper, that on such a day Margaret Moncrieffe became a
happy bride. It will come to you in due time, though the
hour for the sacrifice has not yet been decided; but it soon
will be, and soon after that you may expect to read the
fulsome announcement of a 'marriage in high life.' I
shall be represented, no doubt, as young and lovely, my
cheek blooming, and my heart overflowing with happiness.
The jewels that adorn, and the flowers that decorate me
for the occasion, will claim a place in the description, and,
perhaps, suggest a simile to enliven it. When you read
the sickening details, distrust them all, except the bitter
truth that I have offered up myself as a victim to gratify
parental pride and parental avarice. Believe, that at the
very moment I take upon me the solemn obligations of a
wife, my soul will be dwelling with you. That, though the
fitting words may be spoken, and the trembling form sustain itself unsupported, even at the altar's foot, the gorgeous pageant, the decorated cathedral, and the mitred
abbot who performs the ceremony will be unheeded, and
far away over the broad Atlantic will rise up the plain
and humble dwelling—beneath whose shelter we first met,
and the verandah—upon whose roof we poured into each
other the burning sentences that will live through
the ages in which the soul is destined to
suffer body may be purchased, bargained,
in the may be driven
the the heart ac-

.knowledges no transfer of title, and scorns alike the gold of the trader and the power of the tyrant. That heart is yours, and oh, what a mockery will be the marriage rite that binds me to another! How deep and damning its perjury! How loathsome its fruits! Do you shudder, my own love, at the dismal horrors before me? I, too, shuddered once, but I have looked upon them until I am calm —calm as the lost wretch who knows that he has descended to the lowest deep and quivered through the deadliest agony. I have even ceased to look forward into the future, and speculate upon the consequences that may flow from the gnawing misery of being chained to a husband I detest. Hope was hidden in the bottom of Pandora's box, and when the thousand ills that it contained flew shrieking from its open lid, the gentle goddess followed on glittering wings and dropped a charm for every woe. More terrible than hers, my marriage gift contains no promised gladness to relieve its present sorrow. What have I to expect on earth when every chord that thrills to the touch of joy is broken? and how dare I look for consolation to the Heaven whose holiest laws I have profaned? Profaned at the bidding of an earthly parent—trampled under foot, that the poor customs of society might be unbroken. Yet I, who feel and writhe under—I, who know the dark penalties that wait on obedience to the unnatural demand, have not the resolution to burst the shackles that encircle me and firmly assert the body's right to follow where the heart has gone before.

"Pity me, for I am very weak! Forgive me, for I am very wretched! And oh, do not scorn me, no matter what tale may be borne to your distant home of the vileness of one who loved, who loves, and who will love you with a fervor compared to which idolatry is cold and tame! With you by my side, I should be contented as the tenant

of the humblest hut in America. The toils and hardships
that the poorest undergo would be sweet; and, in the serenity
of conscious happiness, I could look down upon a crowned
empress, and proudly refuse to exchange my lot for hers.
As your wife, I should be gentle, and loving, and good;
humbly returning thanks to Almighty God for the bless-
ings showered upon me, and hopefully looking forward to
the future as a state of blissful regeneration. What I may
be now, let those answer who have made dissipation a
necessity, and excitement of every kind a respite from torture. But whatever may be my fate, let me at least have
the consolation of knowing that you are going on undauntedly to the fulfillment of a glorious destiny. Up to this
time every returning ship has brought tidings of your growing fame—tidings that to me were more welcome than gales
freighted with the spices of Arabia. Let your remembrance
of me nerve you to sterner exertion, rather than sink you
to despondency. Courage and genius never had a nobler
field. Press on in your high career; and when trampled
millions shake their chains in glad rejoicings at your success, I shall feel that I did right to worship the hero whose
sword struck the living waters of freedom from the rock of
tyranny, and vindicated man's inherent right to live, to
labor, to love, and to adore, when, and where, and how, the
soul in its untrammeled intelligence should direct.

"Farewell! In this cold world we shall never meet again.
I do not tell you to forget me, for I know that is impossible. No matter what grief may overshadow me, no matter
what sin or shame may degrade me, I know that you will
love me, and every prayer that ascends for your own redemption will be mingled with a fervent aspiration for the
wretched girl who loved both wisely and well, and yet
loved where it was worse than death to worship."

Alone in his barrack-room, Aaron Burr read and reread

the wild and despairing confession of the wronged and injured girl. The big tears gathered in his eyes and rolled
slowly, very slowly, down his wasted cheek.

"Poor Margaret!" he said, "ours has been a stormy
love—rocked by wintry winds in its cradle, and scorched by
blasting lightnings in its prime. Who would have dreamed
that the meeting of two hearts so young, so loving, so fitted
for each other, could have engendered the mighty woes that
have scarred and blackened both! What had we done to
be marked out as the victims of a curse more terrible than
that which the rebellious angels dragged down on themselves? We met each other, and we loved. If that meeting were a sin, it was not ours. We did not plan it. I
knew not of your existence, and if you had ever heard my
name, it was coupled with the epithet of *traitor*. Well do
I remember the first time I saw you! Well do I remember
how you nestled to the protecting side of Mrs. Putnam, and
glanced at my uniform as at a badge of infamy. The flush
of health and the bloom of innocence were on your cheek,
and when that short visit ended, I was a captive for eternity.
Was that guilt? It was not so esteemed in Paradise, when
the enraptured Adam waked from his long repose and knelt
in trembling ecstasy at the feet of his new-made Eve. It
was not so esteemed when Jesus, on his pilgrimage of atonement, whispered forgiveness in the ears of Mary Magdalene,
because 'she loved much.' Why should the same thing
which wiped out the remembrance of her sins bring sorrow
and tears to us? Oh, how little do we know! how less than
little do we understand of the purpose that placed us here,
and drags us on, blind and powerless, through the fretful
years of a troubled existence! How poor and weak is that
'free will' of which we boast! how dim and undefined the
narrow boundaries of its power! Blown about by every
passion, yielding to every temptation—the sport of circum-

stance and the tool of chance—what is left to our own
choice? what is regulated as we could wish? Free
will, indeed! Is Margaret Moncrieffe free when she
knowingly crushes every bloom of happiness and walks
with open eyes to a living grave? Was I free in that
hour when I forgot that she was the daughter of my country's foe, and knelt and worshiped at her feet? Am I free
now? Can I tear her image from my heart of hearts?—forget her love; forget her grief; forget what she has already
borne; and steel myself against that which she must still
endure? Can I do this, and live? Oh, no! I can bear
disease, and pain, and poverty, and foul suspicion; I can
struggle on even under the maddening knowledge that her
head is pillowed on another breast than mine; but I cannot bear to forget—I dare not cease to love. I know not
what is before me; but I know that when I am called upon
to embark in the shadowy ship that waits for passenger
souls by the shore of time, I shall carry with me a love that
has known no change or abatement from that moment when
our lips' burning vows were sealed and sanctified by our
hearts' enraptured assent. I shall go on, silent and uncom-
plaining, and seemingly contented as the other worms about
me; but there will be an inward longing, a slakeless thirst,
for which ambition has no cure and excitement no relief;
a hopeless gangrene of the soul, rotting and festering until
the confines of life are reached and the freed spirit shakes
off the dust but not the memories of earth.

"'Pity me!' you say, Margaret. God knows, I have deep
need of sympathy for myself! but not so great as yours;
and all that an overburdened heart has to bestow is freely,
fully given. 'Do not scorn me!'—Not I! though you were
stained all over with crimes and vices as black as those that
disgraced the foulest daughter of the Medici. I should
only mourn that man had the power to convert an angel

16

of light into an erring, wicked thing; and shudder at the
inscrutable justice that slumbers while the ministers of hell
are torturing a child of God into crime. Scorn you! What
right has any mortal man to wear that word upon his lips?
Tempt him in the height of his power and the pride of his
wealth, offer him some glittering bauble that he thinks
beyond his reach, and his boasted integrity dies in a night.
Crush out his affections, bruise him, trample on him, and
what does he become? A vile and loathsome thing, wal-
lowing in crime and fattening on corruption. How dare
he talk of *scorn* for the sins of another, whose own are
mountain high, and whom it needs but a breath of temptation to bloat with infamy! Yet it may well be, Margaret,
that you will feel that sting from those who are more guilty
than you are. It may well be that the tyranny of opinion
will drive you from indiscretion into crime, and then judge
you according to that hollow-hearted humanity which looks
only at the fruits, and makes no allowance for the seasons
that produce them. Yours is a terrible ordeal. God grant
that you may pass through it not utterly blasted! But
whether pride and power, or shame and sin shall cluster
about you, there is one heart which will cling to you, and
throb, through every mutation of fortune and of fame, with
a love as undying as your own."

The solitary candle on his camp table flickered in the
socket—a few fitful flashes, and it was gone; the red light
of the fire burned low and dim; but there he sat, rigid and
stony, until the sound of the morning *reveille* roused him
.o life and consciousness again.

CHAPTER XII.

"It was a dreamy mountain land,
Where lawless men a refuge found;
And Murder, with his purple hand,
Reign'd sovereign o'er the bloody ground."

FROM the lines of Westchester Colonel Burr repaired
to Newburg, where he remained for some time the honored
guest of General McDougall. Oppressed by mental anxiety
even more than by physical suffering, he lingered for weeks
on the very verge of the grave. At last his temperate
habits triumphed, and the healthy current began to creep
slowly back to his shrunken veins. In the month of June
the British, in large force, made threatening demonstrations against West Point, and General McDougall, justly
alarmed for the safety of the place, sought by every means
to open communications with General Washington; but
this was a work of no ordinary difficulty, for the British
had so posted bodies of Tories on the roads and among the
mountain passes as to render the destruction of any small
party or the capture of a single messenger almost certain.
General McDougall made repeated efforts to convey intelligence to the commander-in-chief, but all proved abortive.
When these facts came to Colonel Burr's knowledge, feeble
and emaciated as he was, he volunteered to undertake what
so many had failed to accomplish. The general at first
remonstrated, but finally yielded to Burr's urgent solicitations, and, giving him only verbal instructions, dispatched
him on his journey. Well armed, and mounted on a good
strong horse, he set out early in the morning on his dan-

(183)

gerous mission.   Toward nightfall, when approaching one
of the most difficult passes of the mountain, he observed a
man step from the bushes a few yards in advance of him
and turn leisurely up the road, giving, apparently, little
heed to the horseman of whose presence he could not fail
to be aware.   He was dressed in the common garb of the
country, and carried no visible weapon of any kind.   Those
were days when prudent men seldom went abroad unarmed;
but Burr inwardly thought that if any one was justifiable
in neglecting that precaution, it was the powerful figure
before him.   Not more than five feet six inches in height,
his shoulders were of herculean breadth, and over his
ample chest the bones were laid in thick, curved plates
that would have bid defiance to the hug of a Norwegian
bear.   His thigh was so long as almost to amount to de-
formity, and over it was twisted a net-work of muscles as
hard and much more elastic than steel.   The short space
between the knee and the ankle-joint was almost entirely
filled by the swelling calf; and the broad feet looked like
pedestals to a mighty statue.   He raised his head when
Colonel Burr rode up alongside, and exhibited a countenance that would have been singularly pleasing but for the
fierce light which flashed from his dark-hazel eyes.

"Good evening!" he said in a natural, unaffected tone.
"Do you travel far on this road?"

"Perhaps so," was the reply.   "Perhaps not."

"Shy, eh!   Shy and skittish!   That looks bad."

"Why so?   These are not times, nor is this a country
in which a man can safely tell his secrets to every person
he may chance to meet on the highway."

"Well, there is some truth in that; and it was none of
my business, anyhow."

But although thus disclaiming any interest in the motions
of his companion, the sturdy footman kept within grasp of

the bridle-rein, quickening or slackening his pace to suit the gait of the animal. Burr could not fail to notice that, move as he would, the relative distance between them was always the same. His quick eye, too, had detected the butt of a heavy pistol beneath the coarse frock-coat worn by the countryman, and he doubted not that other weapons were concealed by the same friendly cover. Believing from these indications that the purposes of his new acquaintance were in nowise friendly, he thought it more advisable to bring on the struggle at once than to allow his adversary the selection of his own time and place.

"What is that?" he suddenly asked, pointing to a stunted beach-tree on the mountain side. The man turned his head for a moment, and only for a moment, but it was enough. The steed was reined sharply back, and, snatching a pistol from his holsters, Burr leveled it full at the head of his pertinacious companion, at the same time sternly demanding,—

"Who are you? and for what are you dogging my steps?"

The pistol was double charged; it was held by a hand never known to tremble in the hour of danger; the least motion of his arm, the scraping even of a foot, and the giant pedestrian would have been launched into eternity. His eye caught that of Burr as he turned, and his own fierce gaze sank under the overwhelming power of that steady look which no living thing ever encountered unmoved. It was not anger that flashed from those large orbs, nor courage, nor determination merely, but all these combined; and added to them was a nameless spell which carried with it an irresistible conviction that whatever they threatened was certain to be performed. You felt that it was the glance of doom—that there were no chances to

16*

take, no wavering, no hesitation to hope for. You saw
that the man's whole soul was aroused, that all his energies were alive and active, and you knew that it would be
as safe to play with the lightning's forked dart. The bold,
strong animal quailed in the presence of a master-spirit,
and, in a tone resembling the whining growl of a chained
and conquered bear, he answered,—

"My name is Alexis Durand."

"That is little to the purpose. Answer me truly, or,
by the Mother of God, your lease of life will be a short
one. Are you not one of Tryon's Tories?"

"I have no choice, I suppose, but to own it. I am."

"That is enough. I can make out the remainder without your help. Unbutton that coat."

The order was sullenly obeyed, and the open garment
revealed a belt containing two pistols and one of the broad
hunting knives of the day. By successive orders Colonel
Burr compelled him to draw out first one pistol, then the
other, and then the knife, and drop them at his feet. This
done, he marched him forward five paces, counting the steps
and following as he advanced; then he made him lie down
on his face until he leaped from his horse and secured the
arms. This done, he again mounted his horse and ordered
the Tory to rise.

"Where is your troop now?"

"Three miles ahead, in the woods at the back of Jordan's
house."

"Who is Jordan?"

"He is a Tory, and keeps the only public house on the
road."

"That at least tallies with my own information; and
pray, remember in your answers, that I did not come here
in entire ignorance of anything it concerns me to know. I
shall most certainly detect you in any attempt to deceive

me, and then your fate is sealed. Will any of your troop be prowling about before dark?"

"Not on this side. I was sent to watch here."

Burr mused a moment, and then said,—

"Now, Mr. Alexis Durand, I propose to sup this night at Jordan's, and as I do not like solitary meals, I shall take you along for company. As much, however, as I love the society of a single friend, I object decidedly to larger parties, and if any unpleasant intruders should join us, or any other circumstance should occur to mar the festivities of the evening, my dissatisfaction will be instantly manifested by sending a brace of bullets through your skull. You understand me, I hope. Now, forward, march!"

They had proceeded in this way for a little more than half a mile, when they came to a place where a bridle-path led off from the main road through the woods. Here his prisoner indicated a wish to halt, and Burr, reining up, inquired what he wanted.

"I should like to ask you a question, sir, that I hope you will not refuse to answer. I know I am in your power, and you may do as you will; but I swear by all that is holy that it shall do you no harm, to tell me truly whether or not you are Colonel Burr?"

"I do not think I should attach much importance to your oath, if I did not myself feel certain that it can make no difference whether you know me or not. I was Colonel Burr, but I have resigned my commission and left the army."

"Then for God's sake go no farther on this road."

"Why, you told me just now that it was free as far as Jordan's house."

"So it is; but your horse would not be in the stable five minutes before it would be known by those who will compass earth and hell to spill your blood."

"Your care for my blood," answered Burr coldly, "has wonderfully improved in the last hour. Methinks it is not very long since you had some such purpose as murder in your own head."

"I did not know you then, and I suspected you of being a spy of General McDougall."

"And now that you do know me, I cannot understand what has produced so marked a change in your praise-worthy intentions. I am not generally held in high esteem by my country's foes."

"You saved my father's house from being burned; you set a watch over it, to protect my mother from insult; and you fed her starving little ones when you knew us to be friends to King George and enemies to Congress. I am the son of John Durand, of Westchester. Have you forgotten him?"

"No, my good fellow, I remember him well. I remember, also, since you have brought it to my mind, that his eldest son was accounted a confirmed robber and murderer, and while I protected your father and mother as an act of justice, and fed your little brothers and sisters as an act of humanity, I should have taken singular pleasure in hanging you to the first tree that offered."

"I did not begin it, and it is not my fault if there has been a long and bloody account run up between me and those who drove me to take up arms when I was willing to remain in peace with the old folks at home. But, there is no time to talk it over now. The sun is going down. Will you trust me, and follow me? Believe me, there is no other escape from death."

"I will trust you," answered Burr, without the least hesitation. "Lead on. I think you mean well, and if you do not, my hand will be as steady and my aim as certain in one place as another."

Durand turned into the bridle-path, and walked rapidly on until they were entirely out of sight or hearing from the highway. Here again he paused until Burr rode up to his side.

"I am taking you," he said, "to the house of a friend of mine, who is, of course, in British pay. There will be no use in telling him anything we can help, and therefore I should like to ask another question or two. Where are you going?"

"To General Washington's headquarters."

"So I expected. Do you bear dispatches?"

"No. I have only verbal messages."

"That is safer and better. Bill Jenkins's cabin is in less than a mile of us; there you can have your horse fed, get your own supper, and some hours' sleep. After that, I will myself guide you safe beyond danger. I shall call you Mr. Jones, for although I do not fear any treachery from Bill, it is not wise to tempt him too far. Give me my arms; an angel from heaven could not make me hurt you now, and besides averting Bill's suspicions, it may be necessary to use them in your defense."

Colonel Burr promptly complied with his request, rightly judging that he had already trusted him too far to hesitate about any additional confidence. Durand placed the weapons in his belt, and again moved forward with a quick and nervous step. A few minutes brought them to a clearing on a level bench of the mountain, surrounded by a high, strong fence, in which were three or four cabins, irregularly placed, and built so nearly alike that it was difficult to decide which was designed for the use of man and which for the cattle and poultry that lowed and cackled within. The owner of the premises, who was engaged in the unmasculine task of milking a cow, had a villainous, bandit look, and the natural repulsiveness of his countenance was increased by an ugly scar, extending from above the left eye across the nose to the right cheek. He put down his milk-pail, and walked to the gate at the summons of Durand, silencing, as he did so, two fierce wolf-hounds, who were growling and barking furiously at the intruders.

"This, Bill, is my friend, Mr. Jones," said Durand, after shaking the outlaw by the hand. "He wants some supper and a night's lodging, and I have brought him here, knowing that you would give him a hearty welcome for my sake."

"To be sure!" answered Jenkins, extending his horny hand to Burr. "I'm glad to see you, sir, and though I haven't got much, you're welcome to what's here. Aleck," he continued, "take your friend into the house, and build a fire. He looks sick and weakly, and these mountain dews are mighty chilly. I will take care of his horse."

"Rub him down well, Bill," replied Durand, "for he will have to travel hard in the morning. Take your time, I will get supper for you."

Jenkins led off the horse, and Durand entered the house followed by Burr. It was a square one-story log-cabin, covered with boards. Over the joists, for about one-half the length of the room, loose boards were laid, forming a kind of upper room, which was reached by a rough ladder, and was used as a general depository for any and every thing that the owner desired to put out of the way. The floor was of dirt. Over the fire-place, suspended in racks made of forked sticks, were a long rifle, a British musket, and three or four pistols of different size and make, show-ing that they were never intended to match, and indicating pretty plainly that the mode of their acquisition had not been entirely honest. In fact, they had been picked up here and there in the different forays of the present owner, and to some of them tales of murder, as well as robbery, attached. One chair and four or five stools were scattered about. In the center was a rude, square table. In one corner a rough bed, and in the other a pile of blankets, counterpanes, and a miscellaneous collection of other bedclothes, which never came there through fair traffic. By the door there was a shelf for a water-pail, and near the chimney stood a large cupboard made of pine plank, and fastened by a wooden button. There was no window, and no other furniture. Durand had brought in a dry board, which he split to pieces over a large stone that did duty as an andiron, and, raking the embers together, soon succeeded in blowing them into a flame. While he was thus engaged, Colonel Burr had been noting everything in the house, and he now asked,—

"Does your friend live here alone?"

"Not exactly. I am with him a good deal myself; but, if you mean to ask whether he has a family, I answer no. Men like us have no use for women folks about the house. It is bad enough to be harried and burned out when we are alone, without being maddened by hearing the women screaming, and the children squalling besides."

"True," answered Burr, "and there has been too much of that on both sides, in this unhappy war. God knows I tried to put a stop to it wherever I held command!"

"You did, sir; and you owe it to that that you are now safe and sound beneath an outlaw's roof, instead of being bound and bleeding in the hands of men who are deaf to the prayers of mercy. You thought you had me in your power, sir; and while we were upon the highway may be you did; but the moment you had passed Jordan's gate, nay, in the very act of getting from your horse, if your eye had turned from me one instant, you would have been lost. A blow given with half the strength of this arm would crush your ribs like rotten pipe-stems, and it is cer-

tain that I should have found some chance to deal that
blow. It was your eye, sir, that saved you. I remembered my mother's description, and I knew you by that."

"I am thankful the trial was spared us; though I am
not so certain that you, an unarmed man, could have made
me a prisoner when fully armed and on my guard. We will
let that pass, however, for the present, and, as I have been
trusting you more than prudence dictates, while you have
given me no information of your plans and intentions, you
will excuse me for questioning you upon some things which
it imports me much to know."

"Ask me nothing, if you please sir," said Durand, interrupting him. "I know where you want to go, and I intend
to conduct you there in safety or die in the attempt; but
I shall be no more a friend to George Washington and his
cause, when that is done, than I am now. At the same
time I serve you for protecting my mother and her children,
I remember that it was against your friends that protection
was necessary, and I have no idea of sparing the whole
brood of a wolf-bitch because I have found a noble hound
among them. Do not ask me anything, therefore, and do
not tell me anything. Draw that chair nearer to the fire;
it is always cold up here at night. I must get about
supper."

The meal, and the manner of preparing it, was one for
which Burr's experience, notwithstanding his military life,
furnished no parallel. Taking down a small iron kettle,
which was suspended from a cross-piece in the chimney,
he filled it with water and hung it immediately over the
blazing fire; then opening the cupboard, he took there-
from the cold leg of a goat, which he cut into mince-meat;
some slices from a side of bacon were added; two pods of
red-pepper, and an onion chopped fine, some hard biscuit
broken to pieces, and a handful of Irish potatoes, peeled

and sliced thin. All these were stirred together, plentifully sprinkled with salt, and poured into the now boiling water.

By this time, Jenkins had returned. Producing a lamp, and drawing a stone jug from underneath his bed, he invited his guests to partake of some "real old Jamaica"—an invitation to which Durand did double honor; and Colonel Burr, fatigued by his ride, swallowed a larger quantity of the potent spirit, according to his own acknowledgment, than he ever did at any other time in his life.

Those who know nothing of life, except what they have learned in peaceful times, and with carpeted floors beneath their feet, will find little in the foregoing description to please them, and will probably shudder at what is to follow. Three tin plates, or rather pans, were placed on the table by Jenkins; as many iron spoons, tin cups, knives, and forks, some hard bread and cheese, a pitcher of milk, and a gourd filled with salt. The kettle was then removed from the fire, and, hot and boiling as it was, placed in the center of the table, so that each one could help himself; and the three, without ceremony, sat down to a meal that a hungry man would have pronounced savory anywhere. In his old age, Colonel Burr declared that it was the sweetest dish he had ever tasted.

Durand was the first to rise from the table. "You must excuse me, Bill," he said; "I am going to the camp and will not be back until after midnight. Finish your supper, put plenty of wood on the fire, and go to sleep. The sooner the better for my friend Jones. Close the door and bar the gate; do not open either for man or devil, until I return. Call the dogs into the house; they will help you bravely at a pinch."

"What if any of our boys should come along?" inquired Jenkins. "How can I turn them off?"

"They will not; but if they should, pretend not to

17

know them, and shoot the first one that crosses the fence.
Mark me," he continued, observing the astonished stare of
his companion, "if Governor Tryon himself knocks at this
door to-night his welcome must be a rifle-ball. I will
explain to-morrow. Good night!"

With these words he stepped from the door, and was
soon lost among the bushes which grew in rank luxuriance
along the mountain side.

What were the sensations of Colonel Burr when thus
left alone with the ill-favored man of crime, beneath whose
roof he was so strangely sheltered? To fear he was a
stranger; but was there no doubt, no mistrust, no anxiety?
Not a particle. If there had been any purpose to harm
him, he knew that purpose could have been accomplished a
hundred times over. For hours he had been in their
power. There was no necessity for treacherous scheming
to effect either his death or capture. Calm and self-
collected always, the probability is that these reflections
passed through his mind more like the flashes of instinct
than the teachings of reason. Durand's good faith he
could not question, and Jenkins had not given him the
slightest cause to harbor suspicion. Thus far he had done
precisely what his comrade had told him, and done it in
such a way as to make it certain that no sinister design
troubled his brain. Nothing of this was lost upon Colonel
Burr, and after Durand's departure he took his seat com-
posedly by the fire, and began caressing one of the large
wolf-hounds who was gnawing a bone at his feet, while
Jenkins was bringing in some additional logs to heap in
the chimney. After this, the outlaw placed two strong
bars across the door, and, taking a seat, entered into
friendly chat with his guest upon subjects that offered no
chance for party disagreement. At that period of the
American Revolution it was not always safe to ask, much

less to answer, questions, and Jenkins was too well aware of the fact to trouble his visitor with impertinent queries; but what he did say was friendly, and his manner was wholly unembarrassed. Even the dogs seemed to understand that the stranger was to receive none but kindly treatment, for one of them, when he had finished his bone, laid his huge head upon Colonel Burr's knee, and looked wistfully up into his face as if soliciting a caress. Colonel Burr was passionately fond of a good dog, and an excellent judge of his points. The deep chest and sinewy loin of the noble animal supplied him with a subject for conversation until Jenkins rose, and, saying it was time they should go to sleep, spread blanket after blanket, and counterpane after counterpane, on the floor, until he had made a 'pallet" as soft as a bed of down, upon which he invited Burr to lie down and rest until Durand's return. He then sought his own couch, and the dogs unceremoniously disposed of themselves at Burr feet.

It was long past midnight when Colonel Burr was roused by a fierce growl from his four-footed sentinels. The same sound awoke Jenkins, who, springing from his bed, silenced the dogs by a stern whisper, "Hush, Brute! lie down, Cash!" and walking to the door, laid his head against it to listen. The sound of a horse's feet was heard approaching over the rocky path, and soon afterwards Alexis Durand shouted at the gate, "Open, Bill; it is me!"

When the door was opened and Durand entered, Burr discovered that he had added a rifle, together with a bullet-pouch and a powder-horn, to his equipments. His manner, too, was hurried like that of a man whom some danger threatened and who was impatient to be gone.

"It is later," he said, "than I expected it would be before my return. I had trouble to get away, and we may

meet with more on the road.   Get Mr. Jones's horse, Bill;
we have no time to tarry here!"

The horse was brought, and, after bidding Jenkins a
cordial "good-by," the two mounted and rode down the
mountain in a direction nearly at right angles with the
road.   From the many turnings and zigzags made by his
guide, Colonel Burr soon lost all idea of the direction they
were traveling.   Now they were winding among huge
masses of white, rugged rocks; now the bed of a mountain torrent crossed their way; now a deep ravine, black
and gloomy, barred their passage; anon they were skirting
the base of a frowning precipice, and again climbing a
steep ascent, which rose sharp and sudden before them.
Colonel Burr could discover no sign of a path, but his
conductor rode on, avoiding or surmounting obstacles with
an unerring certainty that proved his perfect knowledge
of every inch of the ground.   Toward daylight they descended into the plain, and just as the sun was rising they
emerged from a thick wood in full view of a broad and
beaten road.   Here Durand reined up.

"You are safe, Colonel Burr—beyond the danger of
interruption from our scouts.   That road leads to George
Washington's headquarters, and you are now within a few
miles of his outposts."

Burr turned toward his preserver and said, in a voice
shaken by emotions he did not attempt to suppress,—

"Mr. Durand, you have rendered me a great service,
and I thank you from my heart.   Not, however, for the
life you have probably saved, for of that I take little heed;
but it concerned my honor that the message I bear should
be safely delivered.   Is there nothing I can do to repay
you?"

"I was paid in advance.   The man who saved my mother

from insult has a right to work me in a chain-gang, if he chooses."

"That was an act of common humanity, for which I deserve no particular credit."

"It was a rare one, sir, in those times; and when I forget it, I hope the thunder may strike me. We Tories are human beings, although your Whig friends seldom treat us as such. We have had much to make us bloody, and lawless, and revengeful; and we have therefore done much at which good men must shudder; still, we are better than you give us credit for being, and gratitude is not an obsolete word among us."

"Of that I have ample proof. I wish you would let me show my own, by procuring for you a full pardon for all past offenses, with permission to remain peacefully at home, or join the American standard, as you may prefer."

"You speak in kindness, colonel, and I hope you will not think I meet it rudely in saying that this good rifle is all the pardon I need. As for joining the American standard, I may think of that when I forget the wrongs I have suffered at American hands."

"That there has been wrong on both sides, I know; but surely those who are in arms against their country could not expect to be treated very leniently."

"Your historians, colonel, will tell one story, and ours another. If you succeed, yours will be believed—if we triumph, you will be the traitors. The judgment of posterity, therefore, upon our motives, will be worth just nothing at all; but if an account of the facts could be written precisely as they are, an impartial jury would say that we have been at least as much sinned against as sinning. Take, for instance, the case of Bill Jenkins, under whose roof you slept last night. At the beginning of these troubles, he was just married, and there was not a more quiet, orderly,

17*

industrious young man in the Colony of New York. He
believed, honestly and conscientiously, that King George
was entitled to his allegiance, and refused to join the rebellion.   This subjected him to insult, and, after awhile, to
worse.   He was dragged from his bed at night, tied to a
tree, and lashed like a condemned thief, until the blood ran
down to his heels.   His young wife, who was far gone in
pregnancy, looked on the horrible scene till she fainted, and
died the next day, in giving premature birth to the child
she bore.   Do you wonder that from that day Bill Jenkins
became a house-burner and a murderer?   Do you wonder
that he forgot to distinguish between those who had wronged
him and the party to which they belonged, and inflicted
vengeance on all alike ?"

    "No; but his is an extreme case; there are very few who
have his excuse."

    "Not many, perhaps, who have suffered so much; but all
of us have suffered in some way, and all of us have more
or less to avenge."

    "Your way of stating the case is a strong one, Mr.
Durand, when addressed to the ignorant and the unreflect-
ing; but a man of your education and intelligence must
understand that this is not a personal quarrel.   It is a question of freedom—of freedom for the whole land, and for our
whole posterity.   There may be a dozen, or ten dozen, or
ten thousand bad men among us, who commit wrongs and
outrages upon their fellow-men, in the mere wantonness of
cruelty; but that does not affect the justice of the cause
any more than the bad conduct of a thousand hypocrites
impairs the sanctity of the Christian religion.   You have
no more right to take up arms against your country, because
a Whig has robbed your house, than you have to desert the
cause of Christ, because a professing Christian has cheated
you in trade.   You must remember, too, that the things of

which you complain were, in a great measure, brought upon yourselves. If you had taken sides, in the beginning, openly and boldly, for your country, you would not have been molested. It is no answer, to say that you honestly believed your country to be in the wrong. It is not a case for reasoning about right or wrong. If you saw a strong man beating your mother, I do not think you would trouble yourself to inquire what provocation she had given him. So, in this case, your country is engaged in an unequal war, and whether she is right or whether she is wrong, the arms, hearts, and swords of her sons are her legitimate property. Before the war began, it was your privilege to use argument, reason, and persuasion, if you chose, to prevent it from breaking out; but when it did come, when the blood of your neighbors and friends was poured out like water upon their native fields, patriotism, honor, duty, manliness, all demanded that you should raise your hand on the side of the oppressed."

"We have no time now to argue the point, colonel, and we should probably be as far from agreeing, at the end of the discussion, as we are at this time. It is not safe for me to linger here. Good-by, and if ever you should meet my mother, tell her that her son obeyed her commands and paid a part of her debt. Tell her also that I shall keep on paying it, whenever a proper occasion arises."

"At least," said Colonel Burr, extending a large seal ring as he spoke, "at least accept this, and promise me that if ever you get into trouble you will not fail to let me know it."

"Gladly do I accept the ring," replied Durand; "but as for the promise of applying to you in any coming trouble that may overtake me, you must pardon me for not giving it. It will depend on circumstances, and of those circumstances I must be the judge."

Colonel Burr extended his hand—the sturdy outlaw

almost crushed it in his iron grasp; then, drawing his sleeve across his eyes, as if to wipe away something misty that had gathered there, he turned his horse into the wood and rode rapidly back toward the Highlands.

Colonel Burr had not ridden far, after parting with Durand, before he met a patrol of American horse, by whom he was conducted to the presence of the commander-in-chief. The message he delivered from General McDougall, and his own remarks and observations upon the state of affairs around New York, were considered so important that General Washington immediately marched the largest part of his army to the Highlands, and established his own headquarters at New Windsor, within a few miles of West Point.

The excitement which sustained him under the fatigues of his perilous journey was over, and the reaction proved too much for Colonel Burr's feeble health. He was again prostrated, and, in that condition, was removed to New Haven, where, it was thought, he would have the benefit of better quarters and more regular medical attendance. He was lying at this place upon a bed of sickness when his old enemy, Governor Tryon, at the head of twenty-five hundred men, sailed out of New York, on one of his usual plundering and burning expeditions. His first landing was near New Haven, and the frightened citizens, to whom his former merciless exploits were familiar, fled in all directions to the country. Vehicles of every imaginable description crowded the roads, and women and children ran screaming by the side of their household goods. Immediately upon receiving intelligence of Tryon's landing, Colonel Burr rose from his sick couch, dressed himself, and repaired to a part of the town where he understood the militia were gathering for the purpose of making some show of resistance. He found them assembled together, indeed, but utterly panic-

stricken, and entertaining about as much idea of giving battle to the enemy as a drove of sheep might be expected to
entertain in the presence of a gang of ferocious wolves.
Excited and indignant, he addressed them in the fervent
language of patriotism, urging them to defend their fire-
sides and their altars from an insulting foe, and pointing
out how much better it was to die nobly in a good cause
than to live degraded and debased. The men, however,
were too much under the influence of fear to heed, or even
listen to his stirring appeals. A few gathered around him,
but the greater part began to slink away. Just as he was
about giving up in despair the attempt to infuse some
degree of manliness into their bosoms, he was informed
that the students were forming themselves into military companies on the college green, and thither he rode, followed by
a few of the militia, who had imbibed a portion of his own
courage. Addressing the boys in a few energetic words of
encouragement and commendation, he proclaimed his name
and former rank, and offered to lead them against the enemy.
The little fellows answered with three hearty cheers, and,
wheeling into column, marched out to meet the forces of
Governor Tryon. Shamed into courage by this gallant example, numbers of the militia joined them as they marched
along, and by the time the enemy came in sight Colonel
Burr was able to display so considerable a force that, after
trying the effects of a few shots, Governor Tryon fell back
to wait for his artillery, which he had left behind, in the
belief that no resistance would be offered. By a skillful
disposition of his little force, Colonel Burr succeeded in
keeping the British at bay for hours, and thus enabled the
citizens to remove their valuables beyond the reach of the
marauders. The arrival of the artillery, of course, compelled him to retreat, but it was done in excellent order,
and his regiment of boys was safely conducted from the

town.   In after years there was no achievement of his life
upon which he dwelt with more pleasure; and even in extreme old age his eye would sparkle at the mention of New
Haven College.   But it cost him dear at the time.   He was
carried from his horse to a sick chamber, and continued,
for months, a bed-ridden invalid.

CHAPTER XIII.

"Things done well,
And with a care, exempt themselves from fear;
Things done without example, in their issue
Are to be feared."

WHEN the resignation of Colonel Burr was received at headquarters, Alexander Hamilton could scarcely conceal his joy; and as soon as he could seize an opportunity he went to communicate the glad tidings to Billings. That dark schemer had remained almost constantly with the main army. The principal part of his property was in the City of New York, and while that city was in possession of the British and his own residence occupied, as it was, by a British officer, he had a plausible excuse for remaining in the field. His presence had long ceased to excite comment. In fact he was not only heartily welcome, but his abandonment of the army would have been looked upon as a calamity, for no man ever knew better how to make himself popular than James Billings, when he chose to exert himself for that purpose. Professing to have no home but that where the soldiers of his country were found, he provided himself with a tent and wagon of his own, and whenever the army moved he moved with it. His command of money often enabled him to furnish luxuries to the sick or wounded officers, which were very grateful to them, and were always remembered to his advantage. If the army remained for any length of time in one place, he generally contrived to secure a house, where his judicious hospitalities won for him golden opin-

(203)

ions from all ranks and classes of the soldiery. Besides, it
was known that he had rendered important services to the
cause of the struggling colonists; and he obtained credit
for a great deal more than was actually due him. Sometimes he would be gone for weeks—no one knew where, and
few inquired. During his absence, he would turn over his
field equipment to some necessitous officer, who was in this
way enabled to enjoy a season of comfort that did not often
fall to his lot, and who immediately became the devoted
friend of the man to whom he was thus indebted. On two
or three occasions, he had seized a musket and fought
bravely in the ranks by the side of private soldiers; acquiring a reputation, by so doing, for personal courage as high
as that which was accorded him for patriotism and liberality.
In every respect Mr. Billings was a popular and a trusted
man. Toward Colonel Hamilton, in public, his manner
was always scrupulously polite, and no one suspected the
closeness of the intimacy between them. Their interviews
were never frequent, and were generally contrived at times
to excite the least observation. On the present occasion,
Colonel Hamilton approached him during the day and
said,—

"If you are alone, Billings, and we can be undisturbed,
I will come and sup with you to-night."

"I am alone, or can easily be so. At what hour shall I
expect you?"

"Eight o'clock, if that hour suits you."

"Very well; until then, adieu." And he turned with an
easy, unembarrassed manner, to greet several officers who
came up at the moment.

Colonel Hamilton's impatience carried him to Billings's
door a full half hour before the appointed time. That
worthy, who was something of an epicure, was busy in
giving instructions to his cook how to prepare his favorite

dishes. The entrance of his guest interrupted this agreeable occupation, and, dismissing the man, he courteously invited Hamilton, according to the custom of the times, to join him in a glass of Madeira.

Those who live in camps cannot be very fastidious, and Mr. Billings was forced to be contented with one apartment for dining-room, sitting-room, and bed-room. In this apartment, before supper, the servant was engaged in making preparations for the evening meal, and conversation of a confidential nature was therefore impossible. After it was concluded, and the two were left to themselves, Hamilton opened his budget of news, adding at the close,—

"You see now that I was right in protesting against personal violence. We are rid of him. No one is to blame. We have no cause for self-reproach, and will be annoyed by no fears of a disgraceful exposure."

Billings made no comment on this self-gratulatory address, merely inquiring,—

"Has the resignation been accepted?"

"No; but it will be. Such things are matters of course."

"Study well the letter of acceptance before you send it. Let it be perfectly courteous; but at the same time avoid strong expressions of regret, or strong commendation of his past services."

"I will, if I write it; but the general frequently writes such letters himself, merely directing me to copy. In that case I can do nothing."

"It would not be prudent certainly to show much feeling about it, and it may never be of the least importance. Still, I would like to see that letter before it goes."

"I will gratify you if I can; though I do not understand why you should consider it of the least consequence. He is out of the army—he is out of my way, and I do not

18

care a farthing how much men may praise him for what he has done."

"He is at present out of the army and out of your way; but it is by no means certain that he will stay so. At the expiration of a year, or less, his health may be restored, and he may then come back into the army and into your way too. I have studied his character to little purpose, if he will long rest contented in the walks of civil life when the clash of arms is sounding in his ears."

"You are mistaken, Billings. He cannot come back without entering below those who are now his juniors, and his proud spirit will never consent to that."

"I hope so; but I doubt. I have understood that he did accept the appointment of lieutenant-colonel when the date of that appointment placed him below some who were his juniors the preceding campaign. What he has done once he may do again. At all events, you ought to be careful to do nothing to facilitate his re-entrance into military life. Keep him out by all means. The rewards that will follow success in this contest must be reaped by the sword, or all the teachings of history are false. Let us turn, however, to a question of more immediate concern; I mean the influence this resignation ought to have on your own course. Have you thought of that? Do you propose to remain in your present position, or to exchange it for another?"

"I have not had time to mature my plans. My judgment, though, inclines me now, as heretofore, to seek employment in the line."

"My opinion has long been made up on that point. It must be done some day, and the sooner the better."

"I wish from my heart that it could be done to-morrow; but I foresee that it will be a work of time. The difficulties I mentioned on a former occasion have been increased.

I have become necessary to General Washington, and, in addition to the jealousies of the line officers, I shall also have to overcome his reluctance to part with me."

"There is an obvious mode of getting over that difficulty. Quarrel with him upon some point of etiquette which involves no feeling and will leave no sting behind."

"It may be a long time before any such chance will occur; and just now it would do no good, for he is fixed in his determination not to give staff officers commands equal to their staff rank in the line. I will have a better chance of weakening, if not reversing, this determination by remaining near his person."

"That is desirable, if it can be done; though in your place, I would not wait long in the hope of bringing it about. Where you are, promotion is next to impossible, and it is better for you to accept a place below your juniors than to continue in the staff. In the line, the whole field is open before you. Skill and courage are there certain of their rewards; and now that Colonel Burr has retired from the service, I know no competitor of whom you have reason to fear. You are a better soldier to-day than any general officer in the army, and George Washington knows it; but Congress and the country do not know it, and will not know it, so long as you are tied to the person of the commander-in-chief and are allowed to win no fame except such as is reflected from him. It is better, I repeat, to take any command you can get in the infantry, and trust to your own exertions to rise from it. That you will rise, I know; and every step makes the ascent easier and more rapid."

"I did not suspect you, Billings, of calling my vanity to your aid. Your advice is sound enough to commend itself without such assistance, and I shall watch for an opportunity to act upon it, as impatiently as yourself. My action, however, must not be unduly hurried. It is a maneuver which requires skill and caution, and in such cases time and chance are often our best friends."

"Very good friends they are, if properly improved; and I know of no one better qualified than yourself to make the most of them."

There was a pause of some minutes in the conversation, which Billings employed in helping himself to a glass of Madeira.

"Is there any late news from France?" he inquired, observing that Hamilton manifested no inclination to recur to the former topic.

"Nothing but what you have heard. The treaty is ratified, and we are soon to have a French fleet upon our coast and a French army fighting by our side."

"And I sincerely wish," exclaimed Billings, "that fleet may find its way to the bottom of the Atlantic before it touches these shores. His most Catholic Majesty has thrust his spoon into a dish where he is not wanted. There is no more porridge than will suffice for our own stomachs, and I pray earnestly that he may get well scalded for his impertinence."

"I cannot agree with you, Billings. This alliance was all important. It secures our independence beyond cavil or dispute."

"It was secured without it. England had but one chance from the beginning to reconquer these colonies, and that was thrown away by the foolish statesman who controlled her councils. If she had poured an overwhelming force upon us before the Declaration of Independence; if she had landed an army at Boston, another at New York, and another at Charleston, and marched from each place directly into the country, one-half of the people would have joined her standard, and the other half would have been subdued in a twelvemonth. As it was, they sent over an insignificant

force, which has been confined to the sea-coast, because
they dared not move beyond supporting distance of their
ships, and even there have been compelled to huddle together, lest they should be cut to pieces in detail. The necessary result of such a policy has been to give the republicans
full time to overawe the loyalists, to dissipate their dread of
British prowess, and inspire them with a confidence in themselves which makes reconquest an impossibility. The first
two years of the war achieved the independence of America.
After that, it was merely a question how long British obstinacy would persist in a hopeless attempt at subjugation.
I hoped and believed that it would be ten or twelve years,
and in that time I calculated that the free necks of the
colonists would be pretty well prepared to receive the yoke
of a military leader, under some title, no matter what, so
he had the *power* of an emperor. Now this interference
of France disturbs those calculations, and leaves me at sea,
without a chart or compass to guide me. John Bull's
game is proverbial. He may become incensed at the inter-
meddling of his old enemy, and rouse himself to more
strenuous exertions; but, on the other hand, there is a
chance of his being alarmed at the probability of America
becoming a dependency of France, and he may thus be
induced to conclude a treaty with his revolted subjects as
soon as decency will permit—a result that would put an
effectual extinguisher upon your hopes and upon mine. I
could see my way clearly before; I cannot do so now. The
probabilities are so nearly balanced that it.is difficult to decide which scale preponderates; and therefore I pray that
the French fleet may be met on the ocean, and sunk or
captured, whenever it sails. A great naval victory will so
stimulate the national pride of England, that Parliament
will vote liberal supplies to carry on the war, and ministers
dare not run counter to the national repugnance of the

people to surrender these rich provinces to the fostering
care of King Louis. Every time they beat the French, by
land or sea, the fortunes of Alexander Hamilton will wear
a brighter verdure."

"There is another side to the argument," replied Hamilton, "to which you do not seem to attach sufficient importance. The same success that encourages them will depress
the spirits of our army and people, and dispose them to
return to their alllegiance upon terms of simple forgiveness for the past. You will admit that this would be more
fatal to our hopes than the case you have supposed."

"I wish, Colonel Hamilton," answered Billings, earnestly, "that you would study the history of this people
more carefully than you have done, and make yourself better acquainted with their character. The three tides of
emigration, which have at different periods swelled the
number of inhabitants on this continent, were all singularly alike in one remarkable trait. Obstinacy was the
leading feature in the character of all of them. First,
there came the old Puritans, who, rather than comply with
certain immaterial forms of public worship, abandoned
home and kindred for a residence among savages and wild
beasts. The questions whether a man should repeat his
prayers standing or kneeling, whether he should read them
from a book or utter them extemporaneously from the
lips, whether a minister should or should not wear a gown
of a particular fashion, and the dozen other equally important points of disagreement between the established
church and the dissenters, all seem to my mind unspeak-
ably absurd. Not so thought the Puritans. They had
marked out a particular road to heaven, and were determined to travel no other. A creature possessed of as
much reason as a mad bull, ought to have understood that
it made no difference through what avenue the soul ap-

proached the kingdom of eternal rest. It was foolish to
require them to follow a particular form of worship; but
since that form could in nowise affect their future welfare,
it was the part of plain common sense to yield obedience
to the law. These stern zealots would not look at the
subject in any such reasonable or peaceful light. They
loved opposition for its own sake, and clung to their prejudices the more tenaciously because they were illegal. It
was from this stock—headstrong, obstinate, unyielding,
and unreasonable—that the first colonists sprung. Their
next accession was immediately after the civil wars in
England. Oliver Cromwell had swept legitimate monarchy
from the land, and unceremoniously shortened a crowned
king by a head. The followers of that king, who held out
longest, who were the most determined and unflinching in
his support, whom defeat, confiscation, and the military
execution of their friends, had failed to dismay, refused to
accept the offered amnesty of the great usurper, and came
over here, where they were at least removed from his personal presence. Unlike the Puritans in almost everything
else, they had the same obstinate devotion to their own
opinions, and the same readiness to suffer martyrdom for a
punctilio. When Cromwell was taken away on that tem-
pestuous night which was a fitting close to his wild and
stormy career, the sternest of the regicides, who never
could be brought to acknowledge the lawful rule of the
house of Stuart, abandoned England and hastened hither
to add a new stock of obstinacy to a market already more
than sufficiently supplied with that commodity. The char-
acteristics of the ancestry have not been softened in their
descendants by the dangers and difficulties in the midst of
which they have been nursed. The spirits of such a people cannot be broken. Their towns may be taken, their
armies may be beaten, but they will gather head again,

and, in the end, tire out a foe of more than ten times their
numerical strength. It is immaterial to them whether they
fight for an abstract principle or against the most palpa-
ble and galling oppression. They have no idea of surrendering a principle because it is of no practical importance,
and still less of retracting anything which they have once
uttered. They have declared that "these Colonies are,
and of right ought to be, free and independent States,"
and they will stick to the declaration until England is
compelled to acknowledge it by pecuniary exhaustion.
Bear these things constantly in mind. We do not want
assistance. If your position should enable you to dis-
courage our French allies, in any way, in God's name, do
it! Create jealousies between them and our troops, offend
their punctilious pride, and send them back to France in
disgust, if possible. You and I were not born in this
country; neither of us is tied to it by kindred or by
ancestral remembrances; neither of us is afflicted by Uto-
pian dreams of philanthropy; we are laboring for our own
advancement; the means, though difficult, are perfectly
obvious. When things do not work to suit us, we must
make them; this is no time for doubts or scruples; you
have extended your hand to grasp a scepter, and I have
staked my all upon your success. A failure after so fair a
beginning would be doubly mortifying, and fail we must if
this French alliance brings about a speedy peace. If the
war ends in one year or two years from this date, George
Washington may place a diadem on his head; but it is
doubtful whether it would not be torn even from *his* brow,
and it is certain that if any one else makes the effort, his
reward will be a gibbet instead of a throne. To remove
him now would be of no avail. The army must first get
accustomed to the sound of another name. They must be
taught that another can pilot them through storms as well

as he. They must be prepared to look to that other as an unquestionable leader in the event of his death; and to accomplish these things time is indispensable. A protracted struggle is not merely desirable, but absolutely essential on another account—it is necessary that the people should become so satiated with blood, so weary of plunder and house burning, that they will be reluctant to engage in a new contest, and quietly acquiesce in whatever choice the army may make. You see I deal plainly, and keep nothing back. Situated as we are, we must not only work for the same end, but the means must be also the same. Each one must know all that the other proposes to do, and the way in which he proposes to do it."

"I admit," replied Hamilton, "the general soundness of your reasoning, and I have as little disposition as you have to bring the war to a hasty conclusion; but I have not been, and I am not now, so sanguine of the result. England has not yet put forth a tithe of her strength. She has undervalued the importance of the rebellion from the beginning, and throughout the contest she has relied too much upon Tory assistance. When her eyes are opened to these faults—and the wonder is they have not been opened before now—we shall have an army upon our shores sufficiently powerful to make the assistance of a French force very welcome, if not absolutely necessary to the accomplishment of our independence. The difference between us is, that you underestimate the resources of Great Britain, and overvalue the capacity of the colonies for resistance. In my judgment, we shall stand in need of allies before our independence is acknowledged, and therefore I have been disposed to extend a cordial welcome to the French."

"It is an error, Colonel Hamilton," said Billings, emphatically, "a grievous error. I give Great Britain credit for vast resources, for immense energy, perseverance, and skill in the art of war. I believe there is no power on the globe that is able, single handed, to stand against her. I have admitted that there was a time and a way in which she might have reconquered these provinces. I know that she can still spread desolation and ruin over every portion of the land; but, believe me, Colonel Hamilton, she can do no more. The people of America are now perfectly united; the few straggling Tories in British pay are too insignificant to be counted; the country is too extensive to be overawed by garrison towns; it will, therefore, require as great a force to keep it as to subdue it; and that is a drain no nation can bear or will bear. Depend upon it, we have nothing to fear from the success of England. Our danger lies in the opposite direction; we may triumph too soon."

The strong, direct, and positive reasoning of his companion made a powerful impression on the mind of Alexander Hamilton. He turned the argument over and over again in his mind, and could discover no flaw in it. It was a strong case, strongly put by a strong-minded man. The facts were undeniable, and the argument founded upon them unanswerable. His own experience during the war had dissipated many of his previously conceived opinions of British invincibility. He had seen untrained militia stand up for hours against the utmost might of England's veteran soldiery. True, that militia would sometimes run away when there was no excuse for flight; but they would not run far. The first hill or the first wood was a rallying point. They did not scatter, and desert their standards. In an inconceivably short space of time they collected together again, and, perhaps the very next day, would fearlessly offer battle to the foe before whom they had fled; nor did it unfrequently happen, on such occasions, that they succeeded in compelling that foe to retreat in turn. He had seen these

same men undergo hardships and privations that no regular army could have borne without becoming thoroughly
demoralized, and he knew that a little more service and a
little more training would make them equal to the best
troops in the world. He was thus predisposed to give full
weight to the views urged by his confederate; and after
events proved that he was not unmindful of the sagacious
though villainous counsel that night poured into his ears.

He did quarrel with General Washington upon a trivial
pretext, and rejected the overtures of the general to accom-
modate the difficulty. At the same time he took care that
the quarrel should assume the form of a mere difference
upon a point of etiquette, and managed to retain the good
opinion of the commander-in-chief even while declining to
serve longer on his staff. In a private letter to General
Schuyler, after relating the fact of the rupture between the
commander-in-chief and himself, and his own refusal to
listen to overtures for an accommodation, he wrote,—

"I must assure you, my dear sir, it was not the effect of
resentment; it was the deliberate result of maxims I had
long formed for the government of my own conduct."

In the same letter he speaks of General Washington in
terms which plainly show that he was preparing the way to
undermine his reputation and destroy his influence.

"The general," he says, "is a very honest man. His
competitors have slender abilities, and less integrity. His
popularity has often been essential to the safety of America, and is still of great importance to it. These consid-
erations have influenced my past conduct respecting him,
and will influence my future. I think it necessary that he
should be supported."

The comments of Mr. James Billings on that letter,
doubtless ran in the following manner:—

"*The general is a very honest man. But that is all.*

*He is not at all remarkable for either natural or acquired
abilities.* His competitors are fools and knaves. *Therefore
it is best to keep him in command until I am in a situation to supplant him.* His popularity has helped the cause
of America, and may still aid it; *that is, he has somehow
gained the confidence of the country, and, though a man
of no abilities, we must put up with him for the present.
When his popularity ceases to be useful, we will throw
him overboard.* I think it necessary that he should be
supported—*because by maintaining his authority I keep
down rivalries until I am prepared to meet them."*

Considering the brevity of the foregoing extract, it
would be difficult to find anything in the English language
to equal it in the perfection of "damning with faint praise"
the man to whom he owed everything up to that time, and
whom he was not afterwards ashamed to importune for
great and unmerited favors.

Nor was Hamilton's conduct toward General Washington
the only evidence that the words of James Billings had not
been permitted to fall unheeded to the ground. When
the Count D'Estaing arrived on our coast with a powerful
fleet, General Washington sent Colonel Hamilton on board
his flag-ship to concert a plan of attack upon the British
troops stationed at Newport, in Rhode Island. On his
return, Billings extracted from him a full account of the
intended expedition. In the camp at Valley Forge he
had opened communications with Sir Henry Clinton, and
from time to time had contrived to give that officer much
information that tended greatly to prolong the war. His
absences from the camp had reference to this object. Too
cautious to trust a third person in the conduct of such momentous affairs, he went himself in disguise to the British
lines whenever the object was of sufficient magnitude to
justify the risk. His communications had enabled Sir

Henry Clinton to obtain several advantages, unimportant so far as they affected the general result, but calculated to keep up the spirits of the English troops, and encourage the ministry at home to persevere in their efforts to subdue the colonies. Beyond this, James Billings had no intention to go. If he had possessed the power to betray and destroy the whole American army at once, all the gold of England could not have bribed him to the act. Not that he had one moral or patriotic scruple to restrain him; but he looked to the eventual success of the colonies as the means of realizing the ambitious dreams of his earlier years. Gold had no attraction for him compared with the gratification of resuming his original name, gilded by titles that would hide the memory of the disgrace he had brought upon it. To Sir Henry Clinton he was known only as a common and mercenary informer, and the British commander was sometimes startled by the profound sagacity and stern energy of the man who he believed was playing the dangerous part of a spy for an insignificant bribe. Once or twice these evidences of superiority inclined him to think that a double game was being played upon him. The accuracy of the information he received, however, removed his doubts, and he was left to wonder that a man so much above his fellows in mental acquirements should be so far sunk below them by a sordid love of money as to sell himself to his country's invaders. Billings, on his part, was gradually acquiring a knowledge of all Sir Henry's weak points, and storing up a fund of information which he intended to turn to valuable account at a future day. Heretofore he had caused the capture of a few American posts and the surprise of a few detachments, well knowing that it would have no permanent effect upon General Washington's strength.

The arrival of the French fleet alarmed his fears, as we

19

have seen, and he resolved to spare no effort to insure its destruction. Having obtained from Colonel Hamilton an accurate account of the number and armament of the vessels, and also of the numbers and description of the land forces destined to co-operate with them, he disappeared from the American camp, upon the pretext of making a journey to Philadelphia to collect certain moneys alleged to be due him, and of which he pretended to be in great need. In about two weeks he returned, and soon afterwards came the news of the total failure of the Rhode Island expedition; Sir Henry Clinton having obtained information from some quarter which enabled him to defeat it entirely.

Colonel Hamilton was in total ignorance of his confederate's correspondence with the enemy. The experiment was too hazardous, and its results too uncertain, to have commanded his assent under any circumstances. Billings knew that upon this point he was inflexible, and dared not trust him with the slightest intimation of his own secret operations. He took the whole responsibility upon himself, trusting to his own matchless skill and impudence to escape detection or even suspicion. While, however, Colonel Hamilton would have been grievously offended and indignant if advised of the part that Billings had acted, the results were such as he regarded with great complacency. There is no proof that he had any agency in promoting the jealousies and heart-burnings which broke out between the American and French officers immediately after the failure of the Rhode Island expedition. In this matter, chance may have favored him. It was natural that defeated men should seek to shift the blame from themselves to their allies, and he may have done no more than refrain from efforts to heal a breach which gave to General Washington the greatest concern. But if he was passive at that time, he did not remain so afterwards. His jealousy of French influence, and detraction of everything French, grew into a mania that continued to afflict him during the remainder of his life. For the present, he was relieved from their association. Count D'Estaing, disgusted by his ill success, and exasperated by the quarrels between his officers and his allies, sailed for the South, where, in conjunction with an American force, he made an assault on Savannah, and suffered a bloody repulse. Concluding from the failure of these two attempts that the Western hemisphere was not exactly the theater upon which he was best calculated to shine, he turned the prows of his ships toward the East, and never again honored us with his presence.

After Colonel Burr's resignation, the jealousy of Hamilton slumbered for years. During a great part of the time, Burr was an invalid. He never re-entered the army; and as they seldom came in contact, there was nothing upon which a rivalry could feed. That period of his life, therefore, does not come properly within the scope of this history, and must be briefly disposed of.

After his withdrawal from the staff of General Washington, Colonel Hamilton urgently solicited a commission in the line, which was for some time refused. His wishes were at last complied with, and he again entered the army and served throughout the war, distinguished by courage and eminent ability. At the siege of Yorktown he added still more to his brilliant reputation as a soldier, and stained his character as a man by claiming credit for humanity at the expense of both Washington and La Fayette. This claim, as it afterwards appeared in a "Biography of Mr. Hamilton," is worthy of preservation, if for no other purpose than to show to what a degree of baseness a man undoubtedly possessed of many great qualities could descend, and how reckless he was of the reputation of others when his own might be enhanced by detracting from their just claims to public admiration.

"Previous to the assault," says the Biography in question, "the Marquis de la Fayette proposed to General Washington to put to death all the British troops that should be found within the redoubts, as a retaliation for several acts of barbarity committed by the royal army. The steady and nervous mind of Washington, which was never known to yield to the virtuous prejudice of compassion, gave his assent to the bloody order; but Mr. Hamilton, (the tenderness of whose feelings has led him into error,) after the redoubts were subdued, took the conquered under his protection, and proved to his enemies that America knew how to fight but not to murder."

With this veracious extract, we close the record of Alexander Hamilton, until we again find him the rival and the unscrupulous traducer of Aaron Burr.

CHAPTER XIV.

"The wilder passions work their own decay,
While gentle love woos kindred love to stay."

STRETCHED upon a sick couch, Aaron Burr had ample leisure to reflect upon the past and the future. His affections crushed, his constitution shattered, his fortune gone, and his hopes of military preferment at an end, what was there to save him from the numbing effects of despair? Nothing but the inborn energy of a soul that no human calamity could subdue. Weary months rolled away, and the invalid began slowly to regain a portion of his strength. He had so far recovered as to be able to take exercise on horseback, when, in the summer of 1780, he returned to his native State of New Jersey, in the hope that its old remembered scenes would help to invigorate his frame and bring back the pulses of health. Here he became intimate with the family of Mrs. Theodosia Prevost, the widow of Colonel Prevost of the British army, who had died some years before, while serving in the West Indies.

At the beginning of the revolutionary war Mrs. Prevost was residing at Paramus, in New Jersey, with her two little sons and a younger sister, Miss De Visme. Her husband was then living, and serving in the British army, and it might have been supposed that his high rank would have made her peculiarly the object of suspicion in times when suspicion was a virtue; but the perfect propriety of Mrs. Prevost's conduct not only preserved her from moles-

19*   (221)

tation or annoyance, but made her house the favorite resort
of the American officers who happened to be stationed in
the neighborhood.   Colonel James Monroe, afterwards
President of the United States, was among her warmest
friends and admirers.   At what time Colonel Burr formed
her acquaintance is uncertain.   It is probable that it was
in the year 1777, when he marched from the Ramapo to
Paramus to repel a British incursion from New York.
He is only known to have visited her twice during his
command of the Westchester lines.   Miss De Visme was
then, and long afterwards, supposed to be the attraction
which drew him to her dwelling.   In the letters of his
friends, addressed to him at different times, while Mrs.
Prevost was always mentioned in terms of high regard,
there is no intimation of the least suspicion that he could
contemplate matrimony with her.   All their allusions of
this nature are to her young sister.   Mrs. Prevost was, at
least, ten years his senior; she had two children; she never
had been beautiful, and was disfigured by a slight scar
across the forehead.   She had no fortune to compensate
for these disadvantages, and no one supposed that a young
man whose position and connections entitled him to seek
the alliance of any family in the colonies could contemplate a marriage which, to others, seemed so unsuitable and
impolitic.   They little knew the motives which actuated
him.   Close in his own bosom was hidden the memory of
his early love.   General Putnam was his only confidant,
and he alone might have formed a reasonable conjecture as
to the moving springs of his conduct.   His dreams of rapture were over.   In looking around for a wife, love never
entered into his calculations.   That he knew he would
never feel again.   He sought, rather, an intelligent friend,
in whose society his life might glide peacefully and tran-
quilly along, undisturbed by petty bickerings and unembit-

tered by passionate exactions that he knew himself unable
to satisfy. In Mrs. Prevost these requisites were combined
in a remarkable degree. Although neither young nor beautiful, she was intelligent and refined. Well versed in the
literature of her own and other lands, her conversation
was always instructive; and her criticisms, regulated by
sound judgment and discriminating taste, never failed to
give her hearers a more correct appreciation of the merits
of the volume or the author under discussion. Her education was such as could not be acquired in America at
that day; and her associations, previous and subsequent to
her marriage with Colonel Prevost, had been with the most
intelligent and refined portions of English society. To
these were added a sweetness of temper and a fascination
of manner never surpassed. Colonel Burr, who was himself remarkable for the graceful ease of his deportment,
often declared that he was indebted to her for all his
superiority to other men in that respect. Such a woman
was precisely the companion he sought. He made no
avowals of passion. His courtship was conducted upon
pure and unmixed principles of respect and esteem. Sentiment was a forbidden luxury, and their whole intercourse
was such as might have been expected between friends of
the same sex. Much of the time passed in her society was
devoted to the study of the French language, in which she
was a proficient, and of which he knew but little; and at
such times the lover was completely merged in the pupil.
At other times he would read to her long passages from his
favorite authors, to elicit her comments, which he combated
earnestly when they differed from his own preconceived
opinions; though the discussion generally ended by his
acknowledging the superiority of her taste, and the cor-
rectness of her appreciation of the beauties or the faults
she pointed out. With them there were no moonlight

rambles, no long communings in leafy bowers, where sighs become a language and silence itself is eloquence. Their walks and rides were regulated by a matter-of-fact regard for health; and if they talked of the moon and stars at all, it was to discuss the discoveries of different astronomers, and compare their relative merits. It was, in short, the purely intellectual intercourse of gifted and cultivated minds; pleasing to both, instructive to both, and unalloyed by fiery passions in either. It did not interfere in the slightest degree with the plans he was forming for beginning a new career in life, and neither hastened nor retarded his efforts. These plans were submitted to her as a matter of course, and met her cordial approval.

His reckless generosity had made such inroads upon his fortune, that barely enough remained to enable him to acquire a profession in which his exertions would suffice for a support. He had no time to lose, and as soon as his health permitted, he entered the office of Judge Patterson, of New Jersey, as a student of law. The regular, methodical mode of instruction adopted by the judge did not accord with Colonel Burr's anxiety to hurry into the practice of his profession; and in the spring of 1781 he left him to reside at Haverstraw, in the family of Thomas Smith, an eminent practitioner of New York. Here he devoted himself to study with an assiduity that few men ever brought to bear upon the dry details of that uninteresting science. It was not an unusual occurrence for him to pass twenty of the twenty-four hours among his books, noting down the doubtful and obscure points, and the next day submitting them to his instructor for solution. His close application to the law did not prevent him from writing regularly to Mrs. Prevost. Their letters, like their conversation, were entirely devoid of those soft extravagancies which give such a charm to the correspondence of acknowledged lovers. They were full of keen criticisms of Voltaire, Chesterfield, Rousseau, and other eminent writers; but they contained no burning avowals of affection; none of the gushing tenderness that sounds so sweetly in the ear of beauty and comes so naturally from a heart that is full of the gladness of requited love. Some tenderness there certainly was, but it was the tenderness of friendship; beyond that, their correspondence was a communion of the intellect alone, and it was so understood by both.

After six months of incessant application, Colonel Burr repaired to Albany, to apply for admission to the bar. Here he was encountered by a difficulty which, to a man less fruitful in resources, would have proved insurmountable. He was informed that a rule of the court required candidates for admission to have passed three years in the study of the profession before examination. To this he answered, that he had begun to read law before the Revolution; that he had abandoned his books to take up the sword in his country's defense; that when ill health drove him from the military service, he had resumed his studies; that the rule did not require a continuous application; and that in point of fact it was more than six years since his legal reading actually commenced. His arguments did not satisfy the members of the bar; but, resolving not to be thwarted, he turned his attention to the presiding judge. To him he repeated all that had proved unavailing with others, and added that it was an extreme hardship to deprive a man of privileges he had only lost through devotion to his country, besides being an example that must work injury to the public service. The judge was so far influenced by his persuasions that he agreed he might make a motion for his own admission, and if, on examination, it appeared that he was otherwise qualified, the rule should be set aside in his behalf. The motion was made.

He passed triumphantly through a severe and prolonged examination, and in January, 1782, was licensed as an attorney.

Thus, at the age of twenty-six, he entered upon a new field of action, demanding totally different habits, and calling into play totally different qualities than those through the exercise of which he had heretofore won distinction and renown. In other respects, however, his *debut* was made under circumstances more favorable than usually attend the young practitioner. The legal disqualification of the Tory lawyers had so thinned the profession as to make competition merely nominal. He had a wide reputation as a patriot soldier, and an extensive acquaintance with that class of men most certain to be useful to a professional man. The interruptions and delays incident to the war had caused an immense accumulation of business, and almost from the very first his practice was large and exceedingly lucrative. As a practitioner he never had a superior. There were others more profoundly read in the law; there were others more eloquent and more imposing in their address; but in the skillful management of a cause, in careful preparation beforehand, in the readiness with which he seized upon every advantage against an adversary, and the consummate tact with which he guarded every weak point on his own side, he was without an equal and without a rival. Throughout his long practice he never lost a case in which he had been consulted before the suit was instituted. His soldier life had taught him the advantages of watchfulness, and no adversary ever took him by surprise.

Soon after obtaining his license, Colonel Burr opened an office in Albany, and the first few months of his practice were so satisfactory that he determined upon consummating his marriage with Mrs. Prevost without delay. The arrangements were all made by letter. The style of that correspondence had nothing in it to recommend it to a love-sick couple of the present day, or of that day either. Everything was written in a matter-of-fact, business-like way, that was horridly unromantic. Generally he assumed the positive and decided tone of the husband—never that of the yielding and complaisant lover. At one time he tells her to "deal less in sentiment, and more in ideas." He complains that her letters are too long. Again he says, "don't torment me with compliments." Another letter is devoted to a dissertation on the advantages of a Franklin stove, and he goes on to suggest the room in which she should place it. There were no raptures—none of the fond and endearing expressions so natural and so becoming in two persons who are about to commit to each other's keeping the holiest of earthly trusts. Both had loved once, and both had indulged in all the extravagance to which it gives birth. They knew that such love never comes again. Like the bloom on the peach, it will bear no second handling. Dismissing, therefore, all expectation of joys they knew were beyond their reach, they had calmly and deliberately concluded that the happiness, the tranquillity, and the intellectual pleasures of each, would be promoted by their union; and they walked to the marriage altar under the guidance of an enlightened self-interest, which, after all, is perhaps the surest guaranty of a peaceful and contented life. On the 2d of July, 1782, they were united in marriage by the Rev. David Bogart, of the Reformed Dutch Church. As a woman of the world, and the mistress of an establishment, Mrs. Burr was unrivaled, and their house soon became noted for its profuse and elegant hospitality.

Colonel Burr continued to reside at Albany until the treaty which acknowledged the independence of the United States was signed, and it was there that his only child,

Theodosia, was born. With the birth of that child an entire change came over the man. Upon her he lavished all the overflowing fondness of his nature. The passionate tenderness which had been so long pent up in his bosom showered itself upon the rosy-cheeked child, and the babe became to him an idol, in its cradle. Its mother, too, shared in the newly-awakened sentiment. From that day he became a lover. His letters, when absent from home, were more thickly interspersed with words of endearment, and he no longer checked her most loving expressions. Eight years after marriage, her letters and his replies are full of a warm and glowing affection, to which they were strangers in the days of their courtship. In reply to one of his letters, she says : " Your letters always afford me a singular satisfaction ; a sensation entirely my own; this was peculiarly so. My Aaron, it was replete with tenderness. I read and re-read, till afraid I should get it by rote, and mingle it with common ideas. Profane the sacred pledge ! No, it shall not be. I will economize the boon."

In acknowledging the receipt of another letter, she writes : "What language can express the joy, the gratitude of Theodosia ? * * * * * * * Her Aaron safe ; mistress of the heart she adores ; can she ask more ? has Heaven more to grant ?"

Before marriage he had warned her not to deal in sentiment ; now his soul was athirst for sentiment. " This morning," he writes on one occasion, "this morning came your kind, your affectionate, your truly welcome letter of Monday evening. Where did it loiter so long ?"

Again he writes : " I continually plan my return with childish impatience, and fancy a thousand incidents which render it more interesting."

In another letter, he says : "Be assured (I hope the

assurance is needless) that whatever diminishes your happiness equally impairs mine."

Before this time he had removed his office to the City of New York, and established his residence at Richmond Hill, which had been the headquarters of General Washington during the early part of the revolutionary war. His reputation as a lawyer had preceded him, and he was at once immersed in business. No engagement, however, was ever permitted to interfere with his duties as a husband and a father. No cares or anxieties ever came near the Eden of his home. The two sons of his wife, by her former husband, were considered and treated as his own; and as soon as the little Theodosia could utter a syllable, her education commenced. Courage, fortitude, self-reliance, and energy were instilled into her mind, and formed a part of her character before she knew the meaning of the words. His letters to his daughter, as she grew older, impress the religious reader with the conviction that he laid too much stress upon intellectual culture, and far too little upon that moral training without which intellect becomes a curse. Happily for her she had a mother who, to rare good sense added the merit of genuine piety; and, while the father bestowed his whole attention upon the head, she planted seeds in the heart, which, in good time, brought forth fruits of unsurpassed purity and sweetness. But whatever may have been the errors that developed themselves in the progress of Colonel Burr's system of education, he began right. He made the practice of virtue easy, by implanting in the character those qualities which enable us to reject, at will, whatever is vicious or hurtful. His daughter grew to womanhood a model that the best of her sex might study with advantage.

Colonel Burr's income from his practice was such as to enable him to indulge to his heart's content the boundless

20

hospitality in which he delighted.   The troubles in France
had driven many of her distinguished citizens into exile;
and, entertaining a grateful sense of the services rendered
to us by the French people during our revolutionary struggle, he extended to them a cordial invitation to make his
mansion their home.   Talleyrand, Volney, Louis Philippe,
and others were his guests.   In his family they enjoyed the
satisfaction of meeting persons who could converse in their
own tongue, thus relieving them from the awkwardness of
broken English, and making them feel more completely at
home.   The little Theodosia became the pet of the man
who afterwards, as the minister of Napoleon, swayed the
destinies of the world.   Volney forgot to meditate upon
the ruins of empires, when he twined her silken tresses
around his finger; and Louis Philippe ceased to sigh over
the ruined fortunes of his family, or to pant for the throne
he was destined to fill, when she climbed with childish
familiarity upon his knee, and her joyous smile fell like a
sunbeam upon him.

Dispensing a princely hospitality, surrounded by a loved
and loving family, together with a wide circle of devoted
friends, blessed in all his relations, the life of Colonel Burr
at this period presented a picture of enviable happiness,
far beyond the common lot of humanity.   Thus far he had
avoided the maelstrom of politics.   Once or twice he had
been elected to the General Assembly of the State, but he
took so little interest in its proceedings, and appeared to
be so wholly unambitious of political distinction, that the
impression very generally prevailed that he was unfitted to
shine in parliamentary discussions.   He would at any time
desert the legislative hall for the court of justice, and
leave the interests of the State to other hands while he was
pleading the cause of a client.   This inactivity and careless
inattention in a man so remarkable for restless energy in

whatever he undertook, was attributable to two causes. In the first place, all the time he could, or rather would, spare from his domestic enjoyments was absorbed by his professional engagements. In the second place, there was no theater then open for a man conscious of high capacity and unfailing resources. The United States were lingering out a sickly existence under the old Articles of Confederation. There was no national power; no national center; no enduring bond of Union; no broad and expansive national policy, in the development of which a genuine statesman could make a name for his country and win immortality for himself. Sovereignty was distributed among thirteen independent States, who had no common head—each one of which imagined that its interests were limited by its State lines, and all of which looked upon their sister States in the light of commercial rivals, whose prosperity was just that much subtracted from their own wealth and importance. The admiration of foreign powers for the noble struggle that established our independence was fast changing into contempt for the imbecility that characterized our attempts at self-government, and tyrants were congratulating themselves that a new argument was about to be furnished to the world in support of the inborn right of kings to trample upon the necks of their fellow-men.

During the whole of this gloomy period Aaron Burr confined himself exclusively to the law. He took no part in the public discussions which grew out of the bickerings among the States. He attended none of the public meetings which were called to decide upon the right of one State to pass navigation laws, or of another to tax the commerce of her sister States, or of another to raise and keep up a standing army, or of another to carry on war upon its own responsibility. With all such questions he was thoroughly disgusted, and he kept entirely aloof from the places where they were discussed. The court-house was his theater, and it is upon the records of the courts alone that his name appears. Happy would it have been for him if he had maintained throughout life the same indifference to political honors, and the same disgust of political wrangles !

CHAPTER XV.

"Strange partings hath this world; and yet
Stranger meetings."

DURING the period referred to in the last chapter, one evening as Colonel Burr was about closing his office to repair to his residence at Richmond Hill, he was accosted by a shabbily-dressed man, who inquired if his name was Burr. Upon receiving an affirmative answer, he said that he had called to see him on business of urgent importance, and asked permission to close the door.

"I never attend to business at this hour," replied Colonel Burr. "It is the time at which I always return to my family. You must call again to-morrow."

"I may not be able to call to-morrow, and my mission must be discharged now."

At the same time he raised a broad slouched hat from his head, and exhibited a strongly-marked countenance, rendered still more striking by a deep scar from the left eye to the right cheek.

"Do you know me?" he asked, after allowing Colonel Burr a short time to peruse his features.

"Yours is not a face to be easily forgotten," was the reply, "even if I had less cause to remember it. Your name is Jenkins; and it was at your cabin, in the High-lands, that I was sheltered in times less peaceful than these."

"Your memory is a good one—almost as good as if you had some cause to hate me. Do you recollect also the man who brought you there?"

13*   (233)

"Alexis Durand—my preserver? Assuredly I do."

"Ah! I see he knew you better than I did. I thought you were like the world in general, and in your prosperity would forget, or scorn to recognize, two poor Tories who had helped you at a pinch. He said no. He was right and I was wrong."

"Did he send you here?"

"He did; and here is a token that he said you would remember," replied Jenkins, at the same time extending the large seal ring which Colonel Burr had presented to Durand when they parted in 1779. "He is in trouble," continued Jenkins, "and it is on his business that I wish to talk with you."

"This must be attended to," said Burr, after assuring himself that the ring was the same. "Sit down and wait a minute."

Colonel Burr walked to the door and soon returned with a messenger, to whom he delivered a hasty note to his wife; then, locking the door, he said briefly,—

"Now, Mr. Jenkins, what can I do for Durand?"

"He wants to see you himself."

"Then why did he not come with you?"

"Because he is locked up between four stone walls, with a pair of iron bracelets on his wrists, and another on his ankles."

"In prison! For what?"

"For what he is as innocent of as you are. For murder."

"For murder! How do you know he is innocent, Jenkins? It was said, in days gone by, that he valued human life at a cheap rate, and those who remember him then will believe the present charge on slender proof."

"That is the worst of it, sir. No one can deny that his hand is redder than it is prudent to talk about now, and though he has been pardoned for that, the men who are to try him may hang him upon the old account, when he is innocent of the new offense; for he is innocent, sir; though you must learn the rest from him. I can tell you no more."

"Let us go to him then. I must see him at once."

"I am sorry to let you go alone, colonel, but it is not safe for me to be seen too often near the city prison. I risked it once to-day on Durand's account, but I do not care to risk it again. The fact is, I am not on the best terms with the officers of the law, and do not care to encounter them unnecessarily."

"I understand; but I may need you, and I wish to know where you are to be found."

"That is uncertain. I will come to your house to-morrow night at ten o'clock, if that will suit you; and if you think then that you will have any further business with me, I will leave an address which will enable you to find me at pleasure."

After a moment's thought, Burr replied: "That will do. Here," he continued, extending a handful of gold to Jenkins, "take this and provide yourself with a better suit of clothes."

Jenkins took the money reluctantly, saying, "Necessity, colonel, knows no law. I ought not to take this money, but I cannot serve you as you will expect unless I do; and, besides, as it will be necessary for me to keep very quiet for a time, I may need it for bread."

"Keep it, man, without scruple. The shelter of your roof was once worth more than a hundred times the sum to me. I am still largely in your debt."

When Jenkins departed, Colonel Burr locked his office and walked directly to the city prison. It was past the usual hour for the admission of visitors, but the jailer

abated his rule in favor of a practitioner of such well-
known eminence, and conducted him to the cell of Alexis
Durand.

"I am sorry to see you in this plight," said Burr, taking
the manacled hand of the prisoner. "I hope you have
done nothing to deserve it."

"It is very kind of you, colonel," replied Durand, in-
closing the hand of his visitor in a grasp as hard as the
iron which fettered his own. "It is very kind of you to
come within these gloomy walls to comfort a friendless
man;_ but I always said that you had the best heart
of any man who ever served in George Washington's
army."

"Thank you for your good opinion. Jenkins informed
me tht you were arrested on a charge of murder, of which,
he insists, you are innocent. In that case I want you to
begin at the beginning and tell me everything, omitting
nothing because it may seem unimportant to you. I must
judge of that, and, to judge correctly, I must know the
whol' "

"Well, sir, after I had put you in the Middlebrook road,
I went back to my comrades and served the king faithfully
until the end of the war. I had been too active a foe to
hope for speedy forgiveness; and Jenkins was more obnox-
ious to the victorious Whigs than I was, for he had plundered, burned, and hung without mercy, whereas I had
only killed in open fight. Both, however, were in peril,
and we agreed to repair to New York, enlist in the British
army, and go with it to Europe. Unfortunately, we arrived
too late. They had been gone three days when we reached
here. There was no alternative but to make our way back
to the Highlands, where we lay hid for months, sometimes
sleeping in Jenkins's cabin, and sometimes in the hollows
and lonely glens, with which we were well acquainted.

Occasionally we would venture down to the houses of
known Tories, who lived unmolested in the country because
they had not taken up arms during the war, and from them
we obtained clothing and provisions. In this way months
went over. Our fears had subsided to some extent, and
we now lived constantly in the cabin, trusting to its remote
situation to escape observation; or, if that failed, to our
own watchfulness to guard against surprise. One night
we were alarmed by the barking of the dogs, and had
barely time to escape to the bushes before the house was
surrounded by armed men, who, finding that the inmates
had fled, first stripped it of everything it contained and
then burned it to the ground. I was hid behind the rocks
within one hundred yards of the spot; my rifle was in my
hand; their forms were distinctly marked against the blazing fire—and yet I did not shoot. There was a time when
all of them would not have left that burning pile alive. It
was a sore temptation, but I let them escape, because I
had hopes of being permitted to live in peace in the pursuit of some honest calling, and I did not wish to incur
other disabilities than those which were already hanging
over me. I do not know who was the prime mover in the
business, though I have latterly suspected the man who
will appear as the principal witness against me."

"What was his name?" asked Colonel Burr, for the first
time interrupting the speaker.

"John Roberts. I have no proof against him, and
therefore I have twice kept Bill Jenkins's knife from his
throat. He had been a Tory, but took time by the fore-
lock, and made his peace with General McDougall before
the troubles were over."

"When was that?"

"About the last of 1780. He was a Westchester man."

"I remember him. Go on."

"He knew that Jenkins and I had both saved some money. He knew that we would not keep it in the cabin, or in any other place where it could be easily found. He pretended great friendship for us, and several times sold us provisions. If we were captured, he probably thought he could obtain our secret from us, pocket the money, and leave us to hang. This, though, is suspicion only. I have no proof, as I said before."

Colonel Burr made a memorandum in his pocket-book, and again requested Durand to proceed.

"We remained in the mountains two days, then dug up our money and walked to this city, where we had few acquaintances, and where we thought we would be lost in the crowd of strangers who were flocking here. We took lodgings in a cheap boarding-house close to the water's edge, and in the course of a month I bought a wherry and began the trade of a waterman. Jenkins at first worked with me, and we did very well. At last he became acquainted with a gang of desperate men, and took to worse courses. He changed his boarding-house, and left me. I continued at the business, saving a little each month, and gradually growing contented with my lot. In the mean time I had obtained a pardon for the part I had taken in the war, and had no cause for uneasiness, except on Jenkins's account. His murdered wife was my sister, and from that fatal hour I had clung to him as brother rarely cleaves to brother. I hunted him up, and tried to drag him from the dens of infamy he frequented. He would not hear me. I then learned that John Roberts had also come to New York, and was one of his associates, though Bill seemed to have an instinctive hatred of the man. I don't know what made him suspect him, but he came to me one day and said that Roberts was the man who brought upon us the party who burned our cabin, and that he intended to kill him for it. It took long and urgent persuasion to induce him to abandon his intention. At another time he came to me and said that Roberts must not live. Again I interposed and saved him. This brings me down to the time of the murder; and here I suppose you wish me to be more particular."

"Tell it exactly in your own way, and give me your observations precisely as they occurred to you at the time and since. Omit nothing."

"I lodged in the house of a German, whose name was Franz Klink. It was a two-story house fronting the water, with two rooms below and two above. In the front room below he sold vegetables and groceries of the various kinds used by sailors. The back room was his eating-room, and back of that again was a shed-room, used as a kitchen. He slept in the front room up stairs, and I in the rear. The woman who cooked for us always went home to sleep. There was no other person about the house, which was seldom kept open later than nine o'clock at night. When it was necessary for me to be out later than that hour, he gave me the key of the shed-room, and I entered through the back yard, which was also used as a lumber yard. Just one week ago John Roberts came to see me. It was not dark, though I was lying down, for I had been hard at work, and was very tired. He told me that a man had been knocked down and robbed the night before; that Bill Jenkins was suspected, and that, in consequence, he was lying hid in a house he mentioned, in another part of the city. He said that Bill had sent him for me, and mentioned ten o'clock as the hour at which he would expect me. Before I had time to question him further, Franz came up with a light, and, saying that supper was ready, invited Roberts to join us. He declined, and added that he would wait there until I had finished my meal. When

I came back, he was lying carelessly across the foot of my bed. I suggested to him that it was unnecessary to wait until ten o'clock, and proposed that we should go and see Jenkins together. He replied that he had some business which he must attend to before that hour; moreover, that it would be useless to go sooner, because there would be a number of loungers about the premises, and the landlord would not admit me to the private part of the house. Then, giving me a password, and directions how to find the house, he took his hat to go. I went down stairs with him, and, having still several hours on my hands, I took a seat on the counter and entered into conversation with Franz. Customers were coming in, making small purchases, and going out. Some of these I knew, and talked to them about the news of the day and other indifferent matters. Toward ten o'clock, I told Franz that I was going out, and, borrowing a stout club that he usually kept behind the counter, I took the key of the back shed and left the house. As I did so, a man with the collar of his coat turned up, and buttoned close about his ears, walked quickly by me. From his form and gait, I took him to be Roberts and called him by name. He did not answer, and, supposing that I was mistaken, I walked on. It took me some time, wandering about in a filthy, suspicious locality, to find the house to which I had been directed. Upon knocking at the door, and giving the password, I was admitted to a room in which there were four or five men and as many women, evidently of the worst description, some of whom were smoking and others drinking ale. Not perceiving Jenkins among them, I took the landlord aside and inquired where he was. He replied that he had gone out about an hour before, and left word that if any one called for him, he must wait until his return. When this reply was made, I knew that the man was lying, or that Roberts had lied.

One or the other was certain, for I could not be persuaded that Bill Jenkins would leave the house, after sending for me, before I came. Nevertheless, as I did not know what else to do, I concluded to wait, and, calling for a cracker and a mug of ale, I made myself apparently at home, paying no attention to the scrutinizing glances with which I was conscious the other inmates of the room were regarding me.

"I had no means of ascertaining the exact time, but I am satisfied it was after eleven o'clock when I rose, and, saying that I could wait no longer, paid my score and prepared to depart. The landlord urged me to stay, insisting that Jenkins would certainly be back in half an hour. I cared nothing for the half hour, and would have waited cheerfully, if I had not been sure he was deceiving me. In such cases it is always the safest plan to do directly the reverse of what the deceiver wishes. He wanted me to stay for some purpose of his own, and for that very reason I determined not to stay. I had an undefined apprehension that mischief was afoot, and returned rapidly to my lodging. On approaching the house through the back alley, I observed that my window was up. It had no shutter, and was fastened by a large nail driven above it. I remembered to have seen the nail in its place that day at dinner time. Against the shed-room I have described there was a pile of lumber reaching nearly to the roof. Upon that roof my window opened, and by climbing on the lumber it could be easily reached. Thinking that there might be thieves within, I climbed up to the window and listened. Everything was still. At length I heard what I thought was a faint groan in the other room. I entered, and striking a light went into the bedroom of Franz. He was lying on the floor, in his night-clothes, dead. The groan I had heard no doubt was his last gasp. A large stream of blood ran from the body,

21

and was trickling slowly down the stairway.   I knelt down
by his side to feel his pulse, when I discovered that, besides
a deep wound in his side, his skull was broken.   To be
certain that the murderers were not still concealed in the
house, I went to search the lower rooms.   I found them in
their usual state, except that the money-drawer was broken
open and its contents abstracted.   I returned to the room
where the dead man was lying, and looked around for some
trace of the murderer.   At this time I heard a knocking
at the front door, and, in the agitation of the moment, let
the candle fall.   I have seen blood shed in many ways.   I
have slept among the dead upon the battle-field as soundly
as a king in his palace, and I would not have believed that
these strong nerves could be so shaken by the sight of one
pale corpse and one purple stream.   It was over in a
moment, and I snatched up the candle to relight it.   It
was too late.   The door was broken open, and two men
with lanterns rushed in.   At the same time two more
appeared at the still open window.   To their eager questions of who did the deed, I could only answer I did not
know.   My statement went for nothing, and I was hurried
off to prison as the murderer.   If I had been, colonel,
those four men would never have dragged me ten steps
from the door of that house.   I could have crushed every
bone in all of them; and, if I had been guilty, I would have
done so.   But I knew I was innocent, and did not choose
to make evidence against myself by resistance.

"The next day, when I was allowed to tell my story, I
was afraid of implicating Jenkins, and said nothing about
the cause which took me out, merely relating what occurred
after I discovered the window open.   I understand that
Roberts swore, before the coroner, that he called on me
that night to claim the payment of a sum of money I owed
him, and that I put it off, promising to pay on the morrow

He swore that he met me that night armed with a heavy club, and having my coat collar turned up, so as to hide my face; that he spoke to me, and I did not answer; that his suspicions were excited, and he followed me cautiously; that he saw me enter the back yard and climb in at the window; that he first supposed I had been out for some purpose which I desired to hide from Franz, and had therefore adopted this mode of entrance; that he was about going away when he heard a blow and a heavy fall; that he then became alarmed and ran off for a watchman, who called two others to his assistance, and they proceeded together to the house; that on observing the light, they divided, Roberts and another going into the back yard to prevent escape; that I extinguished the light at the first sound of knocking on the front door; that on entering the house, they found just such a club as he had seen me carrying, lying by the dead man's side all covered with blood; that my knife, bloody from point to hilt, was discovered on the mantle-piece in my room; that my clothes and hands were bloody, and that there were marks of bloody fingers on the money drawer. Upon searching my person they found the key of the shed-room in my pocket, and in my chest a quantity of small change, such as Franz would be likely to receive from his customers. A good deal of this was true, and was corroborated by others. All that was true I could easily explain, but I had no proof to sustain my statement. The money was mine. It had been paid to me for boat fare, and was therefore mostly in small change. The club I had dropped in the pool of blood when I knelt down by the body to ascertain if life was extinct. My hands and clothes were bloodied at the same time. In examining the drawer to see what had been taken out, I had no doubt left the prints of my fingers upon it. The knife was a large hunting-knife I had worn during the war, and had been lying upon the mantle-piece for months."

"Have you no suspicion," asked Burr, "who it was that committed the murder?"

"I *know* who did it, colonel, as well as if I had seen the blow struck; but I can prove nothing, and it will do me no good."

"You may be mistaken. At all events tell me who you suspect?"

"John Roberts. Bill Jenkins had not seen him for days, and did not send him for me. He had planned the robbery before he came, and his visit had a double object; first, to get me out of the way, for he well knew that it was not the safest thing in the world to enter a house where I was sleeping, for any such purpose. His other object was to survey the premises. When I went down to supper, he removed the nail from the window and put my knife in his bosom. He then loitered about in the neighborhood until he saw me depart. The landlord of the house to which he sent me was unquestionably his confederate, and had instructions to detain me as long as he could. It was possible he might fail in this, and therefore it was important for Roberts to accomplish his purpose quickly. My opinion is, that he made his entrance a little too soon; that his fears of my return hurried him, and he did not wait until Franz was sound asleep. I am not sure that he meant to commit murder if he could avoid it, but he went prepared for it. He may only have meant to creep through the room, go down the stairs, rob the house, and pass out of the front door into the street. He must have made some noise, and when Franz jumped up to ascertain the cause, he felled him with a bludgeon and stabbed him after he was down. After that, he robbed the house, placed my bloody knife upon the mantle-piece, escaped through the window, and hid among the piles of lumber until he saw me enter, when he gave the alarm and had me arrested under circumstances which he thought would hang me, and which, I admit, are strangely against me.

"You will not think it strange, colonel, that I should be so positive and precise when you remember that I served for years as a partisan soldier in a country where dark deeds were as frequent as recurring suns. I have tracked out many a one with a smaller clue at the beginning than this; and if I was free for one week, I would prove John Roberts's guilt, or consent to hang in his place."

"That is impossible," replied Burr. "We must trust to what I can do towards untangling this dangerous web; and be assured that I am no novice in the art. Give me the street and number of your lodging-house, and also that of the house to which you were sent by Roberts."

When he had made a note of the numbers, he said: "It will be three weeks before your trial can come on. In that time a great deal may be done. Keep up your spirits. I shall come again in a few days, and hope to bring you cheering tidings."

To the jailor he said, on leaving, "Treat your prisoner with as much lenity as your duty will permit, and allow him all the comforts you can. I will see that you are recompensed."

The obsequious official readily promised all that the great lawyer requested; and in another hour Aaron Burr was mingling with a gay company in his own drawing-room, playing the part of the courteous host with the polished ease of a thorough man of the world, and exhibiting in his countenance not a single trace of the annoying cares that beset his professional life.

To the lawyer society is always unjust. The mechanic who pushes his plane from sunrise to sunset, and receives at night a miserable pittance for his labor, is too apt to murmur when the carriage of the lawyer rolls by him, and his heart is too apt to swell with envy for the wealth which, he thinks, has been so easily acquired. If he could get down into that lawyer's heart and witness the cares and anxieties that have gathered there; if he could follow him to his private chamber, and watch him, as hour after hour, by the lamp's pale light, he taxes his brain to solve some knotty question, upon which the property, the liberty, or the life of a fellow-being depends; if he could see him lying down, hot and feverish, at cock-crow, not to rest, but to go over again in sleep the mental labors which have embittered the long day and the longer night, and rise at last, worn and wearied, from his comfortless repose, to renew the exhausting struggle, until nature rebels against the exorbitant tax, and disease comes in to hurry the neglected body to the grave; if he could witness all this, pity would take the place of envy, and the bread he has earned by the sweat of his brow become doubly sweet from the comparison.

To Colonel Burr the cares of the profession were peculiarly trying. His ardent nature made every cause his own, and in every case he labored as if his life depended upon the result. Yet it was only in his solitary hours that these anxieties were manifest. When he passed from the study to the drawing-room the furrowed brow was left behind him, and he assumed an appearance of gladness that was often foreign to his heart, because he knew it would be a source of gladness to others. The night of his interview with Durand, he was gayer and more brilliant than usual; but when his guests departed and his family retired to rest, he paced the floor for hours in anxious thought. Higher motives than professional pride were at work. He owed his life to that man's grateful remembrance of a kindness; and, apart from this, there was a straightforward manliness about

Durand, there was something so touchingly beautiful in his
affection for his mother, and in his self-sacrificing friendship
for his unfortunate brother-in-law, that would at any time
have commanded the warmest sympathies of Colonel Burr,
particularly when he believed that he had been wrongfully
and maliciously accused of a crime for which there is no
atonement but death. It was past four o'clock when he retired to rest, and before seven he was on his way to the city.
His first care was to examine the house where Franz Klink
had been killed. The blood had not been washed up, and
everything remained as it was on the night of the murder.
On the floor there was a large spot of grease, which seemed
to have been made by the falling of a tallow candle, and
this so far corroborated Durand's story. He next walked
to the house to which Durand had been decoyed, noting
the time it required to go from one to the other. It was
a low ale shop, and the proprietor manifested considerable surprise at the appearance of a guest so much better
dressed than any who were in the habit of crossing his
door-sill. Colonel Burr's chief object was to look at the
house, to see the man, and form some estimate of his character. A few adroit remarks removed his distrust, and
when the man supposed that he was entirely absorbed in
the contemplation of the merits of the ale he was sipping
after the manner of a connoisseur in the article, Colónel
Burr turned to him suddenly, and said,—

"What about this murder, of which people have been
talking so much the past week?"

The man turned deadly pale, and stammered out, "I—I
don't know anything about it. What made you think I
did?"

"Nothing; only I heard that it was done about here."

"No, sir, it was not. It was two squares and a half
from this."

"Well, I heard differently. I heard, too, that one John Roberts was arrested as the murderer. Do you know him?"

"No; and he was not the man. It was a fellow by the name of Durand, who is said to have been a Tory in the Revolution."

"Indeed! Then I think I know him. Was he a low man, with broad shoulders, a tremendous chest, and bright black eyes?"

"That's the very fellow."

"Did he visit your house often?"

"Never but once, and that was the night he done the murder—or is said to have done it."

"I think you said you were not acquainted with Roberts."

This time the eye of Colonel Burr was turned upon him with one of those piercing looks no guilty man ever met without quailing. The cheek of the wretch turned purple, then ashy pale, then purple again. In a tone in which apprehension predominated over assumed indignation, he hesitatingly replied, "No, sir. That is, I am not to say acquainted with him. I know him when I see him, and he has may be sometimes taken a mug of ale in my house. But what is that to you? and what do you mean by questioning me so closely?"

"Oh, nothing," replied Colonel Burr, who had learned all he expected; "only I am a lawyer, and may be employed in the case."

So saying, he threw a silver coin on the counter, and walked away before the astonished proprietor could ask another question.

His steps were now directed to the sheriff's office, where he examined the club which Durand admitted he had carried on the night of the murder. It was very bloody, but none of the dead man's hair was sticking to it, nor was there any evidence, except the blood, of its having been so fatally used. The bloody hunting-knife was also there, and he recognized it as the same Durand had worn in 1779. The scabbard was missing. On inquiry, he ascertained the important fact that it was not upon Durand's person at the time of the arrest, nor could it be found in the house after the most careful search. From the watchman he learned that, when Roberts first came to him, he stated that Franz Klink had been robbed and murdered. Colonel Burr made no comment upon the singular fact that he should have known a robbery and murder had been committed, when, according to his own statement, he had not been in the house, had heard no cry, and was only alarmed by an unusual sound. He gathered nothing else of importance, and returned to his office to digest the information he had acquired and to devise the means of obtaining more.

CHAPTER XVI.

"My wrath is wreaked—the deed is done!
And now I go, but go alone."

IT was ten o'clock on a cold October night. Colonel Burr was waiting at his own house for the appearance of Bill Jenkins, who had promised to meet him at that hour. Throughout the day his mind had been entirely occupied by the dangerous situation of Durand. The observations he had made were conclusive to him of the innocence of the accused, but he well knew they would weigh nothing with a court and jury unless supported by other evidence that he did not see the means of procuring. A good deal would depend upon Jenkins, and he feared that individual stood in too much peril of the law himself to be of any great assistance. He rose to his feet and walked to the door when a knock announced the arrival of his expected visitor, having purposely dismissed the servants in order that their conference should be undisturbed in any manner whatever. When he ushered his guest into the room, he could not help expressing the surprise he felt at the completeness of the transformation he witnessed. Jenkins was dressed with punctilious neatness; the awkward, lounging gait usual to him had disappeared; and, to complete the disguise, the broad scar that disfigured his face was so artistically filled up with some kind of paste as to be almost invisible.

"Upon my word, Mr. Jenkins," remarked Colonel Burr, "you are wonderfully changed for the better. I do not

(250)

think I should have recognized you upon the street, and I am not apt to forget a face I have once seen."

"It is an art that I have been compelled to practice often enough to become a proficient; but I did not design to do more to-night than present such an appearance as would not frighten your family if I should chance to meet them. I proposed also to claim your hospitality for the night, and when I go away in the morning I did not wish that people should think you had given shelter to a beggar."

"Beggar or no beggar," replied Colonel Burr, "the man who sheltered me in the time of my greatest need shall not go away from my roof while he wishes to remain, no matter what people may think upon the subject. I cannot offer you," he continued, "such potent liquor as you once gave me. Here is some Madeira, however, which good judges have pronounced excellent. Be good enough to help yourself as freely and as often as you desire it, for I have many questions to ask; and as you are probably not as much accustomed to doing without sleep as I am, you may need some stimulant before I get through."

"Thank you, colonel. I will do full justice to the wine, though I cannot plead any physical necessity for it. The loss of sleep is no inconvenience to a man of my habits."

At the same time he approached the side-table, and, pouring out a full glass of the generous liquid, swallowed it at a draught.

"Now, colonel, I am ready. Begin your questions."

"Draw your chair nearer to the fire, and tell me in the first place who killed Franz Klink!"

"Didn't Aleck tell you?"

"He told me who he thought did it, but I want to know who you think it was, and your reasons for that opinion.'

"John Roberts is the man. It must have been him or

Aleck Durand; and it is impossible that Aleck could have killed a man for his money. I have known him from infancy, and I know it; though that will not do him any good, I suppose, on his trial."

"Never mind what you think will or will not ·do him good. Give me your reasons, *all* of your reasons, and let me judge what will benefit him, and how it may do so."

"Well, then, to go on. I did not send Roberts for Aleck on that night, or any other night. I was not in hiding for a supposed robbery; none had been committed. I had not been in Sam Larkins's house for a month. I had twice made up my mind to bury my knife between Roberts's ribs, and had been persuaded by Aleck into a promise not to do it. I would not, therefore, go near a house where I was almost certain to meet Roberts, for fear of being tempted to break my promise. Roberts and Larkins were old cronies; they planned the murder, and, knowing Aleck's uneasiness about me, they easily made up a story that they knew would draw him from home. Aleck thinks they did not mean to kill at the beginning, but only to rob. He is mistaken. The murder was deliberately planned as well as the robbery; and one of its objects was to throw suspicion on him, and have him hung if possible. What other motives influenced them I can't guess, but that was one. They calculated that Aleck was so well known as a Tory, that a jury would be ready to believe anything against him; and they judged that very slight circumstances would suffice to hang a man whom they supposed to be entirely destitute of friends among the Whigs."

"Do you know anything else going to establish the guilt of Roberts?"

"Before the murder he was hard pushed for money. Since then, although he has not exhibited any large sum, he has paid his way wherever he went—a thing he never did before. It is said, too, that immediately after the watchmen entered the house Roberts seized hold of the dead body, upon pretense of placing it on the bed. Now it is my opinion that he either knew there were blood-stains upon him, or feared there were, and he took the corpse in his arms to have a plausible way of accounting for them if they should be discovered. I do not think of anything else in particular. From my general knowledge of the man I know he is capable of all manner of wickedness. He has himself made a sworn statement, from which it is perfectly evident that if Durand is not the murderer, he is. That is enough for me, and I do not despair of producing proof, in some way, that will convince others as well as myself. It would help the case mightily if we could get hold of the club with which Franz Klink was knocked down; and, as I could not go about Larkins's house myself, I have put one on the trail who will find out all that can be discovered. They are old birds, however, and will leave few traces of their handiwork."

Colonel Burr's opinion did not essentially differ from that of Jenkins, although he continued until a late hour of the night to question him closely and minutely upon every event of his own and Roberts's life. It pleased him to learn, that although Jenkins's conduct since the war had not been blameless, and his habits were still far from being such as a moralist could commend, yet he had committed no crime which subjected him to the penalties of the law, and the only danger he incurred was the remote one of a prosecution for offenses of which he had been guilty prior to the treaty of peace. He assured Jenkins that he need not be alarmed on account of what he had done during the lawless times of the Revolution; and added, that if any malicious person should institute a prosecution, he had no doubt of being able to obtain his pardon.

"I thank you, colonel, for your offer," was the reply, "as much as if I intended to accept it. The Whigs made me an outlaw, and I do not feel like asking a pardon at their hands. I am going West, as soon as Aleck Durand gets out of this scrape, among a people where I shall not need it. In Kentucky the Indians are troublesome enough to make the addition of a good rifle, a stout heart, and a tolerably strong arm very welcome; and I am mistaken if they require from me any other passport. To a man who expects no rest, and fears no danger, a life in the woods possesses attractions not to be resisted."

"If such is your fixed purpose," said Colonel Burr, "I will not argue against it. Indeed, I think it the best thing you can do. Durand must be acquitted in the first place, however, and you must not let your fear of a prosecution prevent you from going wherever it may be necessary to hunt up evidence in his behalf. I will answer for your safety."

"The assurance is unnecessary. Tell me where you want me to go, and what you want me to do, to help Aleck Durand, and it shall be done, if I hang in one hour afterwards."

"I believe you," said Burr, earnestly. "I believe you fully." Then, after a pause, he added: "It is now late, let me show you to a bed. Remember, that as fast as you gather information, no matter whether you deem it important or not, you are to come to me."

A light was still burning in Colonel Burr's study long after he had shown Jenkins to his bedroom. According to his usual custom he was arranging and classifying the facts and circumstances which had come to his knowledge, and applying to them the law of circumstantial evidence.

For him there was no hour of repose while anything remained to be done.

The next day he called upon Durand, and again questioned him not only upon the events of the murder, but upon many things which apparently had no connection with it. By the time the day of trial arrived, he was armed at all points; prepared to meet every possible attack, and to take advantage of every possible fault in his adversary's management of the case. The watchman who was first introduced as a witness on the part of the prosecution had to undergo a searching cross-examination, from which, however, there appeared little likelihood of obtaining any advantage, for the witness was clearly an honest man who had nothing to conceal, and no motive for telling anything but the truth. Colonel Burr drew from him the fact that Roberts had been the first one to discover the knife on the mantle-piece; that the scabbard was missing, and had not been found upon the person of the prisoner, or in the house; and finally, that the club picked up by the dead body had on it no appearance of hair, although the deceased wore a thick coat of curly hair, a large lock of which had been driven by the force of the blow into the wound on his head. He admitted that detecting, as he supposed, Alexis Durand almost in the very fact, he made no examination to ascertain how far it was possible for any other person to have been the guilty party. The two succeeding witnesses gave almost the same version as the first. The surgeon who had been called in to examine the dead body was next placed upon the witness stand. He described the wounds, and gave it as his opinion that either would have produced death. He was satisfied the wound in the side was made by the knife exhibited in court, and believed that on the head might have been made by the club, although the edges had the appearance of being more sharply cut than is generally the case where a smooth, round instrument is used. At this point, Colonel Burr drew from his desk an eight-square oak club, about two feet in length, with a leathern strap through one end, and heavily loaded at the other.

"Examine this club, doctor," he said, handing the witness the murderous weapon as he spoke, "and tell the jury which of the two would be most likely to make such a wound as you describe."

"Either might do it; but, if I had been shown the two clubs together immediately after the examination, I should have said that the blow was given with the short one."

This decided testimony was strengthened rather than shaken by the further examination of the prosecuting attorney. The attention of the jury was also called to the fact that the club had the appearance of having been washed at the heavy end, and in one or two places scrubbed with sand-paper.

John Roberts was the next witness called. He had been purposely reserved for the last, in order that the deepest impression might be made upon the minds of the jury at the close of the prosecution. Colonel Burr observed that his cheek grew a shade paler when his eye rested on the loaded club. He had not expected to see that instrument there, and knew not what it portended. As soon as he began to give in his testimony, Colonel Burr's eye was fixed upon him with a steady and unremitting gaze. At first he bore it with considerable fortitude, but after awhile he hesitated, stammered, and then trembled visibly. No matter how he turned, no matter which way he looked, that searching eye was never removed from his person—seeming to penetrate to his inmost soul, and read the darkest secrets of his guilty breast. In vain he tried to avoid it; in vain he tried to confine his own looks to the court and jury, or to the prosecuting attorney. In spite of himself his glances would wander to those large and burning orbs that fascinated while they terrified, and compelled attention when attention was torture. His evidence was in substance the same as he had given before the coroner, but his manner of testifying detracted greatly from its effect, and the marked change from the confident air with which he had entered the court-room, to the unaccountable terrors that shook him before the close of the examination, left a most unfavorable impression upon the minds of the jury. Colonel Burr noticed the effect that had been produced, and endeavored to enhance it by an appearance of extreme fairness in his cross-examination. For some time the questions he put were so immaterial, and his manner was so careless, that Roberts regained confidence, and once more looked about him with an unabashed air. After awhile, Colonel Burr inquired in a mild and even tone,—

"What is your trade or occupation?"

"I am a laborer," answered Roberts.

"What kind of laborer?"

"I work on such jobs as I can get; generally loading and unloading vessels."

"Let me see your hand."

It was dirty enough, but smooth and soft, with none of the horny hardness always apparent in the hand of the working-man. Colonel Burr quietly called the attention of the jury to the fact, and resumed his cross-examination.

"Did you ever see this club before?" he asked, handing the loaded club to Roberts.

"I don't know. I have seen a good many clubs like it, and that may have been among them."

"Did you ever *own* one like it?"

"No; I never did."

The manner of the interrogator now changed entirely.

22*

His voice was stern, and again that look of unearthly pen-
etration was fixed upon his victim.

"Did you not carry just such a club as this on the night
Franz Klink was murdered?"

"No, sir," stammered Roberts, trembling in every limb.
"I never carried such a club in my life."

"That will do, Mr. Roberts. You can stand aside."

The court, the jury, and the prosecuting attorney were
all alike surprised at this sudden dismissal of the principal
witness against the prisoner, after so slight a cross-examination; but Colonel Burr had obtained what he wanted.

In his examination of a witness he never asked questions
for the sake of asking them. He never *took chances.* He
had a fixed object, and when it was attained, he knew when
to stop. He did not choose to run the risk of drawing out
something unfavorable to his client, either to show his own
dexterity, or in the mere hope of obtaining something that
would benefit him. Besides, he was satisfied that a practiced and hardened villain like Roberts would come into
the court-house perfectly fortified on all the main points
of his testimony, and that the only result of a prolonged
cross-examination would be to give that testimony greater
strength. He therefore confined himself to questions which
could not have been foreseen and prepared for.

For the defense it was proved that Alexis Durand, ever
since his arrival in New York, had maintained the character of an industrious, sober, and peaceable man. It was
proved that, from his occupation as a boatman, he generally
received exactly the description of money which was found
in his chest; that he had never been known to want money;
that he was on the best terms with his landlord, who frequently left the shop for hours in his charge; that they
had slept alone in the same house for months, and that
Durand had free access both to the sleeping-room of Franz

and the store-room below. Finally, Colonel Burr called to the stand a man by the name of Thomas Winters, who testified that he knew Durand slightly, and Roberts intimately. To a question as to what Roberts did to earn a support, he answered: "Nothing, as I knows on, except gamble, and such like."

In answer to other questions, he said that he was in Larkins's house on the night of the murder; that it was usual at that house to close the doors before ten o'clock, but the initiated, by giving a certain password, could enter at any hour; that Durand came in some time after the doors were closed, and he overheard him ask the landlord for Bill Jenkins; that Larkins replied he had gone out, and directed that any one who asked for him should be told to wait, when, to the certain knowledge of the witness, Jenkins had not been in the house for days; that Durand did wait for a considerable time, but at last became impatient, and determined to go, Larkins still urging him to wait longer. Witness stated that Jenkins was a friend of his, and that after Durand had left, he concluded to follow him and tell him where Jenkins was; that he walked very fast, without, however, overtaking Durand; that, at the corner nearest the house of Klink, he heard Roberts give the alarm to the watchmen; that, in his opinion, it was impossible for Durand to have reached home, committed the murder, and rifled the house, within the time he left Larkins's house and the time he heard Roberts give the alarm. He further testified that the loaded club, exhibited in court, had been taken by him from a room in Larkins's house occupied by John Roberts; that it usually hung on a nail by the door; that he had seen it there several times when he went to Roberts's room to play at cards, and that two days ago he had taken it away, unobserved, at the request of Jenkins, for the purpose of exhibiting it on this trial.

The testimony of this witness was so clear and straightforward, and he maintained, in spite of a severe cross-examination, so much the air of an honest man, that, although he acknowledged himself to be much of a scamp, and a good deal addicted to low and disreputable vices, the court and the jury were inclined to give him full credit; and the pains the prosecuting attorney took to invalidate his evidence proved that he regarded it as exceedingly dangerous to his case.

It was late at night when Colonel Burr rose to address the jury. He began by a dissertation on the nature of circumstantial evidence; admitted that the law held it sufficient to a conviction for the crime of murder, but contended that certain rules were laid down for its government, *all* of which it was incumbent on the prosecution to show had been fully complied with. If any *one* link should be found wanting, the offense was not proved, and the prisoner must be acquitted. The first rule—the groundwork upon which everything rested—was, that the circumstances themselves should be fully established. Not by a mere preponderance of evidence, but by the clear and positive testimony of at least one unimpeached witness. Where a material circumstance depended upon one witness only, that witness must be supported by collateral aid, especially if his former character, contradictory statements, suspicious manner of testifying, or any other cause, raised a doubt of his credibility.

After dwelling upon this point until he had sufficiently impressed it upon the minds of the jury, he asked: "Have the circumstances in this case been established according to the requirements of the law?" Some of them, he admitted, had been. He went over the testimony of the watchmen, conceded that it had been given like honest men, and he believed their statements to be true. But what was it? Unsupported by Roberts, it did nothing

more than raise a bare presumption of guilt; it fell far,
very far short of excluding, to a moral certainty, every
hypothesis but the one that the prisoner was guilty. The
whole case, he contended, depended at last upon Roberts's
evidence alone. Was he supported by collateral aid? No.
Was there nothing to throw a doubt upon the credibility
of the man? There was not only enough for that purpose, but enough to prove beyond all cavil that he was a
base and willful perjurer. He had sworn that he was a
day-laborer, while his hand gave conclusive evidence that
it had long been free from, if it had ever known, the hardening effects of honest toil. He was directly contradicted
also by Winters, who knew him well, who had been his
associate, and who confessed, to his own shame, that he
had participated in his pursuits. He swore that Roberts
was a gambler, and followed no other business.

Colonel Burr then alluded to Roberts's denial of ever
having seen the loaded club, when it was in proof that
it was taken from his room; that it habitually hung
there, and could have belonged to no one else. The jury,
he said, must be satisfied that in relation to this fact, as in
relation to that of being a day-laborer, the witness had
sworn falsely, and common sense, as well as common law,
demanded the rejection of his whole testimony. In two
plain matters of fact, where there was not the least room
for an honest mistake, he had committed unmistakable perjury. It was not necessary, therefore, to refer to the im-
probability of the story itself, to his unexplained wandering about the streets at such an hour, or to the guilty
terrors which shook his frame while the damning perjury
escaped his lips. The positive testimony, apart from all
these circumstances of doubt and suspicion, incontroverti-
bly established perjury upon him; and the juror who could
take away the life of a fellow-being upon the evidence of

such a man, must be dead to all the best instincts of humanity. When that evidence was discarded, what remained? Nothing upon which a verdict of "guilty" could be based. Everything else might be true, and yet the prisoner might be as innocent as the court or any one of the jury now sitting in judgment upon him. To illustrate his meaning, he supposed a case. Aided by the communications Durand had made to him, his supposed case was precisely in accordance with the facts; and this he put to the jury so strongly and clearly, that they could not refrain from nodding assent as he progressed. He dwelt upon the fact, sworn to by Winters, that the prisoner could not have committed the murder and accomplished the robbery within the time that elapsed from his leaving Larkins's house and that when he heard the alarm given to the watchmen, and insisted that he had done much more than was necessary to insure the acquittal of his client. According to the law it was sufficient to raise a *doubt* of his guilt; he had gone beyond the requirements of the law, and demonstrated his innocence. He had said enough for his client's defense, but not enough for public justice. A foul and bloody murder had been committed; it was the work of human hands, and he proposed to track the felon through all the cunning devices by which he had sought to escape from the penalties prescribed for the punishment of his horrid crime.

Here Colonel Burr turned his full front to the witness Roberts, who was leaning against one of the columns of the court-room.

There must have been, he continued, a guilty agent. That agent must have had some motive or inducement to commit the crime, and also the means to accomplish his purpose. He here recapitulated the testimony, showing the total absence of motive on the part of Durand, and the presence of that motive in Roberts. According to

Roberts's own statement, he had called upon Durand for
the purpose of collecting a debt, whereas the proof showed
that Durand was an industrious, laboring man, engaged in
a business whose profits more than supplied his wants,
while Roberts was notoriously penniless. The story of in-
debtedness was therefore too improbable for belief. All
the other facts and circumstances which weighed against
the witness were stated with the concise clearness for
which the orator was so remarkable. Throughout he had
watched the jury with the keen scrutiny of a man accustomed to study every varying shade of the human countenance; and when he saw that their interest was excited to
the highest point, he suddenly seized a candle in each
hand, held them aloft over his head, and, advancing to
Roberts, his eyes burning like living coals, and his voice
ringing as if ordering a charge on the battle-field, he
shouted,—"Behold the murderer!"

The effect was electrical. The jury, by a common impulse, rose to their feet. Roberts shook and trembled as
if the doom of death was sounding in his ears. Gradually
his knees gave way, and he sunk down helpless at the base
of the column. For more than a minute a silence deep
and dread reigned throughout the court-room—judge, jury,
and spectators were gazing in speechless amazement upon
the cowering wretch. It was broken by Colonel Burr. In
a clear and sonorous voice, he exclaimed: "There, gentlemen, is Nature's testimony! There is a confession written
by the finger of God himself! Now write *your* verdict!"

There was another pause; another period of awful sus-
pense, and men drew their breath with a feeling of intense
relief when the orator slowly replaced the candles on the
table and resumed his seat.

He had not spoken more than three-quarters of an hour.
He had not touched more than half the available points

for the defense. A less experienced pleader would have
gone on, and probably ruined a cause already gained, by
attempting to make it doubly certain. Colonel Burr knew
better. He was an adept in the most useful of all knowledge to a lawyer. He knew when to stop. He had
strained the minds of the jury to the highest pitch of excitement, and he knew that under the reaction which must
follow, the concluding argument of the attorney-general
would fall upon dull and listless ears. That officer was
himself embarrassed by a painful consciousness of the same
fact; and the jury, at the conclusion of his address, returned
a verdict of "not guilty," without leaving the box. The
court, of its own motion, immediately ordered the arrest
of Roberts, and his committal to await the action of a
grand jury.

It was some time before the immense throng who had
gathered to witness the result of the trial would disperse;
and the officer in charge of Roberts was standing near the
door impatiently waiting an opportunity to get his prisoner
into a carriage. A tall man, wearing a mustache and immense whiskers, who had given earnest attention to every
stage of the trial, was observed slowly edging his way
through the throng toward the spot were Roberts was
standing. A broad-brimmed slouched hat concealed the
upper part of his face, and a horseman's cloak clasped
around the neck performed the same service for his body.
Watching for a favorable moment, when the crowd around
and in front of him had considerably thinned, he seized the
arm of the prisoner and said, in a hoarse whisper,—

"John Roberts—do you know me?"

There was no response; but a sudden start and an equally
sudden change of countenance told plainly enough that he
was recognized. Instantly a broad steel blade glittered in
the candlelight—a low, dull sound followed its descent; the

officer whose hand was upon Roberts's arm felt him shudder, and heard him faintly murmur, "I am a dead man." Without another word he sank bleeding on the floor. Before those immediately around comprehended the terrible deed which had been committed, the murderer bounded from the door, and was lost amid the crowd.

It was later than usual the next day when Colonel Burr repaired to his office. Durand had been for some time waiting his arrival. After the first salutations were over, he said,—

"I am going beyond the mountains, colonel, and have come to say good-by."

"Going beyond the mountains! For what? The evidence of yesterday showed that you were engaged in a prosperous business, and you surely cannot think that it will be lessened by the events of the trial?"

"No, it is not that. The fact is, the business never suited me. I can work, and have worked, rather than starve or beg; but during seven years' service in the wars a man will acquire habits and tastes not easily shaken off. I am weary and lonesome here in the city, and long to be in the free woods, with a knife in my belt and a rifle on my shoulder."

Colonel Burr was not deceived by the apparently natural reason assigned by Durand for this sudden determination. He remembered what Jenkins had said of a similar purpose, and at once connected them together. He had scarcely any doubt as to who had stabbed Roberts in the court-room, and felt that it would be useless to dissuade Durand from his purpose.

"It seems to me that you have other reasons," he replied; "but I have no right to pry into your secrets, and if your mind is made up upon grounds that you consider sufficient,

I will not attempt to change it. Can I do anything for you before you go?"

"Nothing that I can think of. My money has been returned to me, and I have more than enough to buy two good rifles and such other articles as will be needful in a life among the savages. You must not think, colonel, that I have any secrets I wish to hide from you. There is something on my mind that I doubt whether I ought to tell you; not on my account, but your own. Nor is it exactly my secret either, though to a certain extent I am involved in it."

"I expect I can guess it. Indeed, I know enough to be assured I can. You need not, therefore, say anything about it."

"In that case you must know all. You might guess too much or too little, and think less of me, or of one who is very dear to me, than I would have you do. It was Bill Jenkins who killed Roberts last night while in the hands of an officer of the law. I left the court-room, you remember, as soon as the verdict was rendered, and went directly to a tavern to procure refreshments and a night's lodging. Not long after I got there, the news of Roberts's murder came. My mind misgave me, and I determined to hunt up Bill Jenkins. While in prison he had given me a clew to all his haunts, and I had no doubt of finding him. The only difficulty lay in getting on the street without attracting observation. I was known at the tavern, and the whole trial had been so remarkable, that I was an object of curiosity to every one who came in. The front room was crowded, notwithstanding the lateness of the hour, and if I went out it would be sure to excite remark. I had prolonged my supper, although I had but little appetite, in the hope that they would disperse. Some did go, but many remained. I had ordered a fire to be lighted in my room, and was just about requesting the landlord to show

me to it, when Jenkins himself walked in. I had observed
him in the court-room, so disguised that no eye but mine
could have detected him. His dress was now entirely different. The whiskers, mustache, and wig were gone—the
slouched hat and horseman's cloak had also disappeared.
His manner was easy and unembarrassed, and he congratu-
lated me upon my acquittal in a voice so perfectly natural,
that no one, who did not know him as I did, would have
believed it possible for him to have been an actor in the
bloody scene which had just transpired. He called for a
glass of rum at the bar, invited me and others to join him,
and behaved exactly as a man innocent of any offense, and
rejoiced at the escape of a friend from a great danger,
would be expected to behave. After he had taken another
drink, he said aloud, in the hearing of those present, that
he had come to pass the first night of my liberty with me,
and suggested that as I must have been kept awake by
anxiety for several preceding nights, we had better retire. On entering my room, he locked the door, and carefully sounded the walls to be certain that he could not be
overheard by the sleepers in the adjoining rooms. Then,
approaching where I stood before the fire, he said, in a
fierce whisper,—

"'I have done it, Aleck. I struck down the damned
villain in the hall of justice, and I would have done it if
his arms had been clasped around the holy altar.'

"'I am sorry for it, Bill,' I replied. 'It was a great
crime, rashly and unnecessarily committed. He would have
been hung, at any rate, for the murder of Franz Klink.'

"'It was for that very reason I did it. I had no idea of
being cheated out of my vengeance by process of law. I
could have forgiven him for burning us out of our cabin in
the Highlands; I could have forgiven him—at least I
would not have stricken him—for seeking your death by

false swearing.   If he had done nothing else, I would have been content to leave him in the hands of the law; but there is more to hear.   You remember that he did not join us until the cause of the colonists was at the lowest ebb.   The British had taken New York and chased George Washington through the Jerseys.   Before that he had been a rampant Whig.   While you were in prison, I was charged by Colonel Burr to watch him narrowly, and to engage others whom he would not suspect to do the same thing.   I knew that Winters hated him, for he had been robbed by Roberts and Larkins at cards, and I put him upon the trail.   A week ago he communicated to Colonel Burr nearly all he swore on the trial, and was instructed by him to continue on the watch.   Colonel Burr also supplied him with money to enable him to frequent Roberts's places of resort.   Winters either caught him, accidentally, under the influence of liquor, or succeeded in making him so, and while in that state turned the conversation upon Klink's murder.   He was not so far gone, however, as to be thrown off his guard in reference to so dangerous a subject, and persisted in pretty much the same story he had sworn to before the coroner.   Winters then mentioned my name.   He says he had no particular object, other than to keep Roberts talking, and, for this purpose, he asked if it might not be possible that I had helped you to murder Franz.   To this Roberts answered no, but that I ought to be hung for twenty other things; and went on to say that I carried the mark of his lashes on my back, and that some day he would put a halter around my neck.   When Winters told me this, it was like a flash of lightning suddenly illuminating a dark and murky night, and I could at once account for the instinctive longing I had felt for years to bury my knife in his heart.   Even when we were serving King George in the same company, I am certain I should have killed him if we had been left alone together for a single day. I hated him, and my heart told me I had cause, though I had no other proof. It was all as clear to me as daylight now, and I wondered I had not made the discovery before. I remembered, as distinctly as if it were yesterday, his form and voice among that pack of disguised hell hounds who marked my back with scars that I shall carry to the grave, and murdered my young wife and her unborn babe. I started on the instant to hunt him up. Luckily I did not find him that day, and when the fire in my brain had lost a portion of its fury, I remembered that if I killed him then, it would be charged that you had instigated me to the deed in order to get rid of his evidence on your trial. Two nights ago I met him unexpectedly; we were alone; my hand was on the hilt of the same knife which this night made its way to his heart. I did not kill him, but I hissed in his ear that his hour was approaching, and when next we met the arch fiend himself should not save him. For fear he would have me arrested I hired a disguise, and gave out that I had left the city. Even Winters really supposed that I was gone. I passed him on the street, and spoke to him in bar-rooms, and he did not know me. I went to the court-house to-day, resolved that Roberts should never leave it alive. I could not anticipate his arrest, and when it was done, I trembled lest he should escape me. The crowd did me good service in compelling the officer to stop where he did, and now I can sleep in peace.'

"And he did sleep," continued Durand, "as sweetly as an infant in its cradle, though I paced the floor until daylight. When he awoke, our plans were soon formed, and he is now on his way to Kentucky. I could not go until I had seen you and thanked you for your generous exertions in behalf of a man who is so poorly able to reward you for it."

23*

"Upon that score," replied Colonel Burr, "we are barely even. It is life for life. When do you go?"

"To-night. Jenkins, so far as I know, is unsuspected now, but he may be; and I do not choose that people should be able to get upon his trail by tracking mine. I go alone, and under cover of the darkness. It will be ten or twelve days, and far from here, before I join him. I do not ask you not to betray us—I know you will not; and only hesitated about telling you, because I feared that if it should become known, men might charge you with aiding the escape of a murderer. When I discovered that you already knew the criminal, I could not bear for you to suspect that he had committed the crime for no other reason than because Roberts had sought my life. And now, Colonel," he continued, while large tears rolled from eyes to which tears were strangers, and his giant frame shivered like that of a child in an ague fit, "kindest, noblest, truest, best of men, good-by forever. In this world we shall never meet again; but if I forget you for one day amid all my wanderings and perils, may the lightnings of heaven blast me where I stand."

He was mistaken. They did meet years afterwards upon the banks of the beautiful Ohio, when strange changes had come over the fortunes of both.

CHAPTER XVII.

"I had borne it—it hurt me—but I bore it.
Till this last running over of the cup
Of bitterness."

THE treaty between England, France, and the United
States, by which the Independence of the latter was acknowledged, withered the daring hopes of Alexander Hamilton, and utterly blasted the wily schemes of his unscrupulous confederate, Billings. That shrewd and dangerous
man at once understood that all hope was at an end; yet
he neither cowered nor complained. To all outward appearance his bearing was the same; but notwithstanding the
seeming calmness of the surface, a serpent had wreathed
itself about his heart, whose sting drove him on, and on,
in quest of new excitements, new plots, and new conspira-
cies. In two years afterwards he set sail for France, and it
was long before he was again heard of in America.

Alexander Hamilton was perhaps as deeply wounded
and disappointed as Billings, but for him a theater was still
open in the new world, of which he resolved to make the
most. When the army was disbanded, he turned his attention, like Aaron Burr, to the profession of the law. Like
him he studied hard, and like him he rose rapidly. It was
at the bar, after years of separation, that the rivals met
once more. Here the struggle between them was resumed,
but their rivalry now was divested of the bitterness of former years. It was a war of two giant intellects, in which
neither could stoop to envy, because envy would have been
an acknowledgment of inferiority. Things continued in

(271)

this state until politics came in to imbitter their relations. In the division of parties Aaron Burr took the popular, or Democratic side—Alexander Hamilton the Federal; still their intercourse was personally kind and respectful, until the year 1790, when Alexander Hamilton was Secretary of the Treasury, and his father-in-law, General Schuyler, was a candidate for re-election to the United States Senate, from the State of New York. Aaron Burr became a candidate in opposition to him, and in January, 1791, was elected over the combined influence of Hamilton and Schuyler. From that day the old enmity in the bosom of Alexander Hamilton sprung into a new and more venomous life. Whatever Burr advocated, Hamilton opposed; wherever Burr sought to climb, he found Hamilton in his way. It was impossible that Colonel Burr could misunderstand the extent and bitterness of this opposition; but then, as in the past and throughout his after life, he locked his secrets in his own bosom, and made no complaint.

The career of Colonel Burr in the Senate is too well known to require repetition here. In the third year of his service a great calamity overtook him. The wife who had been to him the best of friends and counselors was called away, and he was left with none but the little Theodosia to enliven his home and soothe him amid the perplexing cares which were gathering thick around him. This blow he bore with his accustomed fortitude; and the only indication the public had of the intensity of his sufferings, was the restless eagerness with which he plunged into politics.

Before the expiration of his term, the State of New York had become thoroughly Federal, and General Philip Schuyler was elected to succeed him. To reverse this state of things, and bring New York into the Democratic fold, was now the cherished object of his life. To this end he devoted all his vast talents and all his tireless energy. He succeeded, after a contest unparalleled in the annals of the Republic, and in the year 1800 he was nominated as the Democratic-candidate for Vice-President, on the same ticket with Thomas Jefferson. This nomination, so gratifying at the time, was the fruitful source of all the woes that afflicted his after years. The result of the election was: Jefferson 73, Burr 73, Adams 65, Pinckney 64, Jay 1. Under the Constitution as it then stood, an election by the House of Representatives became indispensable to decide which of the two highest on the list (Jefferson or Burr) should hold the office of President, and which the office of Vice-President of the United States. Here was a field of operations exactly suited to the genius of Alexander Hamilton, and his conduct during that period was such as to fully justify old John Adams in the declaration that he was the most unprincipled intriguer in America. He writes to leading Federalists to hold out the bait of their support to Burr, but warns them at the same time that that support must not be given to him in reality. He tells them that Jefferson is a libertine in morals, a radical in politics, and an infidel in religion; but adds that Burr is the more dangerous man, and, if elected to the Presidency, that he would conduct the government *a la Bonaparte.* By such low and despicable arts as these he sought the ruin of the rival whose power he had felt, and whose future influence upon the politics of the nation he most dreaded. Colonel Burr did not fall into the trap, and yet he suffered all the consequences that could have followed if he had yielded fully to the temptation. The mind of Jefferson was by some means poisoned against him, and no amount of evidence was sufficient to remove the prejudices then imbibed. In looking back upon the history of that memorable contest, it is difficult to conceive how the belief ever could have obtained that Colonel Burr was willingly the rival of Mr. Jefferson. Yet it did prevail very widely, and none were more fixed in that opinion than Mr. Jefferson himself. It was this belief which in after years led him into the gravest error of his life, and left upon his character the deepest stain it bears.

When the result was almost certainly known, although the returns were not fully received, Colonel Burr addressed a letter to Samuel Smith, a member of the House of Representatives from Maryland, and a devoted friend of Mr. Jefferson. To have sought an election by the House, after the publication of that letter, would have been an act of folly, from which an idiot would have shrunk. He says to General Smith :—

"It is highly probable that I shall have an equal number of votes with Mr. Jefferson; but, if such should be the result, every man who knows me ought to know that I would utterly disclaim all competition. Be assured that the Federal party can entertain no wish for such an exchange. As to my friends, they would dishonor my views and insult my feelings by a suspicion that I would submit to be instrumental in counteracting the wishes and the expectations of the United States. And I now constitute you my proxy to declare these sentiments if the occasion should require."

Notwithstanding the emphatic and earnest disclaimer contained in this letter of all intention to engage in a contest with Mr. Jefferson, the Federal party, for their own purposes, determined to run him. Nothing could have been further from the mind of Alexander Hamilton than a desire to promote the election of his rival, yet nothing could have been more gratifying to him than to see him engaged in a contest which, terminate as it might, was sure to blacken his character and destroy his popularity with the nation. To this end all his powers of intrigue were directed, and he succeeded but too well in the object he had in view. Colonel Burr was no candidate, sought no support, and emphatically disclaimed all desire to receive it. That support was forced upon him, and then he was held responsible for what he had done all in his power to prevent. The world's history does not present an instance of more glaring injustice, nor is there one, in the long list of statesmen who fill its pages, in whose person the blindness of partisan zeal and the merciless nature of partisan persecution is more completely illustrated.

Mr. Jefferson was finally elected. His mind was then just in that state when the fires of rancorous hate are most easily kindled, and there were those about him who did not fail to apply the match. Aaron Burr soon became a marked man, and when it was known that his political destruction had been resolved upon by the President, ten thousand tongues and pens were found ready to assail him. The storm he could not avert; but he neither bent before it, nor cowered at its fury. Calm, and seemingly unconscious of the active malignity of his enemies, he went on to discharge the duties of his high office, with a grace, a dignity, and an ability which has never since been equaled. But Colonel Burr was not idle, nor had he the least idea of falling an unresisting victim. The Vice-Presidency, for a second term, he knew was beyond his grasp. Mr. Jefferson was all powerful at the time, and in that quarter Colonel Burr had no hope. That he would be left off the ticket he never for a moment doubted. Under these circumstances, he resolved to pursue the course he had pursued with so much success on a former occasion, and appeal directly to the people of New York. A gubernatorial election was coming on, and in February, 1804, he announced himself as an independent candidate for the office. The whole weight of the administration was at once thrown against him, and all of Hamilton's talents for intrigue were actively and incessantly employed to insure his defeat. It was a strange union—Jefferson and Hamilton—but *hate* accepts the services of any ally, and both of them hated and dreaded Burr too much to stand on scruples. By their joint efforts he was defeated; and he thus saw go out his last hope of political advancement.

A few weeks after the election, on a balmy night in June, when Colonel Burr was in his own house, surrounded by a select company of friends, as gay and apparently as happy as if nothing had occurred to annoy him, the following note was put into his hands:—

"One who has much to communicate to you in reference to the past, which it concerns you to know, is now stretched upon a bed of death, and earnestly requests that you will come to him as soon as may be."

There was no signature, and, making a polite excuse to his friends, Burr followed the servant from the room to inquire who had brought the note. He was told that the messenger was at the door.

"Then show him into the library."

When the man entered, he asked,—

"Who gave you this note?"

"A man who is dying in my house. I don't know his name."

"Who are you?"

"The keeper of a boarding-house on —— Street, and a friend of yours."

After satisfying himself upon some other points, Colonel Burr said,—

"Tell the gentleman I will call to-night."

"He told me to bring you with me."

"That is impossible. I have company; but say to him I will be there before midnight."

The messenger departed, and Colonel Burr returned to his parlor without a trace of anxiety on his brow. His friends soon dispersed; and about eleven o'clock he knocked at the door of the house to which he had been directed. It was opened with a promptness which proved he had been waited for, and he was ushered at once into the sick man's room. He found him stretched upon a low bed-stead, with a table drawn near, on which a tallow candle was burning dimly, and some phials of medicine were so placed as to be in reach of his hand. The invalid beckoned his visitor to approach, and said, in a feeble voice,—

"Take away the table and draw a chair close to my side, for my voice is very feeble, and I have much to say."

Burr did as he was directed.

"Do you know me?"

"No. I do not remember that we ever met. If we did, it must have been casually."

"Far from it. I am James Billings."

A sudden flush passed over the face of Burr, and he felt something like a pang shoot through his heart; but his voice was steady and unaltered.

"I remember such a man in the camp at Valley Forge —a friend of Alexander Hamilton; but you are greatly altered since then?"

"His confederate, not his friend. In such bosoms as his and mine, friendship never dwells."

He pressed his hand to his brow for a moment, and continued,—

"Listen, and do not interrupt me. The shadows of death are gathering fast around me, and I have no time to waste. When I am through, if I have the strength, I will answer any question you may desire to ask."

Then, in a low but distinct voice, he commenced his narrative. He went over the whole of the dreadful story of

24

Adelaide Clifton's insanity and death. He revealed the source of the vile slanders which had blackened the fame of Margaret Moncrieffe. He told of the unscrupulous and too successful efforts that had been made to prejudice the mind of the commander-in-chief against his listener; of the jealous vigilance with which every step of his military progress had been watched; of Hamilton's daring hopes, and their final frustration by the treaty of peace. The whole dark story was revealed with a distinctness and clearness which left no doubt upon the mind of Burr that every word he uttered was true to the letter. At first he tried to call up facts and circumstances within his own recollection which would confirm or shake the statements of the dying man; but this soon ceased, and his whole attention was given to the dreadful narrative as it progressed. Imperturbable as he generally was—accustomed as he had been to suppress every sign of emotion, this was too much for even his iron will. It recalled all the memories of the long gone past—whatever was dark and bitter in his early career rose up before him, and stung him into madness. Leaning both elbows upon the bed, he buried his face in his hands, while his whole frame shook with the mingled emotions which were struggling in his bosom. That passed away, and raising his head slowly, he inquired,—

"May I ask, Mr. Billings, what has induced you to make these revelations now? Is it from remorse, or in the hope of making some atonement to me?"

"Neither, Colonel Burr—neither. I am not one of those weak things who shrink and tremble in presence of the shadows their own actions have called about them; and to you I know that atonement is impossible. If it be in my nature to feel contrition, the thirst for vengeance has driven it away. I would have Alexander Hamilton disgraced and degraded. In that table drawer you will find a packet containing evidence enough to damn him forever in the minds of his fellow-men. To you I confide it, as the man he has most injured, and now most cordially hates."

The hard breathing of the sick man told that he was terribly agitated, and Colonel Burr paused some minutes before he said,—

"Vengeance! Why, what has he done to you?"

"Stung my pride. Refused to recognize me in public as an acquaintance, and insulted me by the offer of pecuniary assistance in private. But ask me no questions. Let me tell the story without interruption. After that fatal peace, I saw that America was no theater for me, and I embarked for France. It is unnecessary to dwell upon the part I played in the bloody drama which was soon after enacted in the land of olives and of vines. It suited me, or rather it suited the fierce devil who reigned supreme within me, and few hands were redder than mine, in a country where all were red. At length my broken health and shattered constitution, together with the loss of nearly all my fortune, compelled me to seek repose. I returned to America, not doubting that the friendship of Hamilton, who, I was aware, had risen high in the State, and the services I had rendered the American army, or at least was believed to have rendered it during the Revolution, would insure me respect, and a certain amount of consideration during the few years that would intervene before I was consigned to the grave I saw open before me. I sought him out, and told my story and my expectations. He promptly declared that he could not receive me as an associate, or even recognize me as an acquaintance in public; that I was a stranger; my services during the Revolution forgotten; and, if he was seen with me, it would lead to inquiry, and subject him to questions painful to him and difficult to answer; but, he added, if I had need of pecuniary relief, he was willing to relieve my necessities. I turned away and left him. I uttered no threat—gave no warning. It is my habit to strike first, and let the blow prove its own warning. I intended to reveal everything to you at once, but you were so much engaged in the election then pending, I could find no fitting opportunity. In the mean time I was stricken down by the disease that in a few hours more will terminate my existence. As long as there was a possibility of recovery I waited, and I did not send for you until I knew the sands in my glass were nearly exhausted. I have more to say, but no time to say it. I have not ten minutes to live—let me see you secure the papers before I go."

Colonel Burr opened the drawer, and, taking out a carefully sealed packet addressed to himself, placed it in his pocket. A light, almost a smile of satisfaction, played for an instant over the features of James Billings; then came a long-drawn sigh, a gasp, a shudder, and his spirit winged its flight to the judgment bar of God.

Thus, with no one near him but the man he had so deeply wronged, that bold, gifted, and hardened villain passed away. True to the bloody instincts of his nature, his last thought was vengeance—his last feeling that of satisfaction at the prospect of its accomplishment.

Calling some of the inmates of the house into the dead man's chamber, Colonel Burr took his departure and walked rapidly to his own residence. There he opened, with eager hands, the packet which had been placed in his possession, and read over, one by one, the papers it contained. Morning found him still engaged in his absorbing occupation. At breakfast, he contented himself with a single cup of coffee; and, directing the servant to deny admittance to any visitor who might call, again sought his library. With hurried steps he paced the floor, his hand sometimes pressed upon his forehead and sometimes thrust into his bosom, as if he sought to still the throbbings of his beating heart. "Great God!" he muttered, "has this cold-blooded devil been for so many years blasting my prospects, blackening my character, and murdering my hopes, while I, fool, dolt, idiot, that I have been, have gone on in blind ignorance of his machinations? You, too, Margaret—young, gifted, beautiful, and pure then—you, too, he dared to approach, and cover all over with the slime of calumny. And poor Adelaide, his first victim, whom he consigned to a mad-house, in the freshness of her youth and beauty, and who now fills a lunatic's grave. Oh, God! it is an account of crime and horrors for which one life will be poor payment indeed!"

Again he paced the room in silence. Then he paused in the middle of the floor, with his eyes fixed upon the carpet. The furrows of agony had disappeared from his countenance, and he wore the air of a man who was intensely studying some difficult problem. Soon his thoughts took the form of words.

"Yet how, how am I to reach him? How hold him to account, without revealing things it would madden me for the world to know?"

He raised his head as he spoke, and his eye rested upon a paper which was lying on the table. Eagerly he advanced, and picked it up. He had accidentally seen the name of Hamilton, and now he read: "General Hamilton and Judge Kent have declared, in substance, that they looked upon Mr. Burr to be a dangerous man, and one who ought not to be trusted with the reins of government. I could detail to you a still more despicable opinion which General Hamilton has expressed of Mr. Burr."

With a sigh of satisfaction and relief he folded the paper

24*

carefully, locked it in a drawer with the packet he had received from Billings; and, repeating: "That will do, that. will do!" retired to his own chamber to sleep. To sleep! Yes, he did sleep soundly for hours. When he awoke, he partook of a hearty meal, for one of his abstemious habits, and, immediately afterwards, sent for his friend, Mr. Van Ness, to call the next morning and bear to the general a hostile message. Accordingly, the next day, Mr. Van Ness placed in the hands of General Hamilton a note from Colonel Burr, reciting the offensive passages, and concluding with a demand for "a prompt and unqualified acknowledgment or denial" of that which was imputed to him. Hamilton was taken completely by surprise. He had used, on many occasions, harsher phrases, and they had been permitted to pass unnoticed. He hesitated, pleaded important business, and it was not until two days afterwards that he addressed a long communication to Colonel Burr, whose obvious purport was to evade the responsibility of either denial or acknowledgment of the language imputed to him.

Colonel Burr promptly responded that the letter was unsatisfactory; that he could find in it "nothing of that sincerity and delicacy" which Hamilton professed to value, and concluded: "Your letter has furnished me with new reasons for requiring a definite reply."

To this General Hamilton returned no written reply, but submitted to Mr. Van Ness certain propositions as a basis of adjustment. Colonel Burr prepared a letter of instructions to govern Mr. Van Ness in the negotiations; but, wearied by the delays which had already occurred, and fearful that other delays might be interposed, he resolved upon a step that he knew must make a meeting inevitable. About nine o'clock at night, after muffling his face so as to prevent recognition, he walked to General Hamilton's house.

To a question as to whether General Hamilton was in,

the servant who opened the door answered in the affirmative.

"Tell him," said Burr, "that a gentleman wishes to see him for one moment upon urgent business, and as I have no time to spare, he will greatly oblige me by walking to the door."

General Hamilton immediately came out, and Colonel Burr, pulling the door after him so as to exclude the light, and prevent any one within from overhearing their conversation, said in his natural voice,—

"General Hamilton, do you know me?"

"Colonel Burr!" replied Hamilton, in surprise.

"Yes, sir; and I have called to tell you that I did not seek satisfaction from you on account of the petty slanders contained in the pamphlet of Dr. Cooper, however fully you may have authorized their publication. But a few nights ago I sat by the death-couch of James Billings, and heard him go over the whole secret history of the past. He told how Adelaide Clifton was maddened and murdered; how the reputation of Margaret Moncrieffe had withered under the baleful influence of your poisonous breath; how you had pursued me with causeless, bitter, and remorseless hate; and he placed in my hand documents to prove the truth of his story. I did not choose to make these the ground of a message to you, because I did not wish to furnish the gossiping world with all the revolting particulars of that tale of horrors. I sought, and found another pretext. And now, sir, you will understand how useless it is to submit propositions of adjustment, and what consequences will be likely to flow to yourself from a refusal to accede to my demand. Good night, sir. I hope to meet you once more, and but once."

He turned and walked away. Hamilton stood as if petrified. It was long before he shook off the numbing torpor that seized upon every limb; and when he re-entered his own door, the presage of coming doom weighed heavily upon him.

After this some correspondence was carried on between the parties, but it was evident it could have but one termination. It was ended by a peremptory challenge from Colonel Burr, and its acceptance by Hamilton. The day of the final meeting was, however, postponed, at the request of General Hamilton, to enable him to settle up his business and make such preparations as he deemed needful in the event of his fall. The consciousness of the deep wrongs he had inflicted upon Colonel Burr through a long series of years had its effect even upon his daring nature, and he seems from the first to have had a presentiment that his last hour was approaching. Weehawken was the place selected for the fatal encounter; and, according to previous arrangement, Colonel Burr and his second were first on the ground.

When Hamilton arrived he found his antagonist, with his coat off, carelessly breaking branches from the underwood. The two principals exchanged salutations; but Burr observed that the eye of Hamilton fell when it met his own, which was glowing with all the deadly hatred that years of outrage, calumny, and wrong had engendered. Hamilton won both the choice of positions and the word. The pistols were loaded, the two men stepped to their places, announced themselves ready, and the word was given. Both pistols were discharged nearly together—Burr's a little before his adversary's. Hamilton sprang convulsively up, and then fell heavily forward on his face. His second raised him, and the surgeon was immediately by his side. To him he said: "This is a mortal wound;" and sank into insensibility.

Colonel Burr, who was unhurt, was led away to the boat

by Mr. Van Ness, and the two rowed at once to Richmond Hill.

Thus, under the heights of Weehawken, the long rivalry of Aaron Burr and Alexander Hamilton had its bloody ending.

Justice is seldom weighed by human judgment in equal scales. The victor, on that fatal day, labored under peculiar disadvantages. The foul wrongs which Hamilton had committed, the deep duplicity of his character, and the bitter malignity of his nature were known only to his slayer, and that slayer was one from whose lips no secret ever passed. The natural feeling excited in a great party by the loss of its leader, was enhanced by sympathy for the family of the dead, and fostered by reckless misrepresentations of the living. Calm and self possessed, Aaron Burr breasted the storm. He might have forgiven his own grievances, he might have hesitated to dye his hand in human blood for any injury done to himself; but the murderer of Adelaide Clifton and the slanderer of Margaret Moncrieffe was entitled to no mercy, and his fate called forth no regrets. Long years afterwards he stood upon the spot where Hamilton fell. Time had bowed his form and dimmed his eye; but when the recollections of the 10th of July, 1804, came over him, his body swelled beyond the proportions of age, and his eye burned with all the fire of his early days.

"He wronged me," he said, "and I forgave him! He wronged her, and I slew him! If twenty lives had centred in his single body, it would have been a poor atonement! When I saw him fall headlong to the ground, a weight seemed lifted from my breast, and a peaceful tranquillity settled there I never could have known while the same earth sustained us both. He has gone long ago to render his account at that judgment bar before which I too must soon appear. Face to face, in presence of the God who must pronounce our several dooms, I shall say that he deserved the death he received at my hands; and never, for one moment, has a thought of repentance obtruded itself upon my soul!"

Reader, the story of the "RIVALS" is at an end. If it meets with your favor, before long another will follow it, recording the after history of that remarkable man whose whole life was blackened by calumny and imbittered by persecution, and around whose grave still linger the harpies whose presence is pollution, and whose touch is corruption.